# Praise for *Smartbomb*

"Journalists Heather Chaplin and Aaron Ruby . . . take readers on a voyeuristic, enjoyable journey through the bizarre and fiscally fertile subculture of an industry exploding in popularity and relevance. . . . The writing is quick and informative, and the book is a smart read for those who want to learn from the people who keep gamers so entertained." —*Fast Company*

"A history of video games, presented through sharp profiles of their creators."

—*The New York Times Book Review,* Editor's Choice

"*Smartbomb* is a surprisingly poignant book. . . . Here is a book that might have been only an enthralling read about a burgeoning industry, but Chaplin and Ruby have gone one step further and produced something of importance."

—*USA Today*

"If the videogame industry is now eclipsing Hollywood in both financial and cultural power, it's about time someone introduced us to the people behind this amazing revolution. *Smartbomb* is a fascinating and inspired tour through this new creative class—the coders and evangelists and visionaries that are changing the face of entertainment."

—Stephen Johnson, author of *Everything Bad Is Good for You*

"Stimulating. . . . Ventures into that rapidly spreading territory with authority and style." —*The Boston Globe*

"A fine history lesson on the output of highly intelligent minds. Gamers . . . will devour it." —*San Francisco Weekly*

"Like getting a beta of the newest *Halo,* or being set loose at an arcade with a pocketful of silver dollars: a new world opens up, and all you want to do is hang on and race your way into the higher levels. *Smartbomb* is such sheer, entertaining fun it should come with its own joystick."

—David Lipsky, author of *Absolutely American: Four Years at West Point*

"Hackers, geeks and dreamers fill the pages of *Smartbomb,* which engagingly recounts the history of video games from the earliest experiments to today's multi-billion-dollar industry."

—*Paste*

"*Smartbomb* explodes with intelligence, insight, and first-rate writing on every page. Here is your future, in all its fascinating, scary, and very human dimensions."

—Kevin Baker, author of *Paradise Alley*

"The writing is consistently good and the anecdotes are entertaining, which makes *Smartbomb* a welcome addition to the woefully small canon of videogame non-fiction books."

—*The San Jose Mercury News*

"A whirlwind subcultural tour." —*Publishers Weekly*

"Informative and entertaining. . . . The authors trace the videogame's evolution from its exceedingly humble beginnings to its present position as a dominant force in the entertainment industry. They tell the tale with flair and an air of mystery. . . . The best history of the videogame phenomenon since Steven L. Kent's *The Ultimate History of Video Games* (2001)."

—*Booklist*

"My favorite read of the past year was *Smartbomb*. . . . Reading it left no doubt in my mind that videogames will be the dominant art form of the next century."

—John Wray, author of *Canaan's Tongue*

"*Smartbomb* is a riveting, provocative, disturbing dive into the subculture of videogames and the obsessive geeks and visionaries who create them. Chaplin and Ruby describe a virtual reality in which people live fantasy lives—often violent and sexist—inside cathode ray tubes, connected to one another only by their keystrokes."

—Mark Pendergrast, author of
*Mirror, Mirror* and *For God, Country & Coca-Cola*

"Chaplin and Ruby have written an insightful and deeply relevant account of why the brightest minds in videogames are conquering the entertainment landscape."

—Geoff Keighley, editor-in-chief of
*GameSlice* magazine and host of *G4tv.com*

"In *Smartbomb,* meticulous reporting, carefully drawn characters, and beautiful writing sweep you into a world that you did not know existed and could hardly have imagined. Chaplin and Ruby guide you from one terrific story to another and in the process show you a videogame industry full of unexpected delights."

—Alex Spiegel, contributing editor for *This American Life*

"*Smartbomb* puts the gaming explosion in perspective with a look at how far games have come and how far it has to go as it turns into the digital Hollywood of tomorrow."

—Andy McNamara, editor-in-chief of *Game Informer*

# SMARTBOMB

# SMART

HEATHER CHAPLIN

& AARON RUBY

ALGONQUIN BOOKS OF

CHAPEL HILL 2006

**THE QUEST FOR ART, ENTERTAINMENT, AND BIG BUCKS IN THE VIDEOGAME REVOLUTION**

# BOMB

Published by
Algonquin Books of Chapel Hill
Post Office Box 2225 Chapel Hill, North Carolina 27215-2225

a division of
Workman Publishing
225 Varick Street
New York, New York 10014


First paperback edition, Algonquin Books of Chapel Hill, November 2006. Originally published by Algonquin Books of Chapel Hill in 2005.

Printed in the United States of America.
Published simultaneously in Canada by
Thomas Allen & Son Limited.
Design by Rebecca Giménez.

Library of Congress Cataloging-in-Publication Data
Chaplin, Heather, 1971–
Smartbomb : the quest for art, entertainment, and big bucks in the videogame revolution / by Heather Chaplin and Aaron Ruby.—1st ed.
p. cm.
Includes bibliographical references and index.
ISBN-13: 978-1-56512-346-5; ISBN-10: 1-56512-346-8 (HC)
I. Electronic games industry. I. Title: Smart bomb.
II. Ruby, Aaron, 1967– III. Title.
HD9993.E452C43 2005
338.4'77948—dc22 2005047845

ISBN-13: 978-1-56512-545-2; ISBN-10: 1-56512-545-2 (PB)

10 9 8 7 6 5 4 3 2 1
First Paperback Edition

*For Asher Montandon,*

*who knew the value of exploring other worlds.*

# CONTENTS

# ACKNOWLEDGMENTS

We wish to send thanks to the friends and family who supported us through this project: Alix Spiegel, Kevin Baker, Ellen Abrams, Barbara Kammeron, Linda Grant, June Chaplin, all of our siblings, David Aitken, Alison Chaplin, Ardith Ibanez, Autumn Lucas, the Phelps-Walker Clan, Team Oona, Elena Skolnick, the Brooklyn Writer's Space, Duncan Murrell, Chuck Adams, Michael Taeckens, Brunson Hoole, and Daniel Greenberg. We'd also like to thank the hundreds of people who gave their time to help open the world of videogames to us, particularly the following: Will Wright, Ed Fries, John Romero, Sid Meier, Clifford Bleszinski, Alan Willard, Jay Wilbur, Seamus Blackley, Lorne Lanning, Shigeru Miyamoto, Satoru Iwata, Bill Trinen, Trip Hawkins, Bruno Bonnell, Jason Rubinstein, J Allard, Alan Yu, John O'Rourke, Horace Luke, Rich Vogel, Raph Koster, the SWG team, Gaute Godager, Richard Garriott, Gary Gygax, Richard Bartle, David Reber, Redruum, Steve Russell, J. M. Graetz, Nolan

Bushnell, Gary Kitchen, Warren Robinett, Jennifer Pahlka, Douglas Lowenstein, Steven Kent, Leonard Herman, David Kushner, Dean Takahashi, Casey Wardynski, Mike Zyda, Michael Macedonia, Michael Capps, Masaya Matsuura, Tetsuya Mizuguchi, Fumito Uedo, Kenji Kaido, Tetsuya Nomura, Kazunori Yamauchi, Claude Comair, Tom Russo, Geoff Keighley, Adam Sessler, Charles Hirschhorn, Henry Lowood, Edward Castranova, American McGee, Stevie Case, Angel Munoz, Jason Rubin, Andy Gavin, Greg Thomas, David Jaffe, David Wessman, Andrew House, Adam Lerner, Steve Grempka, Brandon and Justin Holt, the Half-Life MOD community, Beverly Clark, Chris Overbey, Lee Rakestraw, James Korris, Jacqueline Morie, Michael van Lent, Elonka Dunin, Paul Provenzano, Stuart Moulder, Billy Pidgeon, Sibel Sunar, James Bernard, Tamara Otto, Chris Olmstead, Julia Roether, Walter Day, the Horde on Stormrage, the Rebellion on Azahi, the Clans on Atlantean, and, of course, Snakeeyes.

# SMARTBOMB

# INTRODUCTION

This is a report from the game front—a place where bleeding-edge computer science and wild creativity have fused to produce a new medium that is poised to dramatically alter not only how we play but also how we communicate and learn.

Until recently, videogames were a boom-and-bust culture, considered by many to be only a notch or two above pornography. Indeed, for most of their thirty-odd years in existence, videogames have been consistently vilified, charged with the corruption of our youth (a role once ascribed to Socrates), blamed for the destruction of our attention spans, and heralded as a precursor to a society of alienated, socially incompetent automatons.

Today, videogames are big business, with annual sales approaching $10 billion in the United States alone. Every day they are changing the profile of our cultural landscape—invading Blockbusters, Barnes & Nobles, and Virgin Megastores alike. Commercials for videogames have escaped from the backwoods of niche cable channels to ride the network airwaves with the big boys. No longer a fad or a novelty, videogames have arrived, and they are here to stay. Meanwhile, the enormous financial success of the industry has overshadowed a much more interesting fact—videogames aren't simply a new medium, they're an entirely new *kind* of medium altogether.

Traditional media like books and movies use descriptions (linguistic, visual, etc.) as a means of representing and communicating ideas. Videogames use models. For example, if people want to learn about the orbits of planets in the solar system, they can consult books, watch educational movies, or even attend lectures. Each of these sources would teach about planetary motion by describing it, using words and/or a stream of sound and images.

Or they could use an orrery, a collection of spheres mounted on a system of armatures and gears. The orrery represents the solar system not by *describing* it but by serving as a *model* of it.

Videogames are like orreries in that they are models—dynamic computer models to be precise. Each videogame, from *Pong* to single-player *Tetris* to the most sophisticated virtual world like *Star Wars Galaxies,* where thousands of players interact simultaneously in a fully 3-D world, is ultimately a model. Videogames allow players not simply to tour a space but to influence what happens in that space. Learning from a model like an orrery or a videogame, or even simply playing with one, requires and encourages very different cognitive skills and imparts a different kind of knowledge than that attained from books or films. In a society in which entertainment has nearly become a secondary education system—studies consistently show that people today spend more time consuming entertainment than they spend with their families or in school—this shift to model-based entertainment will have an undeniable impact on the way people think and communicate. The invasion of the videogame, then, gives new life to the anthropologic saw: "Show me the games of your children, and I'll show you the next hundred years."

Because of this new medium, there are millions of people

around the world who consider themselves citizens of virtual planets; others spend countless hours trying to master tactical combat maneuvers, or even spend hundreds of dollars to hear an orchestra play the score from a cherished videogame. People around the world haunt video arcades, hopping to the electric rhythm of games like *Dance Dance Revolution,* or take their computers to gatherings in giant warehouses where they party and compete against their peers, playing videogames over local networks. Still others have banded together in clans, devoting themselves to the task of using game designers' own creations against them, disassembling popular titles and then rebuilding them as their imagination dictates. The military has gotten in on the game as well, tapping videogame developers to build tools to train soldiers, and those very same tools are then repackaged and sold to consumers.

Indeed, the technology of videogames has made amazing advances since the 1960s and early 1970s, when MIT hacker Steve Russell had the novel idea of using a computer as a toy, and Nolan Bushnell introduced the world to a new business culture with his start-up company, Atari. Nintendo's Shigeru Miyamoto is a present-day Gepetto who dreams of bringing toys to life and is known in his homeland as *sensei*—the master. John Carmack (creator of *Castle Wolfenstein, Doom, Quake*) has made advances in computer graphics that have guaranteed him a place in the history of computer science, while fellow industry "genius" Will Wright is actively trying to build a simulation of Everything—and succeeding.

Colonel Casey Wardynski of the U.S. Army and his colleague Mike Zyda recognized that videogames not only could be used to train soldiers but also could teach kids to become fighters in the first place. Their game, *America's Army,* is now one of the most popular first-person-shooter videogames ever.

("First-person-shooter" refers to the player's perspective in the game, which is typically down the barrel of a large firearm.) Meanwhile, people like Raph Koster and Rich Vogel are fierce advocates of the online communities that have evolved from the first MUDs (multi-user dungeon) to the latest MMOs (massively multiplayer online games), convinced that virtual worlds will force us to rewire our concept of reality.

Yet for all its ascendant power, the videogame industry is a young one, and as a medium videogames are barely in their adolescence, still struggling with the limitlessness of having no established rules by which to play, no real standards by which to measure themselves, where gamemakers must invent the paradigm of their business and their art as they go. These designers, artists, and programmers are a fascinating collection of geeks, mavericks, and geniuses, and they are passionate about what they do. At the same time, the videogame industry has gone corporate faster than any medium that's ever come before, and the tension between the bean counters and the talent is profound.

*Smartbomb* is the story of these people—the people who are living, working, and dreaming at the cultural epicenter of the videogame explosion, the people who make videogames, the people who play them, and the people who stand to profit from them. Their names are not generally known outside the industry, but soon they will be. Their influence will be as great and as far-reaching as that of the people who gave birth to the film industry at the turn of the last century, or to TV in the thirties. *Smartbomb* is the story of tomorrow's Orson Welleses and Alfred Hitchcocks, as well as its George Lucases and Steven Spielbergs; it is also the story of the clans, guilds, and modders who embrace them—it is the story of the people who literally are creating the worlds in which we're going to live and play for the next century.

# 1

## CliffyB and the Dawn of a New Era

CliffyB, or Clifford Bleszinski, as his mom would call him, is getting ready to give a seminar called "The Future Looks Bright." It's May 2001 at the Electronic Entertainment Expo in Los Angeles, California, the largest gathering of the video-game industry in the world. Like anyone who owns a television, CliffyB is well versed in the importance of reinvention in holding the public eye. He turns before the mirror in the men's room. White suit, white snakeskin shoes, hair bleached white to match. *Looking good,* he thinks, although, in truth, his arms and legs are gangly under his suit, his chest thin beneath a black shirt and tie, and his hair, capping a somewhat sallow complexion, is more brassy blond than white.

Ten years ago, CliffyB was that kid on the school bus who got Coke poured on his head and gum smeared in his hair. Back before he was transformed into a pimp-suit-wearing game designer, Cliffy was an acne-riddled, miserable-at-school, small-town kid, filled with unbridled fury at his low status in life—a feeling that years later left him sympathizing terribly, albeit secretly, with videogame fans Eric Harris and Dylan Klebold, the iconic misfits who in 1999 shot up their classmates, their cafeteria, and then themselves at Columbine High School in Littleton, Colorado. It still brings tears to Cliffy's eyes to think about it—not only the horror of the kids who lost their lives, but also how deeply, awfully alone Harris and Klebold most have been to do such a thing. Cliffy thinks he knows exactly how they felt. He still refers bitterly to the hysteria that swept the country afterward as "geek profiling."

"Yeah, but who has the last laugh now?" Cliffy says about his old high school tormenters. "They're all working at gas stations. And look at me." Arms spread wide in his ill-fitting white suit.

Indeed, that was then, and this is now. At twenty-six years old, CliffyB is a nine-year veteran of the industry, lead designer at Epic Games and co-creator with Digital Extremes of the smash success first-person-shooter franchise *Unreal*. This is the year that sales of videogames in the United States have surpassed movie box-office receipts, a stamp of success the industry believes is its passport to legitimacy. People who haven't thought about videogames since their *Space Invaders* days more than a decade ago are saying to one another over coffee and the *Times: Did you know the videogame industry made $6.35 billion this year?* Ads for Sony, Nintendo, Electronic Arts, and Xbox are beginning to creep from cable channels like MTV2, Nickelodeon, and TechTV onto prime-time slots on the networks. Billboards for hit games such as *Grand Theft Auto III* are vying with movies for space on city street corners. Nongamers around the world are awaking, startled, to the ascendance of a medium about which they know little or nothing.

The Electronic Entertainment Expo, or E3 as gamers call it, is the yearly event of the Interactive Digital Software Association, the industry's chief trade group. The gathering was founded in 1995, when videogames got too big to remain an adjunct of the Consumer Electronics Show. E3 is where game publishers, console makers, and related companies show their upcoming wares to retailers and industry press. As CliffyB likes to say, videogames used to be like porn: everyone's got a stack under their bed, but no one admits it. In 2001, however, as young men everywhere are pulling their consoles and games out from under the bed, E3 has come to stand for something much bigger than just a trade show. In 2001, it stands as proof that videogames are here—and aren't going away any time soon.

The enormous lobbies and hallways of the Los Angeles Convention Center, where E3 is held, are tiled with wall-sized monitors, banners of all sorts, and constellations of loudspeakers. The noise is deafening, and the bleating and blinking they emit is potentially epilepsy-inducing. Crouched like a spider beneath its web, a full-scale model of the futuristic Lexus from Spielberg's *Minority Report* guards the escalator to the main convention hall, and a matrix of sixteen or so huge flat-panel screens tease passersby with the images from the videogame of the yet-to-be-released movie. The demos loop over and over, Tom Cruise endlessly fighting off jetpack-wearing attackers. On a wall across the aisle, a digitized Ewan McGregor is firing up his lightsaber above a display for a litany of upcoming *Star Wars* game releases. Though Lucasfilm's digital counterpart LucasArts has been around for more than a decade, in

2001 most movie studios and production houses are just discovering the advantages of tag-teaming their blockbusters with videogames.

On the expo floor, the game companies have gone all out. There are fifteen-foot-tall dungeons and faux Grecian temples surrounded by pillars of red billowing silk that give the impression of flames. There's a small skate ramp in the South Hall replete with professional skaters promoting the newest installment of the multimillion-dollar franchises *Tony Hawk's Pro Skater* and *Tony Hawk's Underground*. The king himself, Mr. Hawk, occasionally steps out from the VIP section to monitor the proceedings, sporting the goofy smile of a tycoon who at heart remains an enthusiast.

When Cliffy gets out of his panel discussion, he chats a bit with reporters and other industry folk outside the meeting room. He bounces on the toes of his snakeskin shoes, excited, as if he can't quite believe he's here himself. Then he heads down to the expo floor.

Cliffy lives for videogames. Time spent on the Nintendo Entertainment System, playing with *Mario* and *Donkey Kong,* forms some of his fondest childhood memories. His preteen years were spent on the PC with *Doom* and *Quake,* and then *SimCity* and the *Ultima* series. By the time he was a teenager, he was making games of his own on a souped-up PC in his bedroom. Cliffy has never had any formal game-design training—until recently the very idea of formal training in game design would have been considered absurd. Nevertheless, Cliffy's been making games professionally since he was seventeen years old. After sending one of his games in a Ziploc bag to a publisher in California, Cliffy found himself a professional game designer before he had even graduated high school.

Microsoft, Sony, and Nintendo, the three console makers of

the moment, as well as three of the biggest software publishers in the business, dominate the South and West Convention Halls, respectively. Each company has an inner sanctum, erected the day before, complete with passageways and little rooms where executives take meetings and give interviews over plates of melon and grapes. Like a solar system with a collection of satellites, each company is surrounded by its subsidiaries, divisions, and allies. Cliffy checks out a couple of displays, and soon spots dozens of people he knows—other designers, gaming journalists, fans of his. People know Cliffy because he makes a point of being known. He accepts panel spots, poses for photographs, and even has a Web site called CliffyCam that lets you watch him while he works, or allows you to rifle through a collection of his photographs, including a prominent one of him in a big fuzzy bunny suit.

After a few minutes of meeting and greeting, CliffyB turns to a friend with the exhausted but excited look of a congressman just returned from a visit with his constituency. Cliffy explains to a reporter that a rumor has been spreading through the convention center like a virus, growing until the grumbling on the subject has become another layer of noise on the expo floor—a rumor that there's been a moratorium on the Booth Babe.

The Booth Babe is a time-honored tradition of E3—to the extent that a tradition less than a generation old can make such a claim—and the Booth Babe issue has everything to do with what videogames have been, and what they're trying to become. Despite the rumored moratorium, Booth Babes appear to be everywhere you look. There's a woman dressed as Lara Croft, the long-legged, gun-toting archaeologist hero of Eidos's *Tomb Raider*. (Angelina Jolie played her in the movie version of the game.) There are women in tiny pieces of chain mail positioned outside elaborate gothic sets, women wandering the showrooms in pink latex bikinis. A group of them outside the South Hall are tossing Hawaiian leis around the necks of pale young men, cooing, "Want to get lei'd?" There would appear to be many, many scantily clad young women, but, apparently, there aren't as many in 2001 as there used to be. And once the rumor takes hold, a dearth of Booth Babes is perceived by one and all, and the judgment of every male queried is that there are not nearly as many as there should be. "Ban the Booth Babe?" you hear in the hallways. "Come on!" People know this is the year the industry is making its big push for the mainstream, and they clearly understand that they aren't to alienate anyone with acts that could be perceived as depraved or immature or in any way foster the general impression of videogame makers as crazed, violent, or immoral freaks. But on the Booth Babe issue, the conventioneers are like dieters looking forward to being thin yet balking at the idea they must disavow pizza.

CliffyB, statesmanlike, sums up the general feeling. "Give me a break," he says. "The Booth Babe is an institution. If people don't have a sense of humor, fuck 'em!"

The irony is that while it's true Douglas Lowenstein, president of the Interactive Digital Software Association (IDSA), hardly wants to project an image of pimply faced boys taking Polaroids with chain-mail-clad young women, he's the last one to hear the rumor. To his knowledge there's been no official moratorium on the Booth Babe. He's certainly issued no such edict. Perhaps the vendors are cleaning up their act on their own, he muses. Perhaps it's been entirely imagined, or perhaps it's a fantasy that became a reality once enough people believed it. Amidst the chaos and clamor of the sprawling videogame shantytown set up by the corporations on the floor of the convention, it's easy to see how that could happen.

Lowenstein is a slender man in his midfifties who favors thin polo-neck sweaters tucked into pleated trousers. He's going bald and has a beak nose. Were his posture to worsen, he would somewhat resemble Mr. Burns from *The Simpsons*. Yet, there's something natty about him—he's polished and professional-looking in a way most people in the videogame industry are not. He shakes Cliffy's hand as they pass in the hall. Lowenstein has his own speech to give. He's a longtime D.C. lobbyist who's had his work cut out for him, trying to transform America's perception of the videogame from that of an artifact of an ailing society to a respectable and fun entertainment product. He's named the 2001 conference "Touch the Future," and, like Cliffy's attempts to vanquish his Coke-wielding demons, he's determined to flip the whole paradigm once and for all. He wants 2001 to be the dawn of a new era. He kicks off E3 with an enthusiastic and statistic-filled address.

"Seven years ago," he says, "videogames were played mostly by teenage boys, usually in the basement or the bedroom. No longer. Today, videogames are mainstream entertainment: they're played by people of all ages; they're played by people of all tastes; and they've become as important a part of our culture as television and movies. . . . They're in the center of the home, they're on the Internet, they're in movies, they're in schools, they're on cell phones; they're on PDAs and airplanes; and they're even in medical research labs. In short, videogames are everywhere."

He chuckles a little, along with his crowd, when he says, "Of course, politicians are still grumbling about videogame violence." It's as if he and the audience were high schoolers, sniggering at a hopelessly out-of-date teacher tramping the halls with toilet paper trailing from his shoe.

Lowenstein is clearly thrilled he finally has the luxury of laughing off angry politicians. The videogame industry has been growing at a rate of 15 percent a year for several years, double the rate of growth for the U.S. economy as a whole during the same time period, and more than double the rate of either the film industry or the computer hardware business. The average age of a gamer has finally exceeded eighteen years—"Please, please, can we put that stereotype to rest once and for all!" Lowenstein mock-pleads. It's predicted that by 2005, videogame consoles will have penetrated 70 percent of all American homes, giving it one of the fastest adoption rates of any consumer appliance in history. The PlayStation 2 alone, for example, made it into 10 million homes its first year on the market, something it took the telephone thirty-five years to accomplish.

Ubiquity is what the industry has been after for years, and ubiquity seems to be what it is finally getting. One study, from investment analysts at Deutsche Bank Alex. Brown, has just concluded that the potential market for videogames had grown from 20 million people in 1980 to 96 million in 2001 and is now growing exponentially—106 million people in 2005 and onward, as every baby born takes to the videogame habit.

"Fun. That's what this . . . industry is about," Lowenstein says. Then he reads from a May 2001 article by Bob Schwabach for the *New York Times:* "'The videogame industry has been on the threshold of seizing dominance in entertainment for several years,'" he quotes. "'Ultimately it will. It's inevitable. . . . I don't see any way out of this.'"

• • •

**THE FOLLOWING YEAR, 2002,** CliffyB's plans for industry dominance aren't panning out quite as he'd hoped. At E3 2001 he'd been riding high on the recent release and resounding success of *Unreal Tournament*. But in the spring of 2002 at the International Game Developers Conference, the release of his next title, *Unreal 2,* is still seven months away, and Cliffy has taken to muttering, "You're only as good as your last game."

If you didn't know that Cliffy introduced a new look at every industry gathering, you might not recognize him right away at the 2002 Game Developers Conference. This year, CliffyB's hair is brown and brushed into his face à la early-*ER* George Clooney. He's wearing a silky shirt and a stiff black leather jacket; a heavy silver chain lies around his neck. Cliffy is well scrubbed and moussed, like someone from New Jersey going to a Manhattan dance club. He's hanging out by the bar of the Fairmont Hotel in San Jose, California, which serves as the headquarters for the Game Developers Conference. It's March, almost exactly one year after the rumored Booth Babe moratorium, and attendance at the GDC, an event as different from E3 as San Jose is from Hollywood, is strong. E3 may be for the companies, but GDC is for the developers. For an industry on the verge of reaching cultural critical mass, it's hard to imagine that a tight sense of community could be maintained among developers, but Alan Yu, the bald, hip twenty-nine-year-old organizer of the event, is doing his best to make that happen. He has a dream of a videogame community that crosses cultural, geographic, and company lines. He's lured designers from as far away as Japan, Hong Kong, Italy, Scotland, France, and England. E3 may shock and awe with its eye-popping display of the electric sprawl of the videogame industry, but GDC opens a portal into the hearts of those who keep it thriving.

Every year, in early March, just before the mad scramble in the months leading up to E3 begins, twelve thousand or so game developers from around the world descend on this four-block stretch of downtown San Jose. They fill up every hotel in the area, every meeting room in the convention center, and every ballroom in the Fairmont Hotel. The hotel's sunken lobby is packed from early in the morning until late at night with designers, programmers, producers, animators, audio engineers, writers, and independent studio CEOs—all the people it takes to put out a modern videogame.

They crowd into seminars ranging from programming with geometric computations, to composing interactive music, to managing online societies, to understanding female gamers. There are educators from universities such as Stanford, MIT, and University of Michigan who want to know how to create degrees in gamemaking and videogame theory. There are business people from wireless companies hot on the trail of multiplayer games that can be played over cell phones. And there are others, like Peter Molyneux of Lionhead Studios (*Black & White* and *Fable*), who are acknowledged masters of this strange universe. GDC is a place where it's possible for the lowest coder to rub elbows with the likes of Will Wright, maker of the most popular PC game of all time, *The Sims,* or Raph Koster, the visionary leader of the current charge into massively multiplayer online gaming, or even Jonathan "Seamus" Blackley, the man behind the Xbox.

The men at GDC—and it is almost exclusively male—are former nuclear physicists, neuroscientists, and linguists; painters, musicians, and illustrators; reformed graffiti artists; professional gamblers; computer scientists who consult with the FBI on the side. BioWare, for example, the Canadian developer known for its hugely successful adaptations of *Dungeons & Dragons* adventures, was started by a pair of MDs bored with designing biomedical software who began building games for a challenge. An even older generation exists, of middle-aged men who were playing text-based computer games like *Zork* and *Adventure* over the Internet a decade before most people could even access it. And perhaps most prevalent are the kids in oversized hoodie sweatshirts, knee-length shorts, and skateboard shoes who have spent their entire lives playing videogames. Essentially the grunts of the industry, these guys—low-level texture artists, game testers, designers without contracts, audio effects hacks, and the like—are simply content to have a job where they can obsess about videogames freely, and an employer who throws them the yearly blowout.

Then there are the Japanese. The Japanese didn't invent videogames, nor were they the first to debut a commercial arcade game or home console. Nevertheless, in the thirty short years or so that the videogame industry has existed, the Japanese have become the undisputed champions of the medium.

This Japanese dominance of videogames is due first to the crushing success of the Nintendo Entertainment System in the mideighties, which effectively disemboweled the struggling American giant Atari and launched what is now considered by many to be the "golden age" of videogaming. During this period companies such as Sega, Namco, and eventually Sony entered the fray so aggressively that by 1990 not a single American firm stood as a major producer of videogame hardware.

The dominance of the Japanese is also due in part to the fact that post–World War II Japanese culture has been especially friendly to technology-based entertainment. It has also been rabid for novelty, and has embraced pop culture to a degree unheard of in the United States except among children. In such a cultural climate did not take long for the dreams of someone like Shigeru Miyamoto (*Donkey Kong, Super Mario Bros., Legend of Zelda*) to find their way in, translated into a near endless stream of 0s and 1s.

The current crop of Japanese game developers has much for which to thank Miyamoto-san, as he is reverently referred to, as well as other veterans, like *Gran Turismo* architect Kazunori Yamauchi, an expert simulation builder who tells a reporter in the lounge of the Fairmont that his greatest goal is to make a simulation of a brain, one that could tell stories to children. Designers like Miyamoto, Yamauchi, and *Virtua Fighter* creator Yu Suzuki have demonstrated an ingenuity, creativity, and versatility that few American or European designers can match.

But while designers like Miyamoto-san are venerated by American gamemakers, it is perhaps the younger generation of Japanese designers that Americans like CliffyB most want to emulate. Tetsuya Nomura, for example, the character designer behind many of Square Enix's *Final Fantasy* blockbusters, is thronged by fans when he goes out in Japan—something that has surprised more than one visiting American designer. It's the same for Tetsuya Mizuguchi, whose music-based games *Space Channel 5* and *Rez* have inspired not only a devoted cult audience but widespread adulation as well.

The highlight of the conference—besides the ubiquitous drinking and schmoozing in the Fairmont lobby—is the Game Developers Choice Awards, held each year in a crumbling palace of a theater across the street from the convention center.

Cliffy joins the flow of people from the Fairmont over to

the awards show. He's dragging his feet, feeling a bit deflated. He had dinner earlier with his boss at Epic, Jay Wilbur, and found himself saying, somewhat plaintively, "We're going to be making *Unreal* for the rest of our lives, aren't we?" After all those years spent dreaming of it, Cliffy is just now realizing that videogame success does not guarantee either cultural adulation or creative freedom.

Cliffy knows he's not the most groundbreaking game designer in the world. "I'm no Will Wright," he says, "no Sid Meier." Cliffy's talent, as he explains it, is being an adept thief, stealing elements from the games that turned him on as a teenager—*Doom, Quake, Wolfenstein 3D*. But recent business trips to Japan and Korea have spurred an interest in history and in cultures other than American. Cliffy has started dreaming about a game that's more than a shoot 'em up. He's been fantasizing about a futuristic World War II–style battle game set in outer space. But one of the hallmarks of this new era of mainstream acceptance for videogames is, like in modern-day Hollywood, the rampant reliance on franchises rather than innovation. It's also an era of extreme consolidation among development studios, and Cliffy knows that Epic is lucky to have a steady moneymaker like *Unreal* on its hands. It's what has allowed the company to stay independent. Cliffy may get to experiment, to make his new game, but it'll depend on how the market holds over the next year, and how well the *Unreal* franchise does.

As Cliffy approaches the theater, he glances at the crowd waiting to get in. It's an interesting-looking crowd, to say the least. There are albinos and men covered in angry red acne. Guys with blow-up plastic dragons on their shoulders, slouchy velvet hats, long ponytails, big fat bellies, tiny concave chests, dandruff on their shoulders, and random piercings. There are grown men wearing top hats and sporting big bushy beards, and women in industry T-shirts worn over ankle-length skirts. There are kids with pink and green hair and hoops through their noses. Girls dressed like anime characters in huge platform boots and spiky hair, and dozens of young men who all seem to be wearing the same oversized, button-down shirts with red and orange flames licking up the bottom. And there are young Japanese men in leather pants and turquoise corduroy, their hair bleached orange, with skinny and chic girlfriends hanging from their arms. The Brits in attendance seem to mostly wear their hair in dreads and swaddle themselves in T-shirts swearing allegiances to different DJs and electronic music labels.

Cliffy cuts through the long line outside the award show and goes directly to the VIP door—as a well-known member of the videogame world, he enjoys the same kind of perks every industry affords its stars. Watching him pass are envious young men, hunched over in their hoodies, who probably work as low-level animators or coders. They aren't going to get in to either the show or the business as easily as Cliffy did. The videogame industry is rapidly becoming the kind of place where publishers will no longer take submissions that come in Ziploc bags.

Once inside, piled into the plush red movie seats, the gamemakers yell and holler and whoop with enthusiasm that is palpable. They can feel the sea change that's taken place over the last year. They can feel the thickness of the crowd—less than ten years ago, the GDC took place in someone's living room. They notice the extra press coverage this year, the reporters stopping to ask them uninformed questions about making games. They all saw Tony Hawk—a man whose mainstream celebrity is almost entirely a product of the videogame industry—guest star on *The Simpsons*. In the spring of 2002, Doug Lowenstein's bold new era seems to be well under way. Three new consoles—the PlayStation 2, the Xbox, and the GameCube—have been launched since E3 2001, stirring up excitement with their technical capabilities, new games aimed at an older audience, and billions of dollars spent on marketing.

It's still an oddly insular world, however. The average guy getting on stage to give or accept an award is most likely known to every member of the audience. And he's probably dressed as casually as those in the audience, his unshaven face, blemished skin, and bad hair projected on big screens at the side of the stage for all to see. He may get a standing ovation here in San Jose, but drop him in any Midwestern Wal-Mart, which may have just sold 100,000 copies of his game, or place him at a Manhattan cocktail party where the people pride themselves on their cultural literacy, and nobody would know who he was.

Event organizer Alan Yu is standing by one of the side doors, a bottle of beer in his hand. He's wearing a red satin cowboy shirt. "This is great," Alan says. "They're having a good time, huh? I just want these guys to have a good time."

Alan scoots away as the contenders for best game of the year are announced. The games up for awards seem to have as much to do with *Pong, Missile Command,* or *Space Invaders* as *Star Wars* does to early cinema classics like *Rescued by Rover.* The best of today's videogames are imaginative and intelligent. As a medium, they have achieved excellence. This is not to say, however, that every game is good. Much like the Hollywood studios in their early days, videogame publishers churn out a constant stream of product, some made simply to meet demand and others with larger budgets and grander aspirations. The AAA games, as the more elaborate entries are called, take years to make, and cost upward of $5 million. They require tightly coordinated staffs of hundreds, and have at their heads men with computer skills that are the envy of government, banking, medicine, and academia. For example, John Carmack, the programmer behind *Doom* and *Quake,* is considered one of the best graphics programmers in the world. Breakthroughs he's made in three-dimensional graphic technology have been used by both the U.S. military, to create training simulations for American troops, and biologists, for 3-D molecular modeling.

As the contenders for this year's awards are announced, the crowd screams, red-faced with excitement and fueled by the cups of beer available in the lobby. They're more like sports fans at a title game than award attendees. They're drunk, and happy, and pumped up. The only difference is they don't really care who wins; they loved *all* the games.

There's *Munch's Oddysee,* the sad tale/adventure game of a one-eyed aquatic creature on the verge of extinction, who must liberate his species, helped by an ex-slave with a pinhead and chronic flatulence named Abe. The game's animation is creative and original, and its story is subversive, at least by mainstream entertainment standards. Its creator, Lorne Lanning, of Oddworld Inhabitants, is a thirty-seven-year-old former painter and hydraulic amusement-park-ride inventor, who does the character animation and voice acting himself. Lanning is six feet three inches, with recently cut-off long black hair, a pointy goatee, and a Cary Grant–like elegance. Ask him what his religious inclination is; "Jedi," he'll tell you.

*Ico* is a fairy-tale adventure game rendered in surreal pools of light and shadow. The game's heavily stylized imagery is a stunning example of what the next generation of gamemakers, with next-generation technology behind them, are accomplishing. *Ico* is the brainchild of Fumito Ueda, a slim, thirty-three-year-old former visual artist from Japan who dresses like a preppy American and slouches like James Dean. *Ico* is the first game Ueda ever made, and it is hauntingly beautiful and well crafted, both in design and gameplay.

*Jak & Daxter* is from a Santa Monica–based studio called Naughty Dog, and it is Disney-esque in its use of anthropomorphized animals chasing each other with mallets while running through stylized cartoon landscapes. Jason Rubin, one of the company's founders, is known for having cashed in, along with Andy Gavin, his partner since Hebrew School days, on the rise of the videogame. Sony bought their company in 2001, reportedly for seven figures. Rubin drives a quarter-million-dollar Ferrari; Gavin collects ancient Egyptian artifacts.

And then there's *Grand Theft Auto III*. The title, from a keep-to-themselves group called Rockstar Games, caught the attention of everyone from TV commentator Ted Koppel to the 12 million people who shelled out fifty bucks for a copy.

What gamers loved about *GTA III* even more than the carjackings and prostitute power-ups was the enormous possibilities the game provided. The game issued players a movielike world of urban mobsters and petty crooks, but the *player* called the action. If players didn't want to follow the plotline that runs through the game, they could cruise the city and decide whether they felt like stealing virtual cars and beating up virtual cops, or driving a virtual ambulance to save virtual pedestrians.

Not surprisingly, many people, both inside the industry and

out, found the content of the game offensive. Ted Koppel was one of them. But ask anyone in that auditorium, and they'll tell you that it wasn't the cop bashing in particular they liked. It was the sense of existing in an alternate universe, surrounded by opportunities to act, and being able to feel the effects of those actions as they played. This freedom simply thrilled them.

When *Grand Theft Auto III* is announced as the Game of the Year, there is wild enthusiasm from the stands—people screaming, whistling, chanting, stomping their feet. Geronimo, one of the grand poobahs of Rockstar Games, takes to the stage, his portly frame packed into a double-breasted zoot suit. He waves the award high over his head. People clap and cheer even louder. Geronimo moves to the microphone and says, "This is to show that videogames don't have to be about hobgoblins and dwarves!" The crowd is silent, unsure about this last bit of heresy. But then they erupt into applause all over again. They can't help it. It was a great game. And if there's one thing the people in this decaying auditorium do care about, it's great games.

By midnight, Alan Yu's post-awards party is in full swing. Winners from the night and others in the know take the Fairmont elevator to the top floor, walk down two hallways to a set of double doors with a plaque beside it engraved with the words FAIRMONT SUITE. Tall and elegant, Lorne Lanning opens the door, drink in hand, relaxed among his peers. There's a fully stocked bar on the left, a marble bathroom to the right. In the main room, Alan is running back and forth seeing to his guests. There are six couches, a grand piano, a view of the San Jose skyline, several small trees, and two bedrooms off to the side. Word at the party has it that the Mexican ambassador to the U.S. has been displaced to another suite on the floor below in order to accommodate Alan and his gathering.

By two a.m., Alan has given up trying to keep the party exclusive, and the place is packed. Cliffy is there, lurking by the doorway between the foyer and the living room. He's clearly tense, which for Cliffy means holding his shoulders high and his lips tight, much like a boxer waiting for the next punch. He fills out his shirt more than he did last year. Indeed, it's apparent he's been working out, lifting weights as part of his path to full CliffyB-dom. He's chugging on a bottle of beer, eyes on a poker table across the room. At the poker table are a group of guys about his age who also have best-selling games under their belts, guys like Jason Rubin of Naughty Dog, who tend to hang out at industry gatherings, forever getting in touch with one another through tiny cell phones. Each has Ferraris, Porsches, or Ducatti motorcycles waiting for them back home. Cliffy himself recently bought a $100,000 2002 Viper, and he drives it around North Carolina, where Epic is based, thinking that surely he is the coolest guy in town.

Still, next to these guys, he feels like the little brother, the tagalong, as they swap stories of bagging PR women in their hotel rooms and partying till dawn at Las Vegas strip clubs. How can you be a sexy rock-star game developer when you've been married to your high school sweetheart since you were twenty-five? Likewise, Cliffy claims he's never taken an illegal substance in his life, although he does drop the occasional comment about "fatties" to keep people off his trail. Like the savviest of marketers, Cliffy knows that image trumps reality every time.

In reality, this party really isn't his thing. He'd far rather be down in the Fairmont lobby, buying drinks for the lower-level programmers from Epic, guys who aren't welcome at Alan Yu's party, but around whom he feels genuinely comfortable. But if he did that, people might get the wrong idea—think *he* wasn't welcome. So he's staying, legs planted firmly, teeth set like a pit bull's, holding his ground in this little corner.

There aren't supposed to be any working press at Alan's party, but by three a.m., their presence is undeniable. One cable TV host is staggering drunkenly around the edges of the poker table, much to the players' annoyance. It's a touchy subject, because last year P. J. Huffstutter, a reporter for the *L.A. Times,* filed a story that included a scene from the Fairmont Suite party that had Lorne Lanning passing a pipe filled with marijuana to the Xbox's Ed Fries.

It's an understatement to say that these guys are touchy about their reputations. The games they've created have been denounced for violent content, and they've been vilified in virtually every newspaper, magazine, and living room in the country, criticized for their marketing practices and held up as a symbol of everything that is wrong with modern society.

So it is no wonder that being pegged as a group of potheads frightened them. Yet it was a stance that drove Montreal game journalist J. F. William to curse in both French and English. William is fortyish, and he can be found stalking industry gatherings dressed all in black, including black sunglasses and a black hat that hangs over long black hair and is held in place by a black cord cinched under his chin. "They need MORE of a rock 'n' roll attitude," he says, or, actually, shouts. "They should have thanked that reporter! Kowtowing to claims of bad behavior!? Do you know what the response to these things should be? These people should say, 'Fuck you! Here we are, we rule, and, and, and—FUCK YOU!' "

**IT'S ONE YEAR LATER,** February 2003, and CliffyB is pulling on a stogie at a bar in the Hard Rock Hotel and Casino in Las Vegas. He's handing the cigar to any girl who wants to take a puff, and he's putting an arm around anyone who gets close enough. He's surrounded by media, mostly guys from G4, a new cable TV station devoted entirely to videogames. They want to provide him with a limousine and follow him around as he paints the town. Portrait of gamemaker as rock star is the idea, and Cliffy is only too happy to oblige.

Cliffy's look for 2003 is grunged-out rocker—dyed red hair made sticky by hair product, raggedy fake-fur-trimmed coat that hangs almost to his knees, and orange-tinted sunglasses. Bicep muscles show beneath his T-shirt, his skin is now flawless, and his eyes shine with enthusiasm.

It's the first night of the Academy of Interactive Arts and Science's (AIAS) third annual industry summit. As the dawn of this new era has brightened into full daylight, the industry is beginning to take on all the trappings associated with the entertainment business. The AIAS wants its summit—called DICE in this acronym-happy world—to be like the Game Developers Conference, but it aims to cater only to the uppermost echelons of the business. Instead of ten or so thousand attendees, DICE is host to a couple of hundred. It's even started its own awards show, in a competitive move that has Alan Yu less than pleased. As CliffyB holds court at the bar, the honchos of the industry, from publishing bigwigs to top-league developers, are flying in from around the world to attend seminars, receive awards, schmooze, and give fifteen-minute interviews in press suites.

Cliffy makes his way around to the other side of the bar to join Ed Fries, one of few men who can actually green-light projects for Microsoft's Xbox. Cliffy's latest game, *Unreal Tournament 2003,* has finally come out, selling nearly one million copies worldwide.

Ed Fries is older and far more mellow in character than Cliffy. In fact, his life as a videogame bigwig is a second career. After more than a decade with Microsoft as a programmer and project manager, Ed could easily have retired. But when the Xbox project came up, he couldn't resist. Ed may favor polo shirts over fake fur and prefer writing poetry to collecting fancy cars, but he loves videogames with the same enthusiasm as Cliffy.

"Videogames are already an alternate place to live," Ed says. "People live alternative lives in these worlds. They become their characters. That's already happening—the rest is just technology. The rest is just how real will it look? Will I stare at a screen? Wear something around my head? Goggles that are really high-resolution monitors? What's state-of-the-art in movies today should be possible in games thirty years from now—worst-case scenario. And the best-case scenario is a whole lot better than that."

Like Cliffy, of whom he's fond, Ed turns a deaf ear to the controversy that has swirled around videogames since people first claimed in the 1990s that Nintendo was stealing the minds of their children. Ed talks about making players feel free, which, he says, "is what videogames are all about." According to Ed, videogames are about having experiences that aren't, or don't feel, earthbound. The fact that people pay about fifty bucks a pop for each shot of freedom—not including the hundreds spent on hardware and peripherals to enhance the experience—doesn't come up too often.

As Cliffy taps Ed on the shoulder, he's bouncing on his toes, an arm half around—and half holding back—a drunk and giggling PR woman. His eyes glint through his orange shades.

"Going to make me the *Halo* of the Xbox 2," Cliffy says, newly expanded chest puffed out to full size. It's an audacious claim. *Halo* is the Xbox's biggest hit, the console's premier title since its release—and it's thought by many to be one of the best videogames ever made. But Cliffy is riding high, too. Not only has *Unreal Tournament 2003* met with resounding success, but also CliffyB has finally emerged as a full-fledged living character. His Web site has been redone by a professional Web designer, the bunny-suit picture exchanged for one of him in a white wife-beater looking knowingly into the camera. He's been featured in *Men's Journal* and *Entertainment Weekly,* looking, to quote Cliffy himself, *"gooood."* And Epic has hired a programmer to head a subsidiary that will continue to spin out *Unreal* titles—leaving CliffyB free, at last, to work on that World War II outer-space epic of which he's been dreaming. If Ed will take it as the premier game for the Xbox 2, Cliffy will switch from PC gamer to console-lover faster than he can change his hair color.

"I might give you that chance," Ed says. And then, to an eavesdropping reporter: "You didn't hear this."

Ed sounds cool, faintly bemused, but then he smiles. Cliffy lets out a celebratory whoop.

The next day, in a hallway overlooking the Hard Rock's complex of faux cascading waterfalls and chemically induced aqua-blue pools, a few hundred men and a handful of women are mingling in between DICE seminars. Cliffy is wearing a black Kangol bucket hat low over his forehead so that he has to tilt his neck back and look down the bridge of his nose in order to see.

Just arriving from Austin, Texas, are industry veterans Raph Koster and Rich Vogel, the maestros of videogame virtual reality. "Virtual reality is just what people call technology they haven't mastered yet," says Rich, who is white as porcelain and has pointy ears like a Vulcan. Raph is a short, plump man with thick glasses and the kind of supercilious smirk sometimes adopted by people who got their asses kicked a lot when they were kids. Will Wright is smoking outside on the Hard Rock's sidewalk, as Raph and Rich pass through. Will's company, Maxis, has just released a massively multiplayer version of *The Sims* called *The Sims Online,* which launched to unprecedented mainstream media coverage, including *Newsweek* and the *New York Times Magazine.* Will's going to be speaking on a panel about massively multiplayer games with Raph and Rich, but he'd much rather talk about a new game he's been working on, which, he says, is a simulation of "all of life."

Seamus Blackley is standing by the glass doors of the Hard Rock accompanied by his brand-new baby of one year and his wife of eight months, Vanessa "Van" Burnham, a former game journalist. Seamus left Microsoft, turning his back on the Xbox shortly after last year's party in the Fairmont Suite, and he's full of fire about starting a new development company to make games the *right* way. Alan Yu admires the baby. Cliffy comes by to say, "Wow, no way," and ruminate as to whether he'll ever be ready to be a father.

It's still early, and people are drinking miniature Cokes and coffee out of little plastic cups with handles. Although most of the action at DICE takes place in the hallways, nearly everyone crowds into the auditorium to hear Yu Suzuki and the reclusive Shigeru Miyamoto talk about their lives as videogame makers. While dogging Nintendo has become an indoor sport for industry folk in recent years, no one ever says a bad word about Miyamoto-san. Bad-mouthing Miyamoto-san would be like saying Homer didn't know how to tell a good story. You just wouldn't do it.

Colonel Casey Wardynski from West Point shows up, accompanied by Mike Zyda, his academic partner on the first-person shooter cum military recruitment tool, *The Official U.S. Army Game: America's Army*. Wardynski and Zyda are here to give a presentation called "Weapons of Mass Distraction—America's Army Recruits for the Real War." All of the game's stunning 3-D graphics are driven by a proprietary engine originally created by Epic Games to power the *Unreal* franchise. Doug Lowenstein, seated in the front row, gets up to tell an anecdote about the bust-up of a Brazilian crime syndicate that had bootlegged the game for training purposes of its own. He gets a good laugh.

At eight p.m., all the gamemakers pour into one of the Hard Rock's bigger venues, the Joint. Big cameras scan the room, and microphones sweep overhead. The place is packed. Free dinner. Open bar. Word has been passing mouth to mouth to "dress as if you were going to a club." The Academy of Interactive Arts and Sciences has been trying to get the show televised since DICE's inception. Now, thanks to the new videogame cable channel G4—as desperate for material as the AIAS is for coverage—the wish has been granted.

Not only is G4 there, along with the usual barrage of industry press, but also in attendance is a reporter from *Entertainment Weekly* who has finally convinced his superiors that videogames are worth covering. There's even a crew from PBS doing a documentary on the life of game developers. All the PR people from all the companies are pleased, as are the presenters and potential award recipients. Even the few plebes in the audience are psyched—nothing creates excitement in a crowd like being recorded.

Backstage, the green room is filled with platters of vegetables, dips, cookies, third-tier actors, and extreme-sports heroes. Tony Hawk is politely talking into the tape recorder of the *Entertainment Weekly* reporter while his Activision PR girl shifts her weight on kitten heels and looks bored. Actresses with recurring roles on the FX Network and WB shows are plumping their cleavage and exchanging secrets on maintaining skin tones. Much to the delight of the videogame makers, Nina Kaczorowski, who boasts a small role in *Austin Powers in Goldmember,* is wearing a red dress that is slashed in the front down to her navel and completely bare in the back. ("Yeah, I threw in a few babes," Josh, the event's talent coordinator, says modestly.)

By some act of God, CliffyB gets to present with Ms. Kaczorowski. He saunters onto the stage, grinning widely, her hand on his arm. When they reach the podium, Cliffy can't help himself. He starts cracking up, laughing uncontrollably at his proximity to the starlet. Then he and the rest of the audience together just start clapping and clapping and clapping.

Blue Man Group is there, too, running around the back halls, wearing their trademark intensely blue face paint. Cliffy complains they're freaking him out. Miyamoto-san, who is presenting an award, is being rushed back and forth, down the narrow hallways, with his usual swarm of interpreter, assistant, and PR women. Vince Neil of Mötley Crüe is there to present an award. He's dressed in a shiny gray suit, and his trademark scraggly blond hair is still scraggly and blond, though his face has wizened. A newly hired G4 anchorperson is being positioned on a balcony overlooking the stage to give his blow-by-blow commentary. Ed Fries is standing around backstage looking awkward and embarrassed. Will Wright, who wins for best massively multiplayer online game for *The Sims Online*—for which he didn't know he was nominated—is being rushed down a back staircase to accept his award. "I really don't deserve this," he is saying on the way to the stage. On the elevator down, Mrs. Vince Neil assures her husband his teeth looked "incredibly white" from the audience.

After the show, everyone—all the presenters and PR people and everybody else in proximity—gather in a tiny room with no ventilation to puff on expensive cigars and drink out of plastic cups. Dave Foley of *Kids in the Hall* and *News Radio,* who was the MC for the night, is walking around the room, his tie undone, announcing "Let the drinking begin!" The industry folk ogle the so-called celebrities, and the celebrities rejoice in being treated like actual stars for the evening. Then a group led by industry veteran Brian Fargo, an old-timer dressed in a Hawaiian print shirt, and Naughty Dog's Jason Rubin pile into taxis and head over to the Bellagio, to an exclusive club called Light.

Of course CliffyB is part of the posse, wearing his Kangol hat and a wife-beater undershirt like the one from his Web site photo, which shows off his newly developed biceps. "She's actually a really nice girl," he says of Ms. Kaczorowski. "She has kids, too! Can you imagine, with that bod?"

The group strides through the Bellagio, with its yellow-and-blue French Riviera–themed casino, and into the dark red mouth of Light. They take an escalator circled with mirrors and rise up, emerging into the club. Cliffy's got his hat pulled down low, his head tilted back, and he seems to be getting friendly with a thin young woman, an industry producer. Brian Fargo ushers everyone into a semi-enclosed plush red banquette and begins ordering $350 bottles of vodka and any fruit juice or mixer that anyone can shout out. A diminutive English fellow named Kos, dressed in a crisp white shirt and sporting a black pompadour, shimmies on the dance floor—clearly delighted to be acting as Hollywood action hero Vin Diesel's personal emissary to the world of videogames.

Cliffy joins Kos on the dance floor. He grinds hips with the young woman, who is now wearing his hat. From the outside, it seems time for an intervention. But in reality, Cliffy is getting that feeling he still sometimes gets: just when he should be feeling like the biggest kid on the block, he feels like the smallest. Surely this should be the peak of his CliffyB-dom so far—his stars obviously aligned by the selection of Kaczorowski as his presentation partner, not to mention the nod from Ed Fries. Surely none of those gas-station-working, Coke-pouring tormenters of his youth have ever had a weekend like this.

Yet it feels nightmarish here on the flashing, noisy dance floor. Cliffy clearly wants to stay. He wants to experience his own apex. But it's the culmination of so many years of dreaming that Cliffy can't quite shake the feeling that he's still asleep. He mentions that it feels kind of like being a zombie.

Finally Cliffy splits, leaving his hat with his dance partner—he doesn't even want it back the next day—and heads down the escalator, and back out onto the Bellagio casino floor. The eternally shining casino lights are bright, the music is blaring, the machines are clinking, and the players are throwing money down on the tables. Alone, Cliffy catches a taxi and is in bed by two a.m. In the morning, he's not sure what was the dream and what was the waking.

Subsequently, Cliffy will tell only a few people that he didn't actually have a good time at the Bellagio. In fact, the whole night will eventually be transformed, assuming the place of treasured memory in his mind. It was, after all, the culmination of all his dreams: acclaim, glamour, wealth, girls, muscles, publicity, good skin. If only he could escape the queasy feeling of being trapped on the edge of a dream state.

And so the videogame industry moves forward.

# 2

## In the Beginning

It was a chain-smoking, Coke-bottle-glasses-wearing nuclear-physicist named William A. Higinbotham who first introduced an unsuspecting American public to the videogame. It was the late fall of 1958, and Willy, as everybody called him, was a senior physicist at the Brookhaven National Laboratory, a United States government office in Long Island, New York, founded in 1946 to study nuclear energy.

Willy had earned his scientific stripes at the Massachusetts Institute of Technology, where he was part of the scientific team that developed radar, and then, under J. Robert Oppenheimer, as leader of the electronics division of the Manhattan Project. It was Willy's timing circuits that allowed the first A-bomb to proceed through its final milliseconds to detonation. Till the day he died, Willy talked about how, through a pair of welder's glasses, twenty-four miles from ground zero, he'd watched the first atomic bomb explode upon the earth.

Decades later, he still recalled the silence in the truck on the way back to the project's desert compound.

In October 1958 Brookhaven was gearing up for its annual open house. Open houses in the past had included posters on the wall that read, "What is nuclear radiation?" and drawings of people hiding behind walls. That October, however, Willy wanted to liven things up. Playing around with an analog computer, an oscilloscope, and an assortment of electromechanical relays—his specialty—Willy devised a game of electronic table tennis. The "net" existed on the oscilloscope's five-inch screen, and the "ball" was a single green blip. Willy attached two boxes with a knob and a button each to the oscilloscope, so that people could control the motion of the ball as it bounced back and forth. They dubbed it *Tennis for Two*.

To Willy's surprise and delight, people lined up to play the thing. They said it was *fun*. Their mouths were agape at the sudden gift of control, at the relationship that sprang into existence between themselves and this machine. True, it was only a little green blip bouncing between two lines on a five-inch screen, but to the children of the first TV generation, controlling the image on the screen in front of them proved to be a wildly satisfying experience. The game was by far the most popular of all the open-house exhibits at Brookhaven. Willy noticed it was particularly popular with teenagers.

After being the hit of two open houses, Willy's invention was dismantled. After all, it didn't serve any practical purpose. In fact, Willy didn't think too much about it again until a reporter called Brookhaven one day in 1983, calling him the "Grandfather of the Videogame." It was David Ahl, editor of *Creative Computing* magazine, who'd also been one of those teenagers in line to play *Tennis for Two* in 1958. He'd never forgotten his first experience with a videogame, and he wanted to write a cover story on its inventor.

At no time, either before he became the "Grandfather of the Videogame" or after, was Willy Higinbotham ever in his life interested in videogames. Although he had to submit his 1958 schematic several decades later for a lawsuit between two videogame makers arguing over which one of *them* had invented the videogame, Willy never took his invention seriously. When his grandchildren began to challenge him to duels on their Nintendo machines, Willy maintained that he would far rather play his accordion.

Willy also never made a dime off videogames. Although he patented at least twenty electronic circuit breakthroughs, he never patented his videogame. "It wasn't something the government was interested in," he said. In fact, he'd point out, the videogame industry is lucky he didn't patent it, because it would have been a very different videogame future if there were a patent out there belonging to the U.S. government. And then he'd laugh. Videogames really meant very little to him. This was a man, after all, who had helped found the prestigious nuclear nonproliferation group, the Federation of American Scientists, and served as its first chairman and executive secretary. The group still exists, operating out of a building in Washington, D.C., called Higinbotham Hall. Videogames were not what Willy wanted to be remembered for. In fact, when, after his death, requests to Brookhaven for information on the "Grandfather of the Videogame" increased, his son wrote a note to the public relations department. "It is imperative," William Higinbotham II wrote, "that you include information on his nuclear nonproliferation work. That was what he wanted to be remembered for."

But a legacy is a hard thing to control. After all, videogames grew out of the same culture that produced the atom bomb, the Apollo, and the Allied code-breaking system of World War II. No one saw that coming.

**THAT SAME FALL** of 1958, a chubby twenty-one-year-old with a buzz cut and a prominent overbite named Steve Russell was getting settled into his new digs in Cambridge, Massachusetts. Russell, or "Slug," as his friends knew him, had just dropped out of Dartmouth College, a few credits shy of a bachelor's degree, to follow his favorite professor, John McCarthy, to MIT. McCarthy was to help found MIT's artificial intelligence lab with mathematics professor Marvin Minsky, and Russell was to be his technician. The lab was going to examine the intelligence possibilities of computers, machines so rare that even MIT, which sat at the apex of artificial intelligence research in the late 1950s, had completed building its first one only six years earlier. In fact, the completion of the machine, the Whirlwind, had landed MIT on national TV.

Like Higinbotham, Russell was intensely curious. He liked to know how things worked. He'd been poking and prodding at outlets, taking apart radios, and building model railroads that put other enthusiasts to shame for as long as he could remember. But unlike Higinbotham, Russell came of age at the same time as the computer. Coming of age at the same time as the computer was like being born in the Promised Land. Here, at last, was a tool to answer questions that no amount of human poking and prodding would ever reveal. The increased speed and ease of problem-solving brought on by the mechanization of calculations was an obvious advantage for any society. Mankind had been working on it for thousands of years before Russell found his way to MIT.

The abacus, named after the Greek word *abax,* meaning

"tablet," is often referred to as the earliest precursor of the computer, and its origins can be traced back to 500 B.C. The abacus allowed merchants and accountants to add, subtract, multiply, and divide easily and swiftly. It changed the nature of business transactions and increased their complexity. In the mid-1600s, natural philosophers of the Royal Academy (the word *scientist* had yet to come into play) began speculating on the possibility of a mechanical calculating machine. And in 1834, London scientist and mathematician Charles Babbage wanted his "Difference Engine"—never completed but an important first attempt to build a general-purpose computer—to do for mathematical calculations what steam had done for manual labor.

By the time Russell got to MIT in the late 1950s, the work done by the wave of pokers and prodders before him—Willy Higinbotham's generation—had invented things like cathode-ray tubes, vacuum tubes, and point-contact transistors, allowing the advent of real and practical computers, advanced enough to be superbly helpful for wartime activities such as calculating ballistic tables, as well as for general government purposes like doing the census. The notion of a computer for personal use—a PC—was not on the minds of even the most forward-thinking technology evangelists. Computers were serious things for serious business. But they were on the verge of becoming perfect toys for people like Russell.

Russell spent his days working under Professor McCarthy on an IBM 704, or "The Hulking Giant," as it was known. The Hulking Giant had cost MIT several million dollars, was housed in a room especially designed for it, and required a custom air-conditioning unit so that its rows of glowing vacuum tubes would not overheat and cause the machine to melt. Russell helped write the first version of FORTRAN on the

Hulking Giant. But Russell's evenings and weekends were spent in a lower-tech environment, albeit one that would ultimately be as important to the future of computers as the Hulking Giant. Russell joined MIT's world-renowned Tech Model Railroad Club, and it's where he found his brethren.

TMRC headquarters were housed in MIT's legendary Building 20, or the Plywood Palace, as it was known to inhabitants. A three-story shack of a place, designed in one afternoon and built in seven months, Building 20 was a wartime facility erected to house developing military technologies. It was home to the Lab for Nuclear Science, the Office of Naval Research, and the Guided Missiles Program. It's where Willy Higinbotham had toiled in "Rad Lab," developing radar. Because it was intended for scientific use, Building 20 was sturdy. Its floors could support 150 pounds of weight per square foot. Because it was only meant to be used temporarily, it was never finished but remained full of exposed ductwork and drooping electrical wires until the day it was finally torn down in 1998. But it was its very lack of style that allowed Building 20's residents to foster the air of intellectual camaraderie and free-flowing experimentation for which it became known. "You might regard it as the womb of the institute," said one MIT professor. "It is kind of messy, but by God it is procreative!" By the time Russell found his way to Building 20 in 1958, it had become a hodgepodge of experimental sciences, student groups for which no other home could be found, and burgeoning new academic disciplines, like a young Noam Chomsky's linguistics department. The Tech Model Railroad Club wouldn't have been the same anywhere else.

Headquarters consisted primarily of a patched-together table in the center of the room topped with a complex layout of model railroad tracks. Nickel-plated HO-gauge trains zoomed through hand-built tunnels and careened alongside papier-mâché mountains. The walls of the room were covered with poster-size maps of the railroad's operating system, which itself hung under the table—an elaborate tangle of wires, switches, and relays as massive as the railroad layout itself.

TMRC members were divided into two groups. There were those who cared about what sat atop the giant table, and there were those whose passions were set aflame by what lay beneath. Russell was of the latter group, a posse of six or seven men in their late teens and early twenties, who all had one thing in common: the tendency to care less about a thing itself, and more about how that thing worked. They sprang directly from the generation of scientists such as Higinbotham who had earned their chops on huge wartime-necessitated advances. Russell and his friends were the next generation of technical savants. They were the very first *hackers,* the originators of computer culture. In fact, it was Peter Samson, one of the group's leaders, who coined the term *hacker* in a dictionary of TMRC-speak the members put together. Out of the culture they were founding would grow everything from the PC to smart bombs to DNA sequencing to videogames.

And in their hacker-speak, as recorded by Samson at the time, can be found a new set of ethics that would come to define a generation. The ethics of the TMRC reflected as drastic a shift away from Higinbotham's generation as one could imagine. The hacker ethic, as summed up by Steven Levy in his 1984 book *Hackers,* went as follows:

1) All information should be free
2) Mistrust Authority—Promote Decentralization
3) Hackers should be judged by their hacking, not bogus criteria such as degrees, age, race, or position

4) Access to computers—and anything which might teach you something about the way the world works—should be unlimited and total. Always yield to the Hands-On Imperative!

The "Hands-On Imperative" was the belief that in the taking apart and putting back together of things, in the discovery of how things worked, lay the truth of the universe. Nothing was more important than getting to this truth. The group patrolled junk shops during the day, and at night roamed the MIT halls "liberating" things like plug boards, phone dials, crossbar executors, and phone company relays. They were obsessed with the phone system, the biggest and most complicated network system of its day. They took locksmith classes so that locked doors at MIT were reduced to distractions. They crawled up through ceilings into the otherworldly infrastructure of Building 20 so they could drop down into vacant professors' offices to "borrow" tools and other supplies. Pete Samson earned the undying respect of his comrades with a nighttime raid on an unguarded IBM 407 electromechanical keypunch machine on which he programmed the club's entire railroad switching system. Russell had walked into a culture of freethinking, future-obsessed, truth-seeking über-tinkerers, unknowingly biding their time until the arrival of a computer that would let them take the "Hands-On Imperative" to a whole new level. That machine was the PDP-1, the world's first minicomputer, and it arrived at MIT in the fall of 1961.

Until then, Russell and his friends had been spending a lot of time with the TX-0, a $3 million computer on loan from Lincoln Labs to professor Jack Dennis. Although the TX-0 still required fifteen tons of air-conditioning equipment to keep it cool, it did not require a specially constructed building or a large staff to run it. It was one of the first transistor computers in the world, and the very first general-purpose computer. The Hulking Giant had required operators to interact with the machine, technicians to keep it running, and programmers to ask it questions. "It wasn't very interactive," Russell said, dryly.

The TX-0 came in an L-shaped console at which three people could sit and work. And, most important to the members of the TMRC, the TX-0 cut out some of the middlemen. Rather than being fed stacks of cards prepared in some far-off classroom and handed to an operator dressed in a white coat, the TX-0 could be accessed by first punching a program into something called a Flexowriter, and then running that work into the TX-0 through a reader. It was the closest to direct interaction with a computer any of the TMRC members had experienced. They hung around the lab that housed the TX-0 all day and all night. Graduate students, who actually had authorized time on the machine, began to complain. No doubt, this was in part because members of the TMRC would lurk in the background, snickering at the students' lack of programming chops. One unofficial TMRC member—a twelve-year-old son of an MIT professor—would infuriate the graduate students by pointing out what they were doing wrong and would then get into their chairs when they got up in frustration, solving their problems while they were in the bathroom or getting a drink of water. TMRC members kept a man posted by the doorway of the TX-0 lab twenty-four hours a day in case anyone actually scheduled for use didn't show.

The arrival of the PDP-1 in fall of 1961 moved them to the next level. The PDP-1 cut out all the middlemen. It cost $120,000 and was half the size of the TX-0. All of its transistors, wires, and boards fit in a cabinet the size of three refrigerators put back to back. There was a bright display screen and a keyboard hooked directly to it. There was no more need for operators or technicians. It was a machine with which a person could actually develop a relationship. With the PDP-1, it was just Russell and the machine, face to screen.

Of course the first question on everybody's mind was, "What should we do with it?" By mistaking a *Y* character for a *Y′* in a program he was writing, Marvin Minsky had discovered early on that the PDP-1 could draw circles. He'd then written a program that made three circles bounce against one another, creating weird swirling shapes. The Minskytron, as the TMRC members dubbed it, mesmerized them. That "You can create art and beauty on a computer," was, after all part of the hacker ethic. But Russell felt the Minskytron got boring after a while. Like cowboys faced with a wild new colt, the TMRC guys wanted to put the PDP-1 through its paces, to see what it was made of, so to speak. They wanted the hack *they* were going to do to push the PDP-1 to its limits. The PDP-1 was an eighteen-bit machine, and they wanted to use every inch of its power and memory. And they wanted to give onlookers an interesting and pleasurable experience. "In short," concluded Russell's roommate, J. Martin "Shag" Graetz, "it should be a game."

The hackers wanted to have fun on the computer. As children of World War II, Russell and his friends sought neither world domination nor a home in the suburbs. What they wanted was to use the computer to extend their intellectual capacity in the same way the car had extended their parents' physical abilities. Their parents found the promise of freedom behind the wheel of a car. The TMRC chose mind expansion behind the keyboard of a computer. They considered themselves pioneers of a bright new future where artificial intelligence would be their spade and shovel for unearthing the mysteries of the universe. Yet, they were studiously whimsical in their work. They wrote programs that changed Arabic numbers to Roman numerals, and one that made the machine play Bach. Both were tremendous feats of programming. Both were utterly insignificant to the future of warfare or running a government. And that was the point. It was the ability to do the hack itself that offered the promise of freedom, not a larger purpose attached to it.

By the time the PDP-1 arrived, Russell was well settled into his Cambridge life. He was living in a bug-infested apartment at 8 Hingham Street, with a couple of other techs from MIT and Harvard's statistical laboratory. Besides artificial intelligence and model railroads, obsessions around Hingham Street included science fiction, folk music, comic books, and Japanese monster movies.

It somehow fell to Russell to be the guy to actually do the PDP-1 hack. As he watched the Minskytron, Russell found himself thinking about the two science-fiction series on which his roommates and he were currently bingeing: *Lensman* and *Skylark,* by E. E. "Doc" Smith (a food engineer by trade, whose main claim to fame was having invented powdered sugar that adheres to doughnuts). Smith's stories thrilled the future-oriented imaginations of Russell and his friends with their epic space battles and campy, larger-than-life heroes. As he watched the Minskytron, Russell thought about "Doc" Smith and about how many times his roommates and he had fantasized about creating space operas of their own. And then he had an idea for a game called *Spacewar!* It would be a science-fiction battle fought between rockets in outer space. When the rest of the TMRC heard about his idea, they were all over him to do it.

The rules were simple: two spaceships, each controlled by a set of console switches, a limited supply of rocket fuel, and the ability to fire "torpedoes" at one another. By January 1962 Russell had come up with two white dots that could be maneuvered around the PDP-1's big round display screen, accelerating and shifting, depending on the operator's whim. By February, the white dots had morphed into two rocket ships, one long and thin like a Redstone rocket and the other short and curvy like a 1930s Buck Rogers spaceship. With a command to the computer, a white dot of a torpedo would shoot from the tip of one ship, and, if it landed in the same place on the computer screen as the other ship, a cascade of white dots would appear, symbolizing that an explosion had occurred. "It really was object-oriented design," Russell said, "but I didn't know it at the time because that vocabulary hadn't been invented yet."

Controls included acceleration, rapid turning, and firing torpedoes. Russell added a few points of light to represent a starry sky. All told, it took him about two hundred hours to program the first version of the game. And when he was finished, he did what hackers always did when they finished a hack: he dropped it into the drawer beside the PDP-1 console, leaving it there for anyone to use at any time, and to improve upon as they saw fit. (Keeping information to oneself—let alone profiting off it!—went directly against the hacker ethic.)

And indeed they saw fit. In fact, *Spacewar!* is probably one of the most well-tested games in videogame history. Pete Samson was offended by the randomness of Russell's star placement. So he added a hack of his own to the game that encoded the entire night sky, including each star and constellation at approximately their actual brightness in relation to one another. Dan Edwards, another tech in the artificial intelligence lab, was offended by the lack of gravity in the game. He fixed the problem by reducing the amount of computations the machine had to make to figure the outlines of Russell's spaceships, which freed up enough computing power to add the dimension of gravity. This allowed for a "sun" in the center of the screen with a gravitational pull over the little ships. Russell's roommate, Shag, thought there ought to be a means of escape, so he added "hyperspace," which allowed players to flee into the "fourth dimension" and then reappear in a different part of the screen. And everyone agreed that Russell's attempt to build in the real-life faults of real-life rockets—like random changes in velocity—had to go. Wasn't that the whole point of computers? To be able to do things better than had been done in real life?

In May 1962 Russell added a scoring system, and the game—all two thousand lines of code—was ready for debut at MIT's Science Open House Day.

For months, the TMRC guys had been experiencing what those who lined up to play Higinbotham's *Tennis for Two* learned—that there was something immensely satisfying about an interactive electronic game. Considering that most people in America had never even seen a computer in 1962, to actually be able to play with one—to control the visual representation on the screen—left them speechless. It also left them with sore elbows from leaning on the PDP-1 console for so long. On the day of the open house, people stood around watching as the spaceships whirled across the monitor screen, firing torpedoes at one another, sailing past the Big Dipper or Orion's Belt, disappearing into hyperspace and then flashing back onto the screen, flying around the sun and using the gravitational force to pick up or reduce speed. The game got so much play that the controls, built with parts from Bell Systems meant to last a lifetime, needed to be replaced within a year.

Digital Equipment Corporation, which made the PDP-1—and had been incubated in Building 20 before taking off as its own company—was so impressed with *Spacewar!* that executives decided to ship a version of the game with each of the fifty PDP-1s they sold. It was how DEC showed clients what a powerful machine they had just bought.

Russell and his friends debated briefly whether they ought to do something with *Spacewar!* In a single conversation they decided that only computer fans would be interested in it. And in 1962, that was a limited market, to say the least. The Altair, the definitive build-it-yourself computer that helped inspire the likes of Steve Jobs and Bill Gates, was still a good decade away. People who were interested in computers were well contained within the military, government, or academia. Even the earliest corporate adopters were just beginning to buy or rent space on IBM mainframes. And even if Russell and his friends had foreseen the public appetite for videogames, their ethos held that the flow of information should be free and unlimited. Besides, how exactly was one supposed to turn a profit on something that might cost a quarter to play, but took a $120,000 machine to play it on? It didn't take a mathematician from MIT to see that that would never work.

Enter Nolan Bushnell.

**LIKE A DOG** with the bite to back up its bark, Nolan Bushnell is one of those people born with an oversized personality, and more than enough chutzpah to carry him anywhere that personality might take him. Born in 1943 to Mormon parents in Clearfield, Utah, Nolan was of the same generation as Russell and his friends. And while they shared the obsession for the taking apart and putting back together of such things as washing machines and radios, Nolan's ethos could not have been more different than that of the TMRC. Russell and his friends were scientists, inventors in the best tradition of American innovation; Nolan was that other great American personality, the entrepreneur. He would push the genius of *Spacewar!* into the culture in the only way that really works in America, by making it financially viable.

Stories of Nolan's audacity begin in his childhood and continue unabated to this day. He was a champion debater and studied philosophy in his free time. There was the time he convinced his next-door neighbor that UFOs existed by attaching a string of Christmas lights to a kite and flying it over the house while he knelt on his roof. There were his days on the chess tournament circuit, when he'd take copious notes after each bad move and hardly any at all after each good one, in direct contrast to the way chess players were taught, a tactic he was convinced won him as many matches as any genius he may have had for the game. "Putting a spoke in the wheels of my competition has always been part of my philosophy," Nolan said.

Nolan hit six feet four inches by the time he was fifteen. That same year, his father, a cement contractor, died. Where other boys might have merely mourned, Nolan went to all of his father's clients and insisted on finishing any uncompleted projects himself. When the time came to go to college, Nolan headed off to the University of Utah to study electrical engineering. It was 1962, just a few years after Russell had begun his career at MIT.

Nolan's penchant for making money showed itself immediately. He put together a calendar of local events and sold ad space in it to local businesses. He built a printing press that rolled out the best fake IDs on campus. (In order to avoid trouble with the authorities, he pretended he was only the middleman for a never-seen, behind-the-curtains mastermind.) With the natural gambler's tolerance for risk, he put his entire year's tuition money into the pot of a poker game the summer after his sophomore year. When he lost, he handled it with equal aplomb, taking a job at the local amusement park, a place called Lagoon, just north of Salt Lake City.

Nolan's job was to operate the ball toss. As usual, he had a strategy: he initially stacked his prop milk bottles so that even the weakest throwers could knock them down. And then, as the dry Utah air breezed over the midway, he collected quarters all night long from unsuspecting young men, lured to his booth by the prospect of easy winnings. Nolan was great on the midway. He'd found his calling in the art of huckstering.

In the early 1960s the University of Utah was one of three premier schools in the country for the burgeoning field of computer science. Graduates after Nolan would include Netscape founder Jim Clark; Ed Catmull, president of Pixar Animation Studios; and John Warnock, cofounder of Adobe Systems. Along with MIT and Stanford, the University of Utah was one of a handful of institutions in 1962 to buy the leading-edge new computer of the day: the PDP-1. And the program that seemed to be running on it more than any other when Nolan first meandered into the computer lab was a game called *Spacewar!* Nolan fell for it harder than one of his midway patsies. He played and played and played. Because time on the computer was mostly available between the hours of two and six a.m., he stopped sleeping, and his class attendance declined significantly. "Hooked and mesmerized" were the words he used to describe his reaction. "I was obsessed," Nolan said, "I mean truly obsessed." My God, he thought, if this were on the midway, I could make a fortune.

Nolan was not a hacker. He was an entrepreneur, and an entrepreneur's natural passion arises not from unraveling a bit of mystery from the universe, but from taking the results of that unraveling and creating customers for it. Sometimes the same person does both, but a quick perusal of America's greatest entrepreneurs—a list on which Nolan Bushnell often figures—shows that more often than not, the man who brings a new invention to the public is not the same man who invented it. William Higinbotham and Steve Russell liked to build things. So did Nolan. Only what Nolan liked to build was not a computer model of the galaxy but rather an economic model of how to profit from that galaxy. How can I sell this? was the question that haunted Nolan.

There are many claimants for the title of "father of the videogame," but Nolan stands alone as the father of the videogame *industry*. In late 1969 Nolan packed up his blue Oldsmobile station wagon and left the Midwest for Northern California—Santa Clara to be exact, the county that would become home to Silicon Valley. Nolan had accepted a position at a company called Ampex, working for $10,000 a year on a high-speed digital type-recording system. The job, with its eight a.m. roll call and day-in, day-out regularity, was not exactly what he'd had in mind. Nolan had a much grander vision for himself—and it was not one that included being out of the house each day by seven a.m. Besides, *Spacewar!* had gotten under his skin.

Just as the Tech Model Railroad Club members were unable to rest until they had mastered the telephone system, hacking their way to the best railway switching system ever devised, Nolan couldn't stop thinking about how to manufacture something like *Spacewar!* inexpensively enough to create a working business. He thought about the midway in Salt Lake

City, and imagined it filled, not with ball tosses and stuffed animals, but with machines that would play computer games. His friends thought he was crazy. But, like his counterparts across the country at MIT, Nolan never worried much what others thought. He knew with the certainty of the genius and the insane that if he could make *Spacewar!* affordable to a mass audience, he'd never have to set his alarm clock again. By 1971 Nolan's two-year-old daughter had been booted out of her bedroom in favor of Nolan's computer game laboratory.

For computers, 1971 was a world away from 1961, when Russell got his first glimpse of the PDP-1. The PDP-1 established the concept of a minicomputer, and ten years later it was apparent that it was a concept with legs. "Smaller and cheaper" had become the mantra. In 1966 a spin-off group from DEC had founded their own company, Data General Corporation, and released an $8,000 machine the size of a small suitcase, called the Nova. In 1968 the Kenbak Corporation started advertising the Kenback-1 in *Scientific American* to a growing group of computer enthusiasts. At $750, with 256 bytes of memory, it was the most successful attempt so far at a "personal" computer. In 1971, when Nolan began tinkering with computer games in earnest, engineers Ted Hoff and Frederico Faggin at another Northern California company, Intel, had just finished work on an invention called the microprocessor. And an IBM team had just introduced the eight-inch floppy diskette to widespread adoration. Power and ease of use were on the way up, and cost was on the way down—fantastic circumstances for a wild-eyed entrepreneur fixated on building the midway of the future.

Nolan quit his job at Ampex, bought a minicomputer from Data General, and began programming a knockoff of *Spacewar!* he called *Computer Space.* The man who'd hired him at Ampex,

Kurt Wallace, predicted in his exit interview that one day he'd be working for Nolan. Despite his former boss's confidence, however, *Computer Space* was a total flop. Much to Nolan's disappointment, the Data General machine just wasn't powerful enough. The spaceships looked bleary around the edges, and their movements were slow and jerky. Also, unless consumers were going to pay twenty-five dollars per play instead of a quarter, it simply wasn't going to make any money. Using an actual computer to build a computer game wasn't going to work. Instead, Nolan built himself a circuit board that was dedicated entirely to running *Computer Space*. "It was the only way to make the math work," Nolan said, "to make it economic." So, he hooked the circuit board up to a black-and-white TV set from Goodwill and gently placed the contraption inside a Plexiglas case. Also in the Plexiglas case was an empty paint-thinner can to catch quarters.

Word spread about his creation, and Nolan's backyard filled up with wireheads, engineers, hackers, programmers, and every other kind of computer savant 1971 Northern California had so far produced. They started coming in the mornings before work to play the game. Nolan made a deal with a local arcade company called Nutting Associates, which agreed to produce 1,500 coin-operated *Computer Space* arcade games and distribute them on its regular pinball machine route. But pioneers are sometimes the guy spread-eagle on the ground with an arrow in the back: 1971 was a little too early for a commercial computer game. Customers found the product, and Nolan's dictionary-sized instruction booklet, completely baffling. Nutting quickly discontinued the product. With the confidence of a born entrepreneur, however, Nolan blamed Nutting for inept marketing and decided to go into business for himself.

On June 27, 1972, Nolan and his new partner, another ex-

Ampex engineer, Ted Dabney, went to the office of the California secretary of state to register their own computer-game company. Their first choice, Syzygy (when three celestial bodies line up in the same plane), was already taken by a candle-making operation in Mendocino, so Nolan and Ted resorted to their backup name, a Japanese word from Nolan's favorite game, Go. Atari, they called it, which means something similar to "check" in chess, but, true to its Japanese roots, is actually a polite warning to one's opponent that he is near capture. Nolan figured naming his company Atari was a good warning to the world at large.

There was something irresistible about Nolan, and he remained a popular figure around the Ampex offices even after he'd left. He would drop by to talk tech shop with folks, knock back beers after work, and "borrow" spare parts. One day he asked Kurt Wallace, the man who'd hired him, to recommend a good engineer for his new venture. Wallace pointed to a burly, twenty-three-year-old former All-State football player named Al Alcorn. Although Al was new to Nolan, Nolan was not new to Al. He mostly remembered Nolan as the man who, before quitting, had convinced a group of Ampex engineers to buy into a stock fund he started but couldn't afford to actually invest in himself.

Over lunch, Nolan told Al that if he joined Atari, he'd be a millionaire before he was thirty. He showed Al the schematics to *Computer Space,* and pitched him on the idea that the future of arcades would not be pinball, but instead games played on TV screens. Al was skeptical. He'd worked his way through high school repairing TV sets in San Francisco's Haight Ashbury, and he explained to Nolan that he'd routinely gotten questions about who was pulling the marionette strings behind the screen. He wasn't at all sure the public was ready.

Nolan waved off his concerns. "We already have a contract with General Electric," he said. He offered Al $1,000 a month and a 10 percent stake in the company. "See that car," Nolan said, pointing to his Oldsmobile. "That's a company car. I don't pay a cent for it. The company, our company, pays for it."

Of course, Nolan was lying through his teeth. There was no GE contract. The Olds was Bushnell's family car. But Al didn't know. It was 1972. The country was still in the grip of the counterculture revolution, which preached that the future was yours for the making. Northern California was exploding with technical advances that made virtually anything seem possible. Al was caught between the absurdity of Nolan's claims and the irrational urge to accept. He'd fought the police in protests against the Vietnam War while he was a student at the University of California at Berkeley; he believed in questioning conventional wisdom. But he was also the first in his family to go to college, and he knew the value of a steady job. Finally, the wild desire to take a chance flashed brighter than any cautionary quivering his gut could muster. Figuring Ampex would take him back when Nolan's venture tanked, Al accepted and became Atari's third employee.

Nolan was thrilled. He told Al to program a simple game of electronic Ping-Pong to fulfill their nonexistent contract with GE. Earlier in the year Nolan had seen Magnavox debut its new interactive TV console, former defense contractor Ralph Baer's Odyssey, at a trade show in Burlingame. The main feature of that machine was a game of electronic table tennis. Though his signature in Magnavox's sign-in book for the event would later serve as evidence against him in a patent infringement lawsuit, Nolan always maintained he'd had the idea on his own while thinking up possible sports games. Nolan had no real interest in electronic Ping-Pong, however. He was busy figuring out how to generate enough cash flow to see Atari through the reworking of a *Computer Space*–type game.

At this point, Atari had moved out of Nolan's daughter's bedroom and into a one-thousand-square-foot space in a concrete office building at 2962 Scott Boulevard in Santa Clara. Such facilities were popping up all over Northern California in order to house myriad new high technology firms. They were one- and two-story light industrial warehouses, cheaply built structures with roll-up front doors and scant windows, occupied by tenants who tended to go out of business long before their leases were up. Nolan put Al into a back corner with a stack of old TV sets, boxes of parts from Ampex, and a Fireball pinball machine to play with when he needed a break. In the front of the office sat Cynthia Villanueva, Nolan's seventeen-year-old babysitter cum Atari receptionist, who made callers wait for the number of minutes Nolan had calculated would convince the callers they'd reached a legitimate operation with a busy, hard-to-reach CEO.

Actually, Nolan *was* busy. Unable to get a bank loan for his start-up, he'd finagled a pinball coin-op route for Atari in Palo Alto. Atari would buy pinball machines from distributors like Seeberg, Williams, or Rockola, and then place them in local bars, coffee shops, pizza parlors, and student unions. Nolan sent Al, when he wasn't working on his Ping-Pong game, to install, maintain, and pick up the machines, as well as to collect the hundreds of quarters every week that became Atari's cash flow. And then Nolan and Ted Dabney, stuck on the reworking of *Computer Space,* began pushing Al to finish the electronic table tennis.

"We want to hear a crowd of thousands!" Nolan told him.

"And we want boos and hisses when people miss!" Ted enthused. "Wild cheers when they score!"

*But one player's hit is the other player's miss,* Al thought. He decided to ignore them. He poked around in the circuitry already in place for about forty minutes until he found a tone that sounded right to him. It went *pong . . . pong . . . pong.* He tossed aside Nolan's illegible schematics—a haze of blue ink and scrawled lines—and focused instead on his own knowledge of transistor-to-transistor logic. He soon had a prototype up and running. It worked like this: on each side of the screen there were lines representing paddles that Al had broken into segments so that the green square that represented the ball would spin off at different angles depending on where it hit. If the ball hit the center, it flew back at a 180-degree angle. If the ball hit the outer edge of the paddle, it rebounded at a 45-degree angle. Al also made the ball pick up speed as the game progressed; included in the program was a clause that instructed the machine to accelerate the green blip after a certain number of hits. Al ran the game through a $75 Hitachi black-and-white TV he'd bought at Payless. He put the TV inside a wooden cabinet, along with a mass of twisted wires soldered onto small boards. Al wanted the game to be so simple that it wouldn't require instructions, but Nolan insisted that all games had to have instructions. After a trip to the local pinball arcade to prove his point, Al capitulated. On a little card he wrote, "Avoid missing ball for high score." He put in a bread pan for collecting quarters, and taped the instruction card to the front of the case.

In September 1972 Nolan took the handmade machine to a bar called Andy Capp's Tavern in Sunnyvale, one of the nondescript towns of Northern California soon to be metamorphosed into a hotbed of high-tech dealmaking. Nolan had seen *Computer Space* tank after being wildly popular with his wirehead buddies, so this time he wasn't taking any chances.

Andy Capp's was a watering hole with a crowd of college kids and recent graduates, the perfect place to test *Pong*. Nolan put the machine, a three-foot square with a glowing center and two knobs, on a barrel in the back of the bar. The first night it was installed, two regulars approached the machine tentatively. One of them inserted a quarter. They heard a beep. The ball darted back and forth across the screen, racking up points first for one player and then the other. The two men watched the screen, not moving, not sure what to do. Other men at the bar came over, attracted by the unfamiliar *pong* sounds emitted by the strange new contraption. The score was three to three when one of the men tried the knob beneath the screen. It was five to four when he first managed to hit the ball with his paddle. At eight to four, his companion began to get the hang of the game, too. By the end of the night, the first two men had spent $1.75. And every other patron in the bar had given it a whirl, too.

Two weeks later, Al got a call from Bill Gattis, the bar's owner. The machine was broken and he wanted it fixed, pronto. Al hopped on his Triumph 650 motorcycle. He was nervous; the machine was just something he'd jury-rigged. And Nolan was at that very moment in Chicago meeting with Bally and Midway, trying to convince one of them to license the game. By the time Al stepped into the darkness of the bar, his heart was pounding. Although it was still afternoon, the place was smoky and smelled like beer. Al headed straight to the back, Gattis at his side. Kneeling by the machine, Al pulled out a wrench and opened it up. The problem was apparent right away. The bread pan he'd used as a coin collector was jammed with so many quarters that they had overflowed into the rest of the machine, blocking the game from functioning. Al smiled.

"Next time this happens," he told Gattis. "Call me right away. At home. This problem, I can always fix."

When Nolan got back to town, he was met with news of people showing up in the morning, before the bar had even opened, to play *Pong*. Having just finished whipping both Bally and Midway into a frenzy of excitement over the licensing potential of the game, Nolan decided Atari ought to manufacture the game itself. Al and Ted Dabney begged him not to, but he waved them away. This was the magic break he'd been waiting for. Each *Pong* cost less than $400 to make—$100 for the circuit board, $200 for the cabinet, and $75 for the TV—and would sell for $1,200 to $1,300. Nolan established a ninety-day line of credit with parts distributors, and the machines sold for cash, upfront. It would be all cash flow and almost no overhead. Nolan called both Bally and Midway and told each one that the other had backed out. In one year, Atari's revenues, based on *Pong,* shot to more than $1 million. The game became such a cultural phenomenon that Nolan got hundreds of letters from people saying they had met their spouses while playing the game.

Nolan soon moved the entire company to an abandoned roller rink a few blocks away on Martin Avenue. There, on the circular wooden floor where teenagers used to hold hands and skating divas once practiced their twirls, Nolan set up an assembly line with rows of plastic cases, circuitry, and boxes filled with random parts. Some new employees came from an assembly worker recruitment agency, but many were picked up by Nolan and Al from the Santa Clara unemployment office. They were a ragtag team of the lost, the experimental, and the disenfranchised. Tattoos, handlebar mustaches, long hair, and bare feet abounded. There were reports of pot smoke wafting over the assembly line and syringes littering the bathroom floor. Nolan installed a keg of beer in his office and had rock music piped in over loudspeakers. There were heroin-addicted employees who fenced TV sets out of the back of the warehouse, and a circuit manufacturer who ripped them off to the tune of forty thousand integrated circuit parts after convincing them they'd cornered the market. And even as *Pong* became a bona fide craze, only three thousand of the twelve thousand machines on the market that first year actually came from Atari. "The good news for Atari was that *Pong* could be built in a garage shop," Nolan said. "The bad news was that anyone else with a garage shop could build them, too."

Still, while most pinball machines were earning $40 to $50 a week, *Pong* machines were bringing in $200 a week. "A lot of people were cheating us," Al said. "We were naive. But we were making so much money, we could afford to be."

By 1974, with other games following *Pong*, Atari's revenues hit $4 million. And since the company got paid up front for every machine it turned out, Nolan never got stuck with unwanted inventory. Even mistakes like pricing their best-selling game of 1974, *Grandtrack 10,* at $995 when it had cost $1,095 to produce, didn't slow the company down.

Atari became as well known in Silicon Valley for its freewheeling culture as it was for the products they were creating. Russell and his Tech Model Railroad Club cronies had defined the earliest ethos of computer culture. Nolan Bushnell and his gang at Atari were establishing the business culture of the computer. People like Bob Noyce and Gordon Moore from Intel stopped by to see what was going on. Office parties were regular happenings. It wasn't odd to see a skateboarder sliding down the old roller rink's aisles balancing parts on his head. One employee, an unwashed nineteen-year-old fruitarian named Steve Jobs, would work a double shift into the evening so his buddy from Hewlett-Packard, Steve Wozniak, could hang out with him, playing on the machines and working on a little project of their own, the Apple computer. Nolan held board meetings in his hot tub, slapping the water with his hand to pass motions like a gavel on a slab of marble. "Work smart, not hard" was the motto.

In 1975, however, Atari began to suffer, in part from Nolan's wild-man style, but mostly from that inevitable demon of all entrepreneurs: competition. Nolan had thought he could keep the "jackals," as he called his rivals, at bay by "out-thinking" them. Atari engineers used obscure parts when building their games to confuse reverse engineers; Nolan and Al kept one nosey gamemaker off their track by convincing him that holograms were the next big thing (they weren't); and Nolan even had his next-door neighbor, Joe Keenan, start a company called Kee Games in order to create the appearance of competition, while in fact it was always an affiliate of Atari. "This was a company started with $250," Nolan said. "We never had any capital. But we learned that stealth and guile can sometimes work instead."

But for all his bravado and brilliance, Nolan did have some weak spots. Not overly keen on the government or paperwork, for example, he tended to shy away from patenting Atari's inventions. And he was abysmal as an international negotiator. After having given the rights to distribute Steve Jobs's game, *Breakout,* in Japan to Masaya Nakamura's Namco, he then ignored his partner's complaints that the *yakuza*, Japan's black-clad mafia, were counterfeiting the machines. As a result, Nakamura, frustrated and unprotected, started knocking them off himself, a fact Nolan only discovered when a friend went to Japan and mentioned seeing far more *Breakout* machines than Atari had shipped. And Nakamura wasn't the only one. Companies in the United States such as Nutting Associates, Meadow Games, and Ramtek were becoming increasingly good at knocking off Atari games. And in 1975 *Breakout* was so successfully faked by an Italian company that the real version could be distinguished only by the address on the back. The Italian models had Atari's current address, while Atari's own models bore the company's old address.

Fortunately, Nolan hit upon the next big thing, again: selling directly to the consumer. The company's internal slogan, after all, had become Innovative Leisure. Engineer Harold Lee managed to re-create *Pong* on a chip so small and high-performance that it worked in a machine the size of a shoebox that plugged into the TV. The company code-named the project "Darlene," after a particularly voluptuous female employee. When Nolan was presented with "Darlene," later rechristened a more appropriate *Home Pong,* he became so excited he ordered the chips without even stopping to consider a marketing plan. Al tried to reason with him, explaining over and over again that the Valley was not about selling consumer products. Although it sounds funny now, it was accepted wisdom in 1975 that Silicon Valley sold to big computer makers like IBM, Honeywell, and DEC, or to the military, but not directly to consumers. "We're going to be billionaires!" was Nolan's only response. His head was full of the bigness of what they were contemplating. Russell hadn't cared if no one had "played" with a computer before, and Nolan didn't care if no one in the Valley had ever taken on this market before. His mind's eye danced with images of a *Home Pong* in every living room, of the possibilities, the incredible, infinite, phantasmal possibilities that arose once you dared to think not only of catching people at bars while they drank, not only at pizza parlors as they awaited their pies, but at *home*. The sheer audacity of it sent thrills down his spine.

Al reminded Nolan about Magnavox's Odyssey. To say people hadn't gotten it would be an understatement. Magnavox had no idea of the confusion people would have over the very notion of plugging something into their TV sets. They advertised the Odyssey as being used with a Magnavox TV, and found themselves faced with widespread confusion over whether it could be used with other brands. People called up the company wanting to know how Magnavox employees knew to move the ball just exactly as they moved their paddles. All told, the machine sold only 100,000 units in its entire life cycle. It was a haunting story. But again, in the world of entrepreneurs, he who wins is not always he who is first. The Odyssey had been an analog affair, but by the time Nolan was fantasizing about invading the living room, the price of digital boards had dropped so low that Atari could use them to make *Home Pong.* Of course, the failure of the Odyssey to hit it big meant Atari couldn't get the toy industry or the electronics industry interested in their product. Finally Sears Roebuck agreed to carry *Home Pong* in the sporting goods section of its 1975 Christmas catalog.

The news of Atari's *Home Pong* spread far and wide, and once again "the jackals" came out. By 1976 there were at least seventy-five other companies producing home videogame machines. The race of innovation was on. Fairchild Camera and Instrument, which had pioneered transistor technology, came out with a machine called Channel F, which could play multiple games—an innovation from which there has been no going back. And when Baltimore, Maryland–based General Instrument announced a five-dollar microchip, Nolan knew it was an entirely new race being run.

And Al had been right about the consumer market being a tricky business. Thanks to its coin-op division, Atari was floating in quarters every week. In the consumer market, it was another story. Now Nolan had inventory to worry about, not to mention reliability headaches—when you sold directly to another company, they had tech departments to troubleshoot problems; but unhappy consumers simply demanded their money back.

By mid-1976 Atari was facing a money crunch again. Nolan thought he had a hot new product up his sleeve, but he had no money to manufacture or market it. The product was a multigame system—this time code-named "Stella," after an engineer's bicycle—and it was built with a general-purpose microprocessor that could allow Atari to produce it for far less money than the Channel F had cost Fairchild. And it came with a new kind of controlling device: the joystick. If Atari could pull it off, Nolan figured, they'd blow Fairchild, RCA, Colleco, Mattel, Milton Bradley, and all their other competitors out of the water. The new machine was officially named the Video Computer System, or VCS, but it became known by consumers as the Atari 2600.

There comes a time in every entrepreneur's life when a certain question arises: Is it time to sell? This was what Nolan had begun to wonder. He thought selling to a bigger company would provide him with an even larger sandbox in which to play. So when Warner Communications in New York City offered Nolan $28 million for Atari, he decided it was time. He bought himself a yacht he named *Pong,* and a mansion that had belonged to Folgers coffee heir Peter Folger. "Finally, when I tell people I'm a millionaire," Nolan said, "it's true."

As happens so often with entrepreneurs, however, everything changes once there is a boss to whom the former owner of the company must answer. Nolan's dislike of authority rivaled that of the Tech Model Railroad Club's. Even as the Atari 2600, in October of 1977, was introducing the world to its first home computer—albeit one disguised as a game box—Nolan was finding his work life becoming unbearable. The new bosses didn't like for folks to smoke joints at meetings. They thought there should be an agreed-upon time at which employees started their day. They thought Nolan was unreliable, unprofessional, and unpleasant. Within a year, Warner Communications gave him the boot—or, alternately, he stomped out, depending on whom you ask.

But Nolan's job was already done. By the time he took off, the world was completely enamored with videogames. In 1978 a Japanese company called Taito struck it big with an arcade game called *Space Invaders*, even causing a shortage in Japan of hundred-yen coins, used to play the game. Midway hit it big with *Galaxian,* and Namco forever hooked the world with *Pac-Man*. And although Nolan, without whom none of this might have started, was gone, Atari's revenues hit $2 billion by 1980, making it, at the time, the fastest-growing company in American history. In 1981 *Time* magazine announced that Americans had dropped 20 billion quarters into videogame machines like *Asteroids, Centipede, Gauntlet,* and *Missile Command*. The Apple II, incubated in Atari's roller-rink offices, had come out to wild acclaim (with joy sticks and a version of *Breakout*), and Radio Shack's TRS-80 became a hit. In fact, this second wave of home computers, the so-called personal computer, caused Atari executives to split as to whether they ought to keep improving on home game machines or throw themselves headlong into the personal computer market. They decided to stick with games rather than word processing. The problem, though, was that by the end of

1982, there were *hundreds* of companies in the field. And as the game machines weren't made with proprietary hardware, there was no way of keeping substandard games off the market.

Movie and TV companies were licensing properties as diverse as *The Towering Inferno, Smokey and the Bandit, The A-Team's Mr. T., The Texas Chainsaw Massacre,* and *Family Feud.* There were games based on the rock band Journey, the Purina Puppy Chow Wagon, and Quaker Oats. Major companies like Gulf + Western, Twentieth Century, and Parker Brothers tried to get in on the action, as did dozens of fly-by-nights with names that flashed before the public's imagination for brief moments before sputtering out just as quickly.

Toy-store bins became flooded with games knocked down from $50 and $40 to $4.99, $2.99, and even $1.99, as consumers grew disgusted with the low quality of games and confused by the sheer number of choices. In December 1982 Atari released a game based on Spielberg's *E.T.* that was so bad that Al Alcorn, who had already quit Atari, wanted to cry when he saw it. Five million copies of *E.T.* sat in an Atari warehouse gathering dust before finally being dumped in a landfill. By 1984 Atari was near bankruptcy. Its president, Ray Kassar, was forced out, thanks in part to talk of insider trading. All but two other console makers had gone under or dropped out, and companies like Toys "R" Us saw their stock pummeled in a chain reaction. By the end of the year, the videogame industry was declared dead.

Nolan, of course, was not dead. In fact, in 1977, after Warner decided the idea had no legs, Nolan hit it big again with an idea for a family restaurant filled with mechanical, talking animals and stuffed to the gills with arcade games. That idea became the Chuck E. Cheese restaurant chain, which still flourishes today. In fact, Nolan went on to found twenty-two more companies over the next three decades. Like Steve Russell with *Spacewar!,* Atari was just one of the things he did. And what both men ultimately had in common was that these things they had done when so young, while not defining who they became as adults, did define the cultural direction in which the rest of us were to head.

# 3

## The Legend of the Last Toy Maker

Shigeru Miyamoto was a small child, with bright onyx eyes and a mischievous smile. He grew up in Sonobe, a small, rural village of rice fields and rolling hills off the coast of western Japan, alongside the Rurikei Valley, which is famous for its unusual rock formations. His parents' paper and cedar house was tiny, even by Sonobe standards. But Miyamoto didn't notice the smallness. The house had sliding shoji doors that Miyamoto loved to pull open slowly—in case another world had appeared on the other side since he'd last checked.

Miyamoto was born November 16, 1952, at a time when Japan was still recovering from the penalties imposed on her as a former Axis power. Shigeru's father earned a living for the family by teaching English. His mother took care of the house and of Shigeru and his siblings. They had neither a car nor a TV, but sometimes they would take the hourlong train ride to Kyoto, the nearest major city, to see the newest Walt Disney movie, such as *Snow White,* which Miyamoto loved.

During school hours, when he was supposed to be studying, he instead drew pictures. At night, when he was supposed to be doing homework, he built models of wood and metal. During meal times, when he ought to have been eating, he longed for his comic books, which his parents thought were particularly bad for him. Sometimes his father scolded him for spending so much time on these things instead of addressing more serious matters. They certainly didn't approve of the flip books he made, but nonetheless Miyamoto thought they were delightful: simply sliding the tip of one's thumb over the edge of the book brought whatever it was he had been drawing to life—creatures jumping, funny men dancing, babies smashing rice bowls on the floor.

It would be a mistake to think that Miyamoto spent all of his time indoors buried in books and drawings, however. Although he did carry drawing pens and paper with him when he left the house, he spent as much time as he possibly could outside. There was a bulldog that belonged to a neighbor that he liked to walk past, to see the dog leap to the edge of its leash. Shigeru would walk as close to the animal as he dared, and although his heart pounded as he did so, he marveled at the dog's curled lip and gnashing teeth, its glittering and narrowed eyes. In the summers he liked to play baseball in the dormant rice fields near his house, climb trees, and fish in the nearby river. Sometimes, when the summer nights grew long, traveling troupes would put on Kabuki plays and long Noh operas for the town.

These festivals made a big impression on Miyamoto—the actors in their billowing black and red costumes, their faces meticulously painted in deep rainbow stripes of color. The starry night sky haunted and enchanted him. At home Miyamoto made puppets and covered them in whatever scraps of finery he could find, and he dreamt of becoming a puppeteer, painter, or some other kind of entertainer.

One afternoon when he was not in school, young Miyamoto made a discovery that was to leave a lasting impression on him. Strolling at the base of the mountains near Sonobe, Miyamoto happened on a cave. It was dark inside and full of echoes, but Miyamoto longed to go inside. He imagined what he might find there—magical creatures, strange crystalline worlds, perhaps a universe governed by rules entirely different from our own. Though he was old enough to know that little boys should not go throwing themselves into unexplored caves, he was just young enough to contemplate doing so anyway. Nearly paralyzed with excitement, hovering on the edge of action, the young Miyamoto drew a breath and then raced home as fast as he could. In bed, the loudest thing he could hear was his own heart pumping away.

The next day Shigeru built a lantern out of some brown paper and headed back to the foot of the mountains. This time he entered the cave, lowering himself in slowly, trembling a bit at first. He found that what lay before him was not a single cave but a labyrinthine network of caves. He was scared, of course—caves are dark, closed-up places—and he had no idea who or what he might encounter around the next corner.

Shigeru ended up spending much of that summer in those caves. He declared one corner the lair of a monster, and another room the summer palace of a creature king. He poked and pressed auspicious-looking crevices in cave walls in search of secret passages, and as he explored, his imagination constructed an elaborate alternate world where there was only granite and limestone.

When his parents decided to move to Kyoto, Shigeru found

things in the city that were delightful, too. Instead of a neighbor with a bulldog, now he had a neighbor with an Akita, a breed of dog that had once guarded royal families, and this thrilled Miyamoto. At his new school, he started a cartoon club and helped put on a show at the end of each school year. He joined a secret society made up of other boys who would meet in people's attics, exchanging code words and foraging for treasure.

When it came time for Shigeru to go to college, he chose the Kanazawa Munici College of Industrial Arts and Crafts in Kyoto. But, just as when he was younger, school was not the primary thing on his mind. Shigeru taught himself to play the guitar and the banjo and put together a duo that played American bluegrass music at local coffeehouses. He wore his hair long, letting it fall backward over his collar. It was quite a statement in 1970s Japan. There, unlike in the United States, long hair was considered neither romantic nor bohemian, just messy. The fact that it took Miyamoto five years to finish college only encouraged the opinions of some of his peers that he was simply a bum. Miyamoto himself didn't know what he wanted to do as a grown-up. The idea of a lifetime devoted to corporate drudgery terrified him.

One day in 1977, the year British and American kids discovered the Ramones and the Sex Pistols, Miyamoto remembered that when his father was young he had been friends with a boy who now ran one of Kyoto's biggest businesses, a company called Nintendo. The company was founded in 1889 by the boy's great-grandfather, a craftsman named Fusajiro Yamauchi. Yamauchi created beautiful *hanafuda,* or "flower cards," out of a paste he initially prepared from the bark of mulberry trees in his backyard. Japanese families bought them for their elegance and used them to play simple matching games. The *yakuza* used them in more complicated bridgelike games in their gambling parlors. The elder craftsman Yamauchi-san became so wealthy manufacturing his *hanafuda* that he eventually bought a castle that had formerly belonged to the fifteenth-century emperor of Japan. In the ninety years since Yamauchi-san had started the company, Nintendo had become quite an institution around Kyoto.

Shigeru's great idea of 1977 was that his father get him an interview with Hiroshi Yamauchi, the elder Yamauchi's great-grandson, with whom Miyamoto's own father had grown up, and who was now running the business. Under the reign of Hiroshi Yamauchi, Nintendo had become a powerhouse of toys. Mr. Yamauchi was a man who very much wanted to leave his mark. He wanted to dominate an industry.

Mr. Yamauchi had turned to toys after trying taxi services, instant rice, and rent-by-the-hour love hotels (of which he was said to be his own best customer). He'd arranged for Nintendo to become the distributor of Disney character cards in Japan, and he brought together a team of toy engineers who have often been described as samurai-like in their fierce dedication to their work and their leader.

Miyamoto's father agreed to approach Mr. Yamauchi about Shigeru. By this time, Mr. Yamauchi knew all about things like microprocessors and what they were doing for electronic games in the United States. He'd even become the Japanese licensee of a machine called the Magnavox Odyssey. Yamauchi-san had begun to suspect the whole notion of toys was changing. He watched with great interest when *Space Invaders* caused a shortage of hundred-yen coins in Tokyo. And when the city resorted to passing ordinances to keep children out of arcades during school hours, he became convinced that a shift in the business was inevitable. Yamauchi had his engineers make him a game machine of his own, called the Color TV 6. It sold rather well, but not well enough for Yamauchi-san. Not well enough for Nintendo.

So when Miyamoto's father approached his childhood friend about a job for Shigeru, Yamauchi simply replied, "We need engineers, not painters."

Nevertheless, as a favor to his friend, Yamauchi agreed to meet with Shigeru. Shigeru arrived for his interview with a bag full of toys he'd designed, child-size wooden coat hangers painted bright colors to look like elephants and chickens. He'd even designed a special way of snapping them to the wall with little hooks he carved out of wood.

It's not clear why Yamauchi-san decided to hire the son of his childhood friend as Nintendo's first staff artist. Maybe he saw a glimpse of a future that would require Shigeru's offbeat brand of enthusiastic creativity. Perhaps it was merely a gesture of loyalty to his friend, Shigeru's father. Nevertheless, when Mr. Yamauchi offered Miyamoto a job at Nintendo, all Shigeru could do was smile. It was a smile that would come to be compared to the cat that has just swallowed the canary—a wide, twinkling smile that would become synonymous with its owner. For his part, Yamauchi-san simply blinked back at Miyamoto from behind his yellow-tinted glasses. Little did he know he had just made one of the greatest hires of all time.

Shigeru worked for almost three years producing art for the sides of arcade game machines and other novelties, until one day in 1980 Yamauchi-san called him into his office. Mr. Yamauchi's engineers had made him an arcade game called *Radarscope,* but the game had not sold nearly as well as Mr. Yamauchi demanded. He was especially peeved because the game was not selling in the United States, a market he was determined to crack. He called in Shigeru Miyamoto because he had no one else to spare.

From across a long expanse of mahogany, Yamauchi-san informed the young Miyamoto that he was to resuscitate the game. Shigeru was ecstatic. He loved arcade games, and he could not keep from bursting out with his own humble opinions on the subject, even against this most formidable of bosses. Shigeru told Yamauchi that videogames had not yet learned from their media cousin, the cinema, how to create memorable characters or how to produce artistically polished products. He said they relied too much on violence instead of drawing from the classic literary themes of good and evil, honor and disgrace, beauty and horror. He brought up Shakespeare; he brought up the Bible; he brought up King Kong. Mr. Yamauchi listened to him in silence and then told him to get busy turning *Radarscope* into something that would sell.

As Miyamoto got to work on *Radarscope,* he couldn't stop thinking that, with the exception of *Pac-Man,* which had been a surprise hit for Namco earlier that year, videogames were painfully unimaginative. He had a vision of a game that would be delightful to play rather than nerve-wracking, with characters that could leap around the screen, like in the flipbooks of his youth. He wanted to make people smile and feel like children again while they played—inquisitive, experimental, capable of being captured by the whimsy of a moment.

The game Shigeru ultimately made for Yamauchi-san had nothing to do with the designs he'd been handed for *Radarscope.* Miyamoto's game featured a protagonist named Jumpman, a mustachioed carpenter who wore bright red overalls and a bright red cap to match. The garish red outfit was not simply the product of whimsy, it was the result of a trick Miyamoto had learned from Nintendo engineers: they'd shown him how bright colors help characters stand out best against the black background of the video monitor. Miyamoto very much wanted Jumpman to stand out so that the player could follow his movements easily during the game. After all, Miyamoto hadn't named his carpenter Jumpman for nothing.

Of course, Jumpman was not just any old carpenter gifted with a vertical leap equal to his own height. He was a carpenter on a mission. Jumpman's quest was to rescue his lovely girlfriend from the clutches of Jumpman's own pet gorilla, who had stolen her away and now stood gloating atop a mountain of metal girders. The challenge for the player would be to race Jumpman up the steel switchbacks while avoiding barrels and other obstacles thrown at him by the errant simian.

To name the game, Shigeru consulted the office copy of an English/Japanese dictionary. Along with the company's export manager, Shigeru selected the name "Kong," which was designed to evoke the runaway gorilla. Next Miyamoto searched for a word to describe the gorilla. Nearly frustrated, he finally hit upon "donkey," which Miyamoto thought would accurately describe the ape's stubbornness and stupidity.

When Nintendo's American sales force was introduced to *Donkey Kong,* they thought Yamauchi-san had lost his mind. They thought the title was stupid and, worse, hated the way the game played. Even the music, which Shigeru had composed himself on a synthesizer hooked up to his computer, was scorned. "Where are the aliens, the ballistic missiles, the nefarious laser guns from outer space?" the salesmen complained.

*Donkey Kong* was unlike anything that had come before. The only arcade game that had even come close to the surreal dilemma of Jumpman was *Pac-Man*. The very first character ever featured in a videogame, *Pac-Man* had been inspired by the image of a pizza pie with a slice missing. Sure, *Pac-Man* had been monstrously successful and had even become something of a cultural phenomeon in the United States, but clearly that was a novelty, *Donkey Kong*'s skeptics explained. *Donkey Kong* had more in common with a Bugs Bunny cartoon than an apocalyptic science-fiction saga, and that made them nervous. Given the choice of preventing Armageddon as a starship commander or playing a pudgy little man with a black mustache and overalls, who would ever choose Jumpman?

Now, it should be noted that Mr. Yamauchi has always contended that he has never played a videogame for fun in his entire life. He claims no interest in them other than as a commodity. Yet the decision of what games went to market always rested solely with him. Yamauchi is known far and wide for never having let anyone talk him into or out of releasing a product. And so it was with *Donkey Kong*. Ridiculous or not, Yamauchi-san decreed that *Donkey Kong* would be the game Nintendo would ship to America. And ridiculous or not, *Donkey Kong,* released in 1981, became Nintendo's first big arcade hit.

Had Miyamoto never made another game, he would still be remembered today as a genius of game design. But it was only after making *Donkey Kong Jr.,* the sequel to his debut smash, that Shigeru began the work that would immortalize him as the Homer of videogame design.

Miyamoto's *Super Mario Bros.,* his first console game, was not complicated, but it certainly was epic. And like most classic toys, the game was based around a handful of small elements joined with an elegance that allowed the sum to far exceed the components. Jumpman would again be the star of the show, but Miyamoto had reworked him into a plumber rather than a carpenter and rechristened him Mario. In addition, he gave Mario a brother, Luigi, who sported bright green in contrast to Mario's red, and was tall and thin instead of short and dumpy.

Miyamoto dropped both of them into an imaginary world rife with gigantic pipes, underground cisterns, caverns, and sewers. The game was again driven by the need to save a kidnapped girl, but this time it was a princess. Miyamoto then populated his world with strange reptilian creatures with funny names like Sidesteppers and Shellcreepers. There were gold coins and magic mushrooms to collect, hidden areas to explore, and each stage ended with a battle against a "boss," who had to be defeated before the player could continue Mario's quest. Like an epic poem, *Super Mario Bros.* was quite long, with many, many stages, and though simple to learn, the game was difficult to master.

Mr. Yamauchi bundled one copy of *Super Mario Bros.* with every one of his samurai engineers' new game machines, which they called the Family Entertainment System. In Japan, it was common for families to sit down and play games together; Mr. Yamauchi saw *Mario* and the Famicom system as the modern-day version of the *hanafuda* cards that had made his great-grandfather rich one hundred years earlier.

What Mr. Yamauchi didn't realize as he prepared for the release of his wonderful new toy was that the videogame industry had begun to fear for its very existence. Soon word flew to Kyoto that videogame companies in the United States were folding like houses of cards, and analysts were beginning to wonder whether the games might just go the way of the hula hoop and the Pet Rock. Yamauchi-san waved away the foreboding news of the "Great Videogame Crash of 1983" like an emperor dismissing a troublesome dignitary. Nintendo went ahead and released the Famicom.

Within hours of its initial launch children began camping

outside stores all over Japan's major cities, desperate for a chance to enter the world of Mario and Luigi. Mr. Yamauchi's factories could hardly keep up with the demand for this new product. At the end of one year, the Japanese had bought three million Famicom systems. The sales were driven almost entirely by *Super Mario Bros.*, and Shigeru Miyamoto quickly became a hero to the children of Japan. In his own neighborhood in Kyoto, children started following him as he rode his bicycle to work in the mornings, chanting, "Dr. Miyamoto, Dr. Miyamoto!"

When Yamauchi-san declared his intention of taking *Mario* and the Famicom into the United States, people thought his arrogance had finally gotten the better of him and had begun distorting his judgment. American retail stores, whether in the toy business or the electronics business, wanted *nothing* to do with the Famicom, now renamed the Nintendo Entertainment System (NES). The name Famicom was abandoned for U.S. retail because though the words *family* and *entertainment* held very positive connotations when combined in Japan, in America the terms were viewed as incongruous, and "family entertainment" was often applied as a euphemism for "boring." Entertainment in the United States, Miyamoto had noted, was something the different generations did not like to share. The name change also helped Yamauchi-san let American consumers know about his company. For while Nintendo had become famous in Japan, it was almost completely unknown in the United States, a situation Yamauchi-san very much wanted to change.

After 1984 it had become all but common wisdom in the West that videogames were a fad whose time had passed. Much hype was being made over the *next* big thing—personal computing. Just to get Miyamoto's first masterpiece and the

NES into stores, Nintendo had to make all kinds of unusual promises. For example, they were forced to agree to buy back any units that did not sell, and managing in-store displays was left almost universally to Nintendo's sales force. Nintendo even added a foot-high plastic robot to the package called the Robotic Operating Buddy, which though not particularly engaging to play with, reinforced the image of the NES as a toy that technophobic parents need not fear.

*Mario* and the NES finally debuted in the United States in 1985, and by Christmas 1986, Yamauchi could boast a penetration rate of 1.9 million American homes. And the numbers kept growing: 5.4 million units sold in 1987; 9.3 million in 1988; and onward. What a time that proved to be for Miyamoto! *Mario* was a global phenomenon. By 1990, Nintendo had claimed more than 80 percent of the entire videogame market. People around the world fell in love with the little plumber with the twitching mustache. Enthusiasts dubbed *Mario Bros.* a "platformer," because gameplay largely involved guiding Mario or Luigi through a series of jumps, bumps, and leaps in order to progress through the game world, all the while negotiating a near endless onslaught of kooky enemies. The game also came to epitomize the "side-scroller," since Mario and Luigi's journey always led them from the left edge of the screen to the right. Though David Crane's *Pitfall* for Atari was the very first side-scrolling videogame, it was Miyamoto who mastered the technique, and it lent his game a sense of continuity and size that was truly epic.

Within five years, one in every four American households had bought an NES and *Super Mario Bros*. There was no more talk about the videogame industry being dead. There was only talk about Nintendo and Mario. There were Mario dolls, magazines, action figures, cereal, clothing, a TV show, and movies.

Nintendo put out game sequels as fast as they could make them, and even gave Mario's sidekicks games of their own. Between 1985 and 1991, Miyamoto made eight Mario games—which altogether sold almost 70 million copies. In fact, Mario became such a phenomenon that parents all over the country grew alarmed by their children's overwhelming love for the plumber and his strange cast of friends, and they formed groups to protest him. They thought Miyamoto was trying to rob their children of their attention spans as well as their pocket money. These sorts of accusations pained Miyamoto, and made him look deep into himself, and think about what it was he was doing. When children approached him for advice on how to play Mario, he would always tell them the best thing they could do was play outside whenever they could. When parents approached him, he would not answer directly, but often would tell them the story of his own parents' distrust of comic books, as a gentle reminder that the fear of one generation is often the quaint nostalgia of the next.

By 1990, polls showed more American schoolchildren recognized Mario than Mickey Mouse, which Miyamoto, who often wore a Mickey Mouse tie to work, had great trouble accepting. *Fortune* magazine writer Susan Moffat predicted: "Just as Mickey Mouse helped pioneer the animated picture in the 1930s, so might Mario help establish a new medium called interactive entertainment."

**ONE DAY, TUCKED** away in his office at Nintendo, Miyamoto found himself thinking about a tiny garden that could fit inside one of his desk's drawers. While most game designers will start with, say, a monster or a great weapon, Miyamoto often started his game design with a location. A snowy mountain, a sewer system, a contained garden. With a controller in his hand, he'd start the design right on the monitor and say to himself and his team: "Okay, where is the fun here?" And they'd play around until they created an image, or a sound, or a particular move that Shigeru felt was truly delightful. It was the same way with *The Legend of Zelda,* the game Miyamoto built from his idea about the garden in his desk drawer. Like *Super Mario Bros.,* it was created around a small number of elements that could be combined to give players enough choices, enough possible connections between elements, that the game world would feel limitless. Like its gameplay, the story in *The Legend of Zelda* was simple, too, and reflected Miyamoto's strong belief in the power of mythology. The game is the folktale of an all-too-ordinary boy named Link, who becomes stronger and more heroic by undergoing a series of challenges until finally his strength serves to benefit not only himself but also his community.

**EVEN TODAY, WHEN** the average game is several hundreds of times more complicated than Miyamoto's early efforts, *The Legend of Zelda* is still considered one of the greatest videogames ever made. Children often take a toy, like a tin soldier, which is a kind of model, and they play with it. They build their own world rules based on the musings of their imaginations. Out of something very small, as small as a tin soldier, they create in their minds something very big. What Miyamoto was able to do with such mastery was make a model of an entire game world and present it to kids as a toy. Though gamers often talk of "beating" a game like *The Legend of Zelda,* they really just mean that they've completed the game's main quest. You can't really "win" a game like *Zelda* because it's not designed to be a competition. Rather it's much more like a toy model, where the joy of playing comes from engaging one's imagination and delighting in the play that comes from manipulating the model. Many gamers who played *The Legend of Zelda* when it came out say it was the first videogame that ever made them cry. They cried for the little boy hero, Link, and they cried for the sheer joy of playing.

In 1994 Shigeru flew to America to attend the Consumer Electronics Show, which is where game designers used to debut their creations before the videogame industry demanded a tradeshow all to itself. Nintendo was introducing its newest machine, the SNES ("Super" NES), and of course Shigeru's newest game, *Super Mario World,* was bundled along with it. Although the cast of characters was the same, the next generation of technology had allowed Shigeru to take his notion of what a videogame should be even farther. And with each iteration—for that is what videogame makers had begun to call each new version in a series of games—not only had Miyamoto become a better craftsman, but also he'd become far more ambitious in his game designs.

Although his games were incredibly successful and were now universally known, Miyamoto himself was not. Miyamoto relished the opportunity to investigate firsthand the ideas and designs his colleagues had come up with. He strolled through the convention halls, stopping at different booths to examine games that piqued his interest, until eventually he was accosted by one of the few people there who knew who he was. The man who stopped him was Steven Kent, who would eventually become one of the premier historians of videogames, and Mr. Kent was a huge fan of Miyamoto. Some people say there is a kind of pixie dust Miyamoto sprinkles over his games, and that you can immediately feel its presence or its absence. This is precisely how Mr. Kent felt. He spoke to Miyamoto and was surprised when Miyamoto told him that if Nintendo were to disappear that day, he would not keep making videogames. This was not at all the response that Mr. Kent expected. Most gamemakers Mr. Kent had interviewed said they would keep making games even if the sun burnt out like a used match. But Miyamoto seemed to think videogames were not so important. He told Mr. Kent that if it all disappeared tomorrow, he would go back to his original dream of being a simple toy maker.

Rather than implode, however, the videogame industry only expanded, and by the time Nintendo released its next game machine, the Nintendo 64—or N64 as nearly everyone took to calling it (which had a 64-bit processor—more than anyone would have thought possible a mere decade before!)—Miyamoto was ready. *Mario 64,* Mr. Kent says, "was truly a Miyamoto project," even though he had a team of seventy-five people to work with. The technology of Mr. Yamauchi's samurai engineers now let Mario's world be three-dimensional. Now Mario leapt and jumped not only left to right but right to left, forward and backward, up and down as well—truly covering the entire screen the way Shigeru had always imagined. It was so much fun to play that gamers everywhere slapped their foreheads in disbelief. Now Miyamoto was credited with defining another videogame genre: the 3-D platformer! While he thought he was just doing a job, to the rest of the world, Miyamoto was building miracles.

When *Mario 64* debuted, players had never seen a completely realized 3-D game world like this before. Indeed, Miyamoto had anticipated that gamers might be intimidated by the revolutionary change in game design, so he adjusted the game's difficulty curve accordingly. Though he wanted his new game to be challenging, he did not want gamers to be discouraged simply because they had no experience with playing in three full dimensions. So Miyamoto made the game much easier at the beginning than he would have otherwise. It was beginning to seem as if Miyamoto's games had no weak links, that his vision was limitless. His games were crafted more finely than anything that had come before, and they shone like freshly cut diamonds in a field of coal.

**IT'S HARD TO SAY** exactly how what happened next happened. Perhaps it was that Miyamoto's games were now so numerous and of such high quality that fame was unavoidable. Perhaps Mr. Yamauchi saw what success his competitor Sega was having promoting its own top gamemaker, Yu Suzuki, and realized that people liked to associate a face with a company. Perhaps the time had simply come for gamemakers to start getting recognized. For whatever reason it was during the reign of the N64 and the glory of *Mario 64* that Miyamoto went from being a Japanese local hero to Miyamoto-san, the greatest game designer of all time. Attending game shows and wandering the floor on his own would no longer be part of his future. The next time Mr. Kent saw Miyamoto, in 1996, he bowed low and called him *sensei,* which means "master" in Japanese. Shigeru blushed to the roots of his hair. This was not a level to which he had necessarily aspired.

Today, Miyamoto-san is rarely seen with less than four or five people in tow—publicity specialists from both sides of the Pacific, translators, assistants, and other executives. They surround him like a bevy of white-collar bodyguards, keeping fans, journalists, and colleagues at bay. If you passed Miyamoto-san in the hall of a videogame conference today, you could not reach out and touch him. You probably could not even see him amidst his entourage, except possibly for a glimpse of his shaggy head or his enormous grin bobbing down the corridor.

Today, getting to spend time with Miyamoto-san is like being granted an interview with the Queen of England. Nintendo guards him as if he were their crown jewels, doling out the minutes of his day as if each were a precious gem to be appreciated but never fully shared.

When the Academy of Interactive Arts and Sciences began giving out awards in 1998, Miyamoto-san received the first lifetime achievement award. It was presented to him by one of his dear friends in the U.S. industry, a man named Will Wright. Miyamoto-san was now the first inductee of the Video Game Hall of Fame. People stood and cheered until all Miyamoto-san could do was clutch his little prize and grin his famous grin, his hair still falling messily over the back of his collar just as it had when he was a college student. Miyamoto-san was very pleased by the honor of the award and the applause of his peers. He would hold the memory close to him as one of his finest.

At the dawn of the twenty-first century, although people continued to revere Miyamoto-san, there began to be whisperings among some gamemakers that Nintendo games were only for children. Over drinks at videogame conferences, people began to speculate that Miyamoto-san's pixie dust was sprinkled too thin. It was true that Mr. Yamauchi, who was getting on in years, decided that the wisest thing to do would be to have Shigeru teach all the other game designers at Nintendo to make games that *seemed* like Miyamoto-san games. Although people said you could feel the absence of the master's touch, it is also true that Nintendo games to this day have a feel that can be described as Miyamoto-esque. Games like *Animal Crossing,* which was not designed by Miyamoto, are set in a seemingly self-contained world where players plant trees, do aerobics with their animal neighbors, fish at the beaches, and start butterfly collections. The game world looks like it is crafted from Filo clay, and animal characters chide the player if he's playing late at night or too often. Even *The Legend of Zelda: The Wind Waker,* though a continuation of one of Miyamoto's most personal stories, was not made by the *sensei* himself.

Gamemakers also began to wonder whether Nintendo was too old-fashioned, that its refusal to follow the trends of photorealism, gritty violence, and voice acting would be its death. People even laughed behind their hands at the GameCube, Nintendo's new console—which Miyamoto-san had been very much involved with creating—because it was small, and came in purple plastic, and could be carried around with a little handle. It was cute. *It looks like a TOY!* gamemakers hissed to one another, as if there were no worse insult. Even little boys in Blockbuster Video stores around the country shook their heads at Nintendo boxes, eschewing them in favor of *Grand Theft Auto III* or *True Crime,* saying Nintendo games were "too kiddy," even though they themselves were kids. Even Epic Games designer CliffyB, who passed some of the most pleasant days of his youth playing Miyamoto's games, was critical: "Dude, you've got to take your old-school sensibilities and move them into the new school of what it takes to make a game in 2004!"

The biggest game of 2004 was *Grand Theft Auto: San Andreas.* How much its makers at Rockstar Games owe to Miyamoto-san! Was it not the same sense of freedom within the game universe that made both *Super Mario Bros.* and *Grand Theft Auto* great? The feeling that it was up to you to play with the given elements as you so desired? And yet how different the game was. It was as if Rockstar had taken a beat-up old Toyota with a tooting horn and pimped and pounded the little car until it became a Cadillac. The guys at Rockstar even incorporated digital prostitutes into their game as power-ups. And although they were careful who they told, many people thought that Miyamoto was simply behind the times.

Miyamoto-san is in his early fifties now. Age has left him with heavy lines around the eyes and mouth, in the manner of one who has laughed a lot in his lifetime. While people still like to describe him as childlike and innocent, they are foolish indeed if they do not also see that he is a tired man. In 2002 Mr. Yamauchi retired. In a final act of imperial petulance, he fired his son-in-law, Minoru Arakawa, the heir-apparent, when he refused to move back to Japan from America, and instead named a relatively unknown former gamemaker, Satoru Iwata, to head the company of his ancestors—the first break in the family line since his great-grandfather founded Nintendo more than one hundred years ago. And Miyamoto-san, as Nintendo's most valuable asset, remains at Mr. Iwata's side, helping to lead the company he once dreamed of working for.

Many people who know him well wonder why Miyamoto-san agreed to take on so many managerial responsibilities when they know him to be so creatively driven. People who know him less well joke that Miyamoto-san is an indentured servant of Nintendo's, because he has never earned more than a mid-level employee's salary, and most of his financial rewards will not arrive until he retires. In fact, Mr. Yamauchi used to delight in telling people that the great Miyamoto-san, the *sensei* of game design, worked for him, and for a pittance! But for Miyamoto-san, loyalty to one's company is an important value, even if that means subordinating oneself to its needs. Miyamoto-san loves Nintendo, unquestioningly, the way a small child loves a parent, or a parent loves a child who has grown up to be something quite special.

And so Shigeru has taken up swimming and gardening to maintain balance in his life, and he still likes to play music. Sometimes, at night, he still dreams of the caves of Sonobe. He returns in his mind to those dusty passageways and hidden rooms as if they hold the key to the very nature of imagination. Miyamoto-san still says—and those who know him believe him—that no matter how big a business videogames become, his goal has always been to make games that make players more creative rather than less so. When people ask Miyamoto-san about the fierce competition among videogame companies, Miyamoto often closes his eyes for a moment, before explaining, politely, that this is a question that exists only in the minds of journalists and analysts. The real question of game design, he insists, is one of competition with oneself to come up with new ideas no one has thought of before.

But the modern-day videogame industry is growing up, and, like teenagers eager to disengage from their childhood, the videogame industry is obsessed with its new, "mature" self. As the entire world has shifted its gaze to this pastime, once the sole domain of kids and oddballs, many in the industry have become dazzled by the attention.

On stage at the DICE summit in 2003, Miyamoto talks about his design process—he talks about drawing right on the monitor with a magic marker; he likens his process to that of working with clay rather than chipping away at stone; he explains that he depends on feedback from Nintendo testers the way an art student waits for and depends on his professors' and peers' criticism. He warns the roomful of game developers that they will lose the "core element of fun" if they focus too much on being "realistic." Game design is like casting out a net to catch fun, he continues.

And what is fun but an ephemeral mist, as Will Wright likes to say. The more you try to grab it, the more diffuse it becomes.

But videogames have become an industry that, like the movies, does not want to rely on that which cannot be easily quantified. The more ephemeral a quality is, the less the industry likes it. The harder to name, the more suspicious it becomes. Miyamoto-san is far too polite to say explicitly what he often seems to be implying—that game designers, and American game designers in particular, focus far too much on technical prowess and far too little on creativity.

Very quietly, at the end of one of his long responses to a typical question about the dangers of videogames for children, Miyamoto-san looks down at his hands and says he has begun to wonder if videogames are "okay even for adults to play." He says it almost to himself. Miyamoto-san is so well known for his quasi-poetic musing that no one seems to notice. The questions go on. And then he's whisked off by his Nintendo team, who meet him at the side of the stage in a tightly formed huddle. They move him through the crowd, past all the people who seem to want something from him. Past the people who don't have the nerve to say his reign is over, but have forgotten it might not be, past the people who built their careers on the vocabulary he established, and into an elevator, which takes him up, up to the highest floors of the hotel, where the clouds float by his window. The elusive Miyamoto-san vanishes. But though he may no longer be the king of the videogame world, or even its crown prince, Shigeru Miyamoto will still be remembered by history, kindly, as the Geppetto whose genius and imagination turned a heap of technology into a living world of delight.

# 4

## Dallas: First-Person-Shooter Capital of the World

Angel Munoz has a dream. A forty-two-year-old retired investment banker, and a longtime Dallas resident, Angel has replaced the gray pinstripes of his former profession for a new kind of uniform entirely. Today, he wears jeans with a clean T-shirt tucked into them that says CYBERATHLETE PROFESSIONAL LEAGUE. In 1997, thirty years after first discovering *Pong* in a local pizzeria in the Puerto Rican neighborhood where he grew up, Angel founded an association of professional videogame players. And Angel's players aren't just a bunch of random arcade jockeys. They're first-person-shooter players. And not just any first-person shooters. They're the best of the best. The elite.

**IF YOU'VE NEVER** heard of any other videogames, you've at least heard of first-person shooters. When people are wringing their hands about the horrors of videogames, they very well may be talking about this one category. In fact, they may be talking, without realizing it, about only a handful of games. The ones that started it all. *Return to Castle Wolfenstein. Doom. Quake*. These are the games that end with blood splattering the walls, organs flopping on the floor, devil people, and monsters dredged up from imaginations bred on horror movies. These are also the games where your view is down the barrel of a shotgun—or any of a number of powerful firearms—hence the name *first-person* shooter. Your sole mission is to kill whatever monster, terrorist, or machine is trying to kill you.

If the name *Doom* or *Quake* rings a distant bell, perhaps it's because those are the games Eric Harris and Dylan Klebold, the Columbine shooters, were so into. They are also the games Senator Joseph Lieberman used to bolster his reputation as a family-friendly entertainment vigilante. And they are the games that left the videogame industry staring down the barrel of a multimillion dollar lawsuit in 1999.

After Columbine, the first-person shooter became, in most people's minds, what videogames are. What most people don't know, however, is that every single one of these games—*Wolfenstein, Doom, Quake*—was created by the same group of people, in a shiny black box of a building in the suburb of Mesquite, just outside Dallas. The ones that have come since—*Unreal, Half-Life, Counter-Strike*—are all basically offshoots. Dallas folks, some living in different areas, some still there, all working off the same paradigm, the same aesthetic, that *Doom* established. Insiders call them the Children of *Doom*.

For his part, Angel couldn't have cared less about the world's fear and fury. Angel looked at *Doom* and saw a damn fun game, and he saw dollar signs buzzing in his head. So today, in convention centers all over the world, Angel holds tournaments, attracting thousands of contestants and tens of thousands of viewers over the Internet, to crown the world's best first-person-shooter players.

**ANGEL'S MAIN EVENT,** the World Cup of first-person shooters, takes place every year in Dallas. The fourth annual tournament is in the downtown Dallas Hyatt Regency in July 2002. It's so hot out that even with fully blasting air-conditioning you can't keep your legs from sticking to the seat of your car. Angel is in action. He's running wild with a cordless microphone in one hand and a pile of T-shirts over his shoulder. All the way to Texas, to the sweltering heat and empty streets of Dallas in July, teams from as far away as Norway, Australia, and Brazil have come. There are representatives from sixty-three different countries. And it's a strange scene in the lobby of the Hyatt. There are good old boys with big bellies and straw cowboy hats eating pizza slices and drinking Dr Pepper alongside groups of Asian kids, with slick, bleached hair, and wide-eyed Norwegians, who seem to be all legs and narrow chests.

In Angel's tournament, the kids play in teams. *Doom* was the first videogame that made real the dream of playing with other people in a completely 3-D environment over the Internet. The game Angel is using this hot Dallas weekend is *Counter-Strike,* a popular post-*Doom* game from a Seattle company called Valve, which pits terrorists against counterterrorist military teams. Teams are dropped into a mazelike environment where they run, armed to the teeth, through amber-toned concrete alleyways and bombed-out buildings. If they're on the terrorist team, they must plant a bomb. If they're on the counterterrorist team, they must defuse the bomb and kill all the terrorists. Games are played in three-minute rounds, with the best of thirteen winning. Any team good enough to qualify for CPL membership probably practices thirty or so hours a week *minimum* over rented high-speed servers that can cost several hundred dollars a month to maintain. That wouldn't seem to leave much room for a social life, if it weren't for the fact that first-person shooter clans are so numerous, so well-organized, and so dedicated that the pastime offers a social life as complete as that offered by any bowling league or country club. A Brazilian player with a St. Santio medal and a green Team Brazil soccer jersey even claims that his luck with the girls has been vastly improved since his team won Brazil's national championship earlier in the year. (Their parents also perked up when they started bringing home high-end computer gear as prizes.)

The basement of the Hyatt is cold and dark, just the way gamers like it. There are long rows of tables, stretching in banks of eighty or a hundred feet across the span of the room, with PCs every four feet or so. An Internet radio booth is streaming a live simulcast of the proceedings near an area roped off for competitors and journalists. Still Angel is not even remotely satisfied. Angel wants to build a Cyberstadium. *A Cyberstadium*. That is his dream.

"This isn't how this should look!" he cries. "Not these crazy tables and wires all over the place. I want it to look like it had some thought put into it. " He waves his arms about. "I want a huge structure! There should be all different types of food vendors, and permanent stations for our sponsors. We should have a tournament area surrounded by an arena!"

Angel seems shocked by the question of where he might locate his Cyberstadium. His eyes simmer with incredulity for a moment before replying. "Dallas, of course," he says. "Dallas is the first-person-shooter capital of the world."

**THE WHOLE THING,** the whole reason several thousand teenagers are in a basement in this Dallas Hyatt, and a man like Angel dares to dream about a Cyberstadium, is because of two guys, both named John. When they met, John Romero was a charismatic twenty-two-year-old with jet-black hair down to his ass, obsessed in equal parts with *Super Mario Bros.,* his Apple II, *The Texas Chainsaw Massacre,* and Black Sabbath. John Carmack was a tight-lipped, formerly troubled youth from Missouri who spoke little and worked, as friends say, "like a machine."

The friendship that sprung up between the two men—if *friendship* is quite the right word—is the stuff of legend among videogamers. The story of John and John and id Software and *Doom* is the founding myth of first-person-shooter culture. The Johns, as they became known, were like opposing forces of nature, creating an energy—a *synergy*—between them that somehow was bigger than either could muster on his own. Products that grew out of the Johns' relationship sent repercussions rippling through the culture at large—aesthetically, economically, and even politically.

**THE DALLAS HYATT REGENCY** is a shield of silvery glass on the very edge of the southwesternmost part of Dallas. To the east are skyscrapers, Neiman Marcus, and museums. About half a mile to the west and under a freeway ramp is a row of bail-bond firms, hamburger joints, questionable-looking bars, and a minimum security state penitentiary. The hotel is right on the line between the part of Dallas where one goes, and the part where one doesn't.

The particular weekend that the Hyatt is hosting Angel's Cyberathlete tournament happens to fall smack in the middle of a monthlong Mary Kay Cosmetics convention. Every week, groups of seven thousand Mary Kay ladies have been shuttling in and out of the air-conditioned suites of local hotels. The day that the cyberathletes arrive, a Saturday, turns out to be the same day that one battalion of Mary Kay ladies are sent back to their homes across America, and a new battalion arrives. The curb outside the valet's stand is swarming with ladies in pink-and-purple suits. Their hair is teased and sprayed in a style popular in Dallas but no longer seen much in the rest of the country. Many of them carry white tote bags with hot pink piping, or plastic bags with images of Mary Kay models shining through. They wear big badges on their blouses like ruffled horse ribbons proclaiming them Future Managers, Grand Achievers, and Unit Queens. Their lapels are covered with little pins: rhinestone Cadillacs, intertwined hearts, red enamel lips attached to enamel lipsticks, little glazed portraits of Mary Kay herself. Even though it's near 101 degrees by ten a.m., they all wear pantyhose, heels, and blazers. Their faces are, of course, fully made up.

As the Mary Kay ladies wait for their taxis, the cyberathletes are beginning to unload their stuff. Behind the valet podium, a kid in khaki pants, cut off but still dragging across the floor, and a black T-shirt with a single red box containing the word RAGE, is smoking. The kid next to him wears a name tag that says NUTZ. Brandon and Justin Holt, brothers, fifteen and twenty, respectively, have just driven for six hours from San Antonio in a Ryder truck, with eight other friends following in a caravan of cars. Brandon is in line at the Hyatt concession stand to buy a three-dollar bag of chips. "Nah, I'm not competing," Brandon says. He's small, muscular, has black hair that stands straight in a wave that peaks at his forehead. His mouth is tight, and his eyes, although a lovely shade of green, are narrowed into what seems a permanent state of suspicion. "Have you seen those guys down there? I'd get raped," he says. "Getting raped" is the universal term among shooters for being in over your head.

This is actually Justin's first cyberathlete tournament, and not competing is doing nothing to lessen his fun. Beside the sheer fact of being away from home, he's psyched to hang out with other *Counter-Strike* fans, to stay up twenty-four hours—the game room in the basement is open from Saturday morning until Wednesday night, when the tournament shuts down—and to collect high-tech goodies such as bootleg DVDs of Vin Diesel movies. Brandon isn't so sure, though, about the attitudes of some of the other guys at the event. "I said to one guy, 'Hey, it looks like you've got a scratch on your computer,' and he just turns to me with this look and goes, 'Dude, this is the most beautiful PC *you're* ever going to see.' " Brandon shakes his head from side to side and grimaces, then drops his wraparound sunglasses back over his eyes. It's so hot this Dallas morning that even in the lobby of the Hyatt people are wearing sunglasses. "Got to run," he says.

**IT WAS THE SUN** that eventually brought John and John and the rest of what became id to Dallas. In 1990, Romero and his buddy, Jay Wilbur, were living in Shreveport, Louisiana, a piss-poor town that had collapsed when its oil wells dried up in the seventies, and working for a company called Softdisk that sold subscription CD-ROM magazines. Romero wasn't crazy about the gig, but he was devouring information, learning everything there was to know about the PC, after having mastered his first love, the Apple II. Then Softdisk agreed to start a game division and to hire another programmer.

In dropped John Carmack, an underground legend of a programmer who'd been hoofing it around the Midwest since dropping out of college, making a living at convenience stores, and lavishing attention on his Apple II as if he expected a genie to pop out.

Romero and Jay had seen a piece of programming Carmack had done and literally begged him to come. Carmack blasted into their lives like a twenty-first-century man dropping back in time with a laptop and a Landcruiser. The things he did on that Apple, and then on the PC once he got his hands on that, took people's breath away. He could squeeze power from a computer like juice from a lemon.

One morning, shortly after Carmack's arrival, Romero walked into his office and discovered an unmarked floppy leaning against his keyboard. On the disk was something Carmack had made the previous night. Romero popped the disk into his computer, and his jaw went slack. Somehow Carmack, along with another Softdisk programmer, Tom Hall, had re-created the entire first level of *Super Mario Bros.,* but instead of running on Nintendo's proprietary console, the side-scrolling platformer ran on Romero's PC. "OH . . . MY . . . GOD!" shouted Romero. He knew every PC game that had ever been made up to that point, and he knew that no one had every done anything remotely like this.

Romero knew that a side-scrolling game like *Super Mario Bros.* required an entirely different kind of graphics engine than a vertically oriented, top-down game like *Space Invaders.* Making vertically scrolling graphics requires changing a single variable for every screen line you redraw. But in 1990, you could only get eight-pixel columns at a time moving horizontally. As a result, creating side-scrolling graphics on DOS-based computers was daunting to say the least. But Carmack had figured out how to tell the computer monitor to shift the display—what the viewer sees—by a single pixel without having to actually touch the display's memory, which would have required a lot of CPU and slowed the computer down. This allowed for smooth horizontal scrolling. It was a feat Romero almost couldn't believe.

Romero grabbed Carmack when he arrived at work the next day. "Dude, we are out of here!" But Carmack was nonplussed: "Whatever," he replied. "I just wanna program."

Romero was unrelenting: "Dude, that is the coolest shit I have ever seen anywhere in my whole life! Don't you see? We're going to take over the world!"

Carmack just turned back to his computer.

During the day, Romero, Carmack, and Wilbur worked at Softdisk. But at night, they loaded up Softdisk's computers into the back of Romero's car and took them home to the Lake House, a big, one-level affair the three had rented from a dentist they called Dr. Bob. The house sat alongside Cross Lake, and had a Jacuzzi in the master bedroom and a keg in the refrigerator. Together the Johns and Wilbur held marathon *Dungeons & Dragons* campaigns, watched *Evil Dead* on the VCR, played Nintendo, listened to Iggy Pop, Queen, and Nine Inch Nails, and swam in the lake. But mostly, they made videogames.

Then one day Romero realized that the fan mail he'd been tacking up above his computer and making everyone read was all coming from the same address: Garland, Texas. He called up the sender to say, "Leave me alone, you psychotic bastard," but it turned out the guy was a man named Scott Miller, the founder of now-legendary PC game company Apogee. Miller deftly defused the situation by offering Romero $2,000 to make any kind of game he wanted. Make three games, Miller said. We'll give the first two away and sell the last one—Miller was at the forefront of what's now known as a shareware model of distribution. So Romero, Carmack, and Tom Hall spent three months making a trilogy called *Commander Keen* about a little boy who saves the universe. One month after being uploaded, the Shreveport guys had a royalty check for $10,500. One year after that, they were settling into new digs in Dallas.

**BY NOON IT'S 108°F** outside, and cyberathletes are still pouring into the Hyatt lobby, brushing past the Mary Kay ladies, lugging monitors as big as their chests, carrying armloads of keyboards, cords dangling to their knees. In the lobby, the air-conditioning drops the temperature down to somewhere south of sixty-five. The shooters look around them, take in the chandeliers, the high ceilings, and then hop on the escalators down to the basement. The basement is all Angel, pre-Cyberstadium, was able to procure. But it's theirs for four days.

It's even cooler in the hotel's basement. Anything over fifty-nine degrees and the cyberathletes start squawking. (With so many people and so much overclocked computer equipment humming, buzzing, and whirring nonstop, the room must meet near-refrigeration temperature standards.) There are huge bags of food, stacks of caffeine drinks. Coolers block the aisles.

In the back, still unpacking, is Beverly Clark, who just drove in from Springdale, Arkansas. A *Doom* fan for about six years, Beverly has come with her husband, Vince, an ex-marine who's now a programmer with IBM, and her son, who's celebrating his twelfth birthday. Beverly made sure her posse arrived early so she could snag the back row for her family and the fourteen friends with whom they traveled in a caravan to the event. Beverly unpacks cans of Pringles, and huge bags of M&Ms. She's been shopping and cooking almost nonstop for two weeks. She's got trail mix, peanut brittle, chocolate chip cookies, turtle brownies, and her specialty, homemade peanut-butter cups. A kid with a handful of headsets stops by and puts an arm around Beverly. "I love you," he says, with only a hint of sarcasm before grabbing some snacks and moving on. "And I love you," she calls after him. "They call me Quakemom," she says, sounding pleased.

One of the friends with whom Beverly came to the Summer CPL is Lee Rakestraw, who has made a Computer-on-a-Stick, which he hopes will capture the top prize in Angel's BYOC (Bring Your Own Computer) custom computer contest. Pieces of computer hardware stick out at crazy angles, held by clamps to a pole, which stands about four feet high. Somehow the contraption is completely functional. There's a photograph taped to the thing of John Romero in a red shirt posing next to it.

Lee Rakestraw has been coming to Angel's CPL events since they started. In fact he's a little worried the thing is getting out of hand. He's concerned there won't be a place left for someone like him, a guy who comes not to compete but only to be a spectator. Lee himself stopped competing after he lost it during a match and smashed his keyboard over his knee. Still, Lee is happy to make the cross-country trip every year anyway. "This is my vacation," he explains. "I come down here to let my hair down. You walk in here and it's like, my God, these are my people. It's just *right*. It's like walking into your own house."

Lee is also a card-carrying member of the Senior Gaming League, a relatively new enterprise of his buddy Chris Overbey's, thirty-seven, who's sitting at the table right behind him. Overbey felt guys over thirty having to compete with guys under thirty wasn't fair, and he's been working ever since to establish a separate league. His argument is that it's not fair to expect a guy older than thirty—with family responsibilities and real work commitments—to compete with some nineteen-year-old with nothing but time on his hands. Overbey looks like a character actor hired to play a mean cop. He's big, and kind of burly, with a close buzz cut, a little mustache, and slittish eyes. So far the Senior Gaming League has had only a minitournament at Quakecom, a rival tournament; he's been having a hard time breaking in.

A kid squeezes through the aisle between the tables where Lee and Chris are sitting. He's wearing a white T-shirt that says ANGEL MUNOZ IS MY HERO in fuzzy ironed-on letters. Lee and Chris exchange a friendly nod with the kid as he passes.

**MOSTLY, WHEN THE** two Johns and the rest of their team arrived in Dallas, Carmack sat with his back to the door, programming. "Carmack is a robot," John Romero says. "The dude just works. Okay. He never stops. Okay. He didn't even have a mattress or a bed." Occasionally, one of the others would toss a blanket or a pillow into the room, on the off chance Carmack wanted some sleep. Usually, he didn't. Eventually, Romero got him a mattress. ("I was like, Dude, you need to sleep like a normal human being.") Occasionally, Carmack would emerge from his room and toss the guys a bit of programming, and the guys would holler and swoop down on it.

They had actually sent Carmack's version of the side-scrolling *Super Mario Bros. 3* on the PC to Nintendo in a bid for a contract. But Nintendo had responded to the technical feat with a letter saying they would never put Mario on anything but a Nintendo system.

After that, the guys had figured, *fuck it,* and were making their own kind of game. It was a remake of an old Apple II game called *Castle Wolfenstein,* and it was about Nazis and prison camps and vicious dogs and lots of other good stuff that turned Romero and his partners on. They worked sixteen-hour days, and business manager Jay kept them stocked with the essentials: junk food, toilet paper, and computer disks. If you can't join 'em, beat 'em was the operating attitude at id. On hindsight, of course, that's how it often is with these high-octane bursts of creative or technological energy that set a culture on fire—people saying *fuck it* and just doing it their own way. But at the time, it was just the Johns, a couple of guys cooking up their own version of the great garage band of American entrepreneurial lore.

When id uploaded *Wolfenstein 3D,* word shot through the hardcore gaming community. People started to know there was something crazy going on in Dallas. This time the group found themselves with a first-month royalty check for $100,000.

Jay moved the id crew out of the five connecting apartments in the La Prada Club apartment complex where they'd been living and working and into the sixth floor of that black cube of an office building off the LBJ Expressway in Mesquite. One year later, they had built *Doom*.

*Doom* was to be a crazy, "beat-back-the-minions-of-hell type of game," Jay said. The attitude that had cemented the id team together in the first place was translated into the game's design. It was a horror-movie heavy-metal aesthetic on top of a videogame experience. Instead of designating difficulty levels with labels like "easy," "medium," and "hard," players were asked "How Tough Are You?" and options ran from "Can I Play, Daddy?" to "Death Incarnate."

There was only one advertisement for *Doom,* which came out on December 10, 1993. The word of mouth, however, proved so effective and efficient that marketers have been studying it ever since. They call it *viral marketing* now. Jay Wilbur sat with the game as it uploaded. And the very minute the last bit of data was up, ten thousand gamers hit the site, causing the entire network to collapse under the pressure. The guy who was running the network in Wisconsin called Jay on the telephone. "Oh my God," he said, "I've never seen anything like this." The game spread like the flu in February.

When *Doom* came out, everything in the world of videogames changed, instantly and irrevocably, overnight. The engine Carmack had built for the game maximized power and allowed for a speed of game play that had never existed before on a PC. The balance between speed and high resolution is the perpetual struggle in game design. A game like *Myst* produces gorgeous, elaborate images, but moves at a snail's pace. *Doom* was so fast it made novices dizzy. (By 1996, the medical profession was recognizing DIMS, or *Doom*-induced motion sickness, as a medical term.) You roared through the dungeons of hell at the pace of a locomotive, mowing down everything in sight at rapid-fire speed, and were into the next corridor before the mutated beast you'd just blasted away had even finished its dying spasms.

*Doom* was totally immersive. You heard a simulation of your own breathing. The monsters you fought had scales and slime and rolling eyeballs. There was blood. Hard industrial-rock music blasted in the background. It was the thing for which people had been waiting, without even knowing it. No more monkeys swinging from trees collecting coconuts. Parents had been worried that too much Nintendo would harm their kids. Now those kids had become teenagers, and they were playing as heavily armed mercenaries, fighting it out with every kind of sick and demented monster a guy like Romero could come up with. The tone of the game was dark in a way that frightens grownups, because it laid bare their children's ability to tolerate something that to them is a total assault on the senses.

The ante had been raised. Completely alienating to the older generation, it was completely energizing to the younger. It was the creative culmination of the wrath of a generation of ignored young men. There were parents' groups, lawsuits, stories in *Fortune* and *Forbes*. *People* magazine named John Romero one of the sexiest men of the year. Carmack was a god among his high-tech brethren. The two Johns bought matching Ferraris.

**BY SATURDAY EVENING,** Angel is running around the Hyatt basement with his benign smile and frantic forward posture. He's almost completely hoarse. They're having problems because the kids have been ordering pizzas and not picking them up, so there's a logjam of pizza delivery guys in the Hyatt lobby. Angel is disheartened. "Please, if you've ordered a pizza, you must come pick it up!" he announces into his microphone. *This is why we need the Cyberstadium,* every look from Angel seems to convey.

The kids are starting to amble out of the basement—many of them haven't left it in eleven, twelve hours. They've got laminates around their necks that display their names and announce them as professional cyberathletes. There are lots of baggy shorts, oversized sweatshirts, and bad posture. There's a musical "event" happening this opening night. The CPL's first ever. And it's upstairs, in the Reunion Ballroom, out of the basement. Angel is quite excited.

Two cops guard the ballroom's entrance. One leans over to the other: "Whatcha have here is a bunch of people who need to get to work," he murmurs. When they get into the ballroom, all the kids pile into the back. Angel in black shorts, a black polo shirt, and a black baseball hat is up on stage begging the kids, in a determinedly upbeat way, to move to the front of the room. "For those of you up against the wall, please come join us," he calls. But the kids are refusing to sit up front. Someone runs onstage and gives Angel a note. He claps his hands together. "CNN is coming!" he cries as the kids filter in, carrying pizza boxes and crates of Bawls, an obscenely thick and sweet guarana caffeine drink—and a tournament sponsor. Angel is bending his knees and coming as close to shrieking as a man who's almost entirely lost his voice can, "You're going to be on national television!" The crowd is clearly psyched. A couple of lighters can be seen flickering across the room. Angel stands up tall. "This is now a worldwide recognized sport!" he cries. "And we are *here,*" he adds, "to make sure you get the media attention you deserve!"

Intel, the CPL's major sponsor—who do you think buys all those high-margin, high-powered CPUs?—raffles off a Pentium 4 processor.

Then, Angel is joined onstage by a young woman in tight jeans and a big black motorcycle jacket. She's got short blonde hair, huge round breasts, and what's got to be the sweetest, brightest smile in Dallas. Every single boy in that room knows who she is. She's Stevie "Killcreek" Case, the girl who beat John Romero in his own Quake Deathmatch in 1997 when she was twenty, and now claims the title of girlfriend and business partner. Stevie was actually one of the original founders of the Cyberathlete League. Her baptism into the world of shooters had come as a *Doom II*–addicted college freshman, and her passion for the genre led her to found the notorious Impulse9 clan.

Stevie asks the audience to "say hi to John Romero," who it turns out is sitting in the audience. He stands up, about three-quarters of the way, waves a quick hand, and hunkers back down in his chair. There's a kind of hush, as if the kids aren't sure how to react. Some of them are a little too young, some just weren't expecting his actual presence—Romero can have that effect on people, generating a sort of shock that he actually exists.

**SOME PEOPLE THINK** John Romero should have died young, crashed one of his fast cars off a Dallas freeway. Romero rose too far too fast—and his obvious enjoyment of his success irked people. He was everywhere you looked: online, in magazines, at events, always with his long, black hair swinging, his mouth working intelligently but overtime. He was having the remarkable experience of being exactly who he was and being richly rewarded for it—a crystalline moment in time when he was so good at simply being himself that the world around him exploded in excitement. Romero had a kind of rock-star charisma that made certain people shiver.

But, like the movie industry, the videogame industry is very much a "What have you done for me lately?" kind of business. When Romero plummeted back to earth, the industry fairly hummed with glee.

Like many who have enjoyed meteoric fame, John Romero is far smaller in person than pictures of him would indicate. He's good-looking in an off-kilter way. One of his eyes heads off in its own direction, making him look a bit like a miniature Keanu Reeves who's just taken a hard knock to the head. In fact rumor, which Romero denies, holds that his walleye is the result of having had his head bashed against a videogame machine by his stepfather, who had forbidden him to enter arcades.

Romero's childhood and adolescence were not the stuff of happy memories. He grew up in Rocklin, California, a suburban wasteland outside Sacramento. His stepfather was a former drill sergeant with his own ideas about discipline, although apparently he wasn't very successful in this respect with John. By the time Romero was a teenager, he was into comic books, vandalism, graffiti, and fighting. In fact, John's penchant for trouble didn't abate until he discovered the Apple II. At that point, Romero began channeling everything into his computer—all his pent-up rage, unrecognized intelligence, and dormant creativity. Once he'd discovered this digital machine on which to learn, play, and build, his sights shifted from petty larceny toward designing videogames. He made dozens of them, selling them on his own to tiny publishers and computer stores. The Apple II had set him free.

**UPSTAIRS IN THE** Dallas Hyatt bar, the bartender is insisting on three forms of ID. "My boss said he'd fire me if I don't." It certainly seems to be doing the trick. There is only one person at the bar, a hefty young man wearing a black visor low on his head and a collection of black rubber bands on his arm. His name is Frank Rivera. He's a first-generation American, the leader of his own FPS (first-person-shooter) clan, and he's having a whiskey and water on the rocks.

Frank, twenty-one, is down from Arlington, Texas, for the tournament. Frank's clan is called D4W, which stands for "Down for Whatever." He formed the clan three years ago with some guys he recruited over the Internet from Omaha, Nebraska. He even convinced a couple of them to move down to Texas. "They were working for Intel, they had the money, they were down for it," Frank says. Things went really well for a while. Practices were regular and disciplined. But lately, Frank's been having some trouble with his players. They're not listening, skipping practice. He takes his role as squad leader as seriously as any boot camp sergeant, so the lack of dedication among his troops demoralizes him. He feels it's his responsibility to motivate them. "They don't *listen* to me as much they should," he laments. "Sometimes I just have to *tell* people to take their *heads* out of their *asses* and PLAY."

This year, D4W isn't competing. Frank doesn't think they're ready. But they better be, and soon, because Frank's life ambition is to be a top-ranked clan leader. "People always ask me, 'Why are you so interested in this game?'" Frank says. Christian friends, especially, have been on his case. "I just say, 'Hey, that's what your good at—quoting scripture, reading the Bible. And that's cool. But this is what I'm good at.' You know?"

Frank admits he initially got so wrapped up in the first-person-shooter *lifestyle* that for a while he let both his financial and familial obligations slip. "There was a time when I didn't go *to work,*" he says. "I wouldn't show up because I *had* to play." He stopped going to church, didn't go see his mom. "I needed to *chill,*" Frank says.

Now Frank is a waiter at Chili's at the Dallas/Fort Worth International Airport. He goes to church; he has dinners with his mom. But his dream is the same. He thought about joining the Air Force—similar skills, he figured—but a dream can be a hard thing to squelch. He doesn't care that he's older than most of the top clanners, that the ranked players practice far more than the six hours a day he squeezes in, that maintaining a seven-gigabyte team server is expensive. "This is what I'm good at," Frank says.

So far D4W has done all right in random matches online and at a couple of LAN parties, which is when the kids hold tournaments for themselves, getting a server and linking together their PCs in rented warehouses or abandoned buildings. "We get respect," Frank says. "I don't have the best people in my clan. But I have *smart* people." Smart is the ultimate compliment among first-person shooters. Saying someone is smart is saying *he's got it.* In the theater, they call it talent. In sports they call it heart. But for shooters, it's not the ability to relate with an audience or deliver some feat of impossible athleticism that earns respect. Rather, shooters value the ability to make accurate decisions at breakneck speed while juggling multitudes of variables in a simulated life-or-death situation. That's what makes you *smart.* Period.

**BY 1995 *DOOM*** mania was at its peak, and id was raking in money hand over fist. Annual revenues had gone from a couple of hundred thousand to about $17 million in three years. And because the company had never borrowed a dime, and still adhered to the shareware model, which sold directly to the consumer, it was all theirs. By the time they were working on *Quake,* their followup game to *Doom II,* there were an estimated 20 million shareware games of *Doom* installed around the world, and two million games sold. These were unthinkable numbers for a computer game at that time.

But the tensions at id had begun to show, like cracks in a cheap cement wall. Carmack was being hailed as the most important 3-D graphics figure in the world. Romero was known as the "ego of id." Romero took to wearing ostrich boots and having custom race cars built. Carmack got an apartment less than half a mile from the offices so he wouldn't get hurt driving home exhausted from several days of programming.

Romero wanted *Quake* to be a complete departure, a totally wild, new thrill ride of a game that neither looked nor felt like *Doom* or *Doom II.* Carmack himself didn't care what the game looked like. In fact, Carmack wasn't even playing videogames anymore. The *Quake* engine, his twentieth, was taking him a painfully long time to finish. He had begun dreaming about polygons in space, then waking up covered in sweat. Carmack became so consumed with the idea that those around him weren't working hard enough that he set up his workstation in a hallway where he could monitor the team's habits. He had all the walls in the office torn down so that everybody had to work together in one big room. You still meet people at game gatherings today who labored for id during this period, and they shudder at the memory of life in what came to be known as the War Room.

Carmack was particularly suspicious of Romero, who it was rumored spent much of his time organizing death matches with fans over the Internet rather than getting much work done. Carmack wrote a hack that reported to him every time Romero logged on to and off of his computer. The results weren't flattering. Finally, one day in June 1996, not too long after *Quake* was released, John Carmack fired John Romero. Carmack gave his partner his walking papers in a small room with Adrian Carmack (no relation) and Kevin Cloud, two of the original id members, sitting right there, feeling like shit, but afraid not to back Carmack up. Although the original id team members were supposedly all partners, the fact of the matter was Carmack was truly king—it was his technological prowess that was irreplaceable.

"Look, the fact is, John Carmack is going to go down in history as one of the brilliant programmers of our day," says Henry Lowood, the curator for the History of Science and Technology Collections at Stanford University. "John Carmack's work on matrix math, searching algorithms and collision algorithms was very important. The problems he solved are real technical problems, far more than just game design problems."

That's a hard guy to be partners with.

**SOME OF THE** American kids at the Hyatt are growing concerned about the international competition this year. A crisis bloomed last year when 3X, the top-ranked American team, famously split up in a fissure that sent one half of the team to DoP (Domain of Pain) and the other half to 3D (Desire. Discipline. Dedication.). Frank Rivera, for one, is still mourning 3X's break up. He still studies matches of theirs that he downloaded from the Internet. "They were so *intelligent,*" he laments. But what's done is done. DoP and 3D are this year's top-ranked American teams, and many at the tournament have their hopes firmly pinned on one or the other. Nevertheless there's a lot of speculation in the basement that even 3D and DoP don't have what it takes to bring down the Northern Europeans.

Schroet Kommando. A top contender from Sweden. SK—part of choosing a clan name is realizing that whatever the name, it will inevitably be abbreviated to four or fewer letters—is led by manager Andreas Thorstensson, who's twenty-three and arrives in low-slung jeans, with gorgeously tussled blond hair. The team, which has a German and a Scandinavian branch, is backed by a sponsorship from Intel and has a reputation for "just raping you." Their clutch player is a tall boy of Asian descent, Jorgen Johannessen, aka XeqtR, with cheekbones to rival Faye Dunaway's and hair that he's gelled into spikes lying forward and framing his face. When Schroet Kommando move through the hotel, people stop talking.

Spacebar. Norwegian. Only ranked twelfth, but thought to "rip." They're a dream team, an amalgamation of top players from Norway. The most conspicuous members of Spacebar are a pair of friends seen together throughout the tournament, one short and fat, wearing a Nike sweatshirt and a Rastafarian sham throughout the proceedings, the other three feet taller and reed thin, with an angelic face framed by white blond hair.

GoL. Another Swedish team. The word on them is that they're good. Real good. GoL is not a dream team. No stars, standouts, or rejects. They're just a collection of good, tight players.

Steve Grempka, of American hopeful Domain of Pain, says Spacebar is the team to beat. Steve says all the European teams are really aggressive; it's just the Euro style. First-person-shooter games are big in Europe, especially in northern Europe and the Scandinavian countries, because, or so people speculate, the long winter nights leave them little else to do.

Steve is a recent graduate of Northeastern Illinois University in Chicago and is waiting until after this competition to get a full- time job. He has extremely good manners, is solidly handsome, and clearly exercises and eats his vegetables. He majored in business and hopes to get a job in marketing at a computer company. Hardly the picture of a game-addled loser, Grempka's articulate, rational. He's been on DoP for about a year and a half, but he only actually met his teammates—from Orlando, Alabama, Dallas, New York, and St. Louis—at last year's CPL. So far, DoP has won about $5,000 in prize money. It's not much, but Steve's not complaining about earning an extra grand. And in any event, tournament purses seem to be following a Moore's law of their own, rising almost exponentially each year. Plus, they get to travel on someone else's tab—in Domain of Pain's case, a chain of gaming cafes in Seattle and British Columbia called Nerve.

Steve says the community of top-notch players, the ranked,

the truly elite, is so insular that if someone unrecognized shows up at an LAN party and does really well, everyone will assume they're cheating. "You just couldn't be of a certain level and not be known," Steve says, "unless you're from Dallas. Which I guess is a whole category unto itself."

**THE DISSOLUTION OF** the original id team hit the gaming world the way the breakup of the Beatles had shattered rock fans twenty-five years earlier. The community reacted with grief, anger, and shock. People took sides, made assumptions, assigned blame. There were Carmack supporters and Romero apologists. But whatever side people took, everyone pretty much agreed that the industry had suffered an enormous loss. Apart, neither of them was capable of achieving the kind of brilliance they'd displayed together. In some ways, however, it didn't matter. By then, first-person-shooter culture no longer belonged exclusively to them.

So while the industry churned with rumors over his firing, Romero happily accepted $25 million in start-up money and a publishing deal from English publisher Eidos. He rented the glass-roofed penthouse of the prestigious Chase Tower in downtown Dallas, and formed Ion Storm, where the motto was "Design is law." Ripe with attitude reminiscent of the early days of id, Ion Storm ran ads saying, "John Romero Wants to Make You His Bitch," with a tag line that said, "Suck it down."

The early days of Ion Storm enjoyed all the glory of Marc Antony in Rome. Money flowed freely through Ion Storm's coffers, and everyone in the world who dug first-person shooters wanted to work there. Hundreds of ambitious FPS fans and would-be developers poured into town. Dallas was

Mecca, and id and Ion Storm had established themselves as its competing temples.

Ion Storm alone had 120 new positions to fill, and id had already been spawning for years. Cygnus Games came down to do subcontracting work for them and spun off into Rogue Studios. Scott Miller had spun off part of Apogee into 3D Realms, which hit with the FPS-parody *Duke Nuk'em*. There was Ritual Entertainment, Terminal Reality, Rebel Boat Rocker, and Ensemble Studios. The development houses were like so many amoebas, splitting and dividing, sloughing off daughter cells in droves. Dallas soon became to first-person-shooter culture what Seattle had been for pop music in the late 1980s and early '90s. Dallas was where you went if you wanted to be where the action was.

**ON MONDAY, THE** third day of the summer CPL competition, there are sixteen teams left. By Tuesday evening, there will be only three, and on Wednesday a new CPL champion will be crowned. So far, there have been no big surprises. DoP is still in, Spacebar, Schroet Kommando, 3D. Generation X, the cute Brazilian team, has been knocked out, and the guys are trying to keep up each other's spirits for the rest of the tournament.

Brandon Holt, the fifteen-year-old from San Antonio, is still running strong. He's only been sleeping about five hours a night, he says. He's amped up on Bawls, the "energy" drink whose marketers are giving away cases of the stuff to attendees. (Hardcore gamers are well versed in the art of swag collection.) When he's at home, Brandon practices with his older brother, Justin, daily. During the summers, drills start at eleven a.m. and often don't end until eleven or so at night. They play games of five-on-five with friends whose computers are networked together. They practice weapon handling—pistols, grenades, and machine guns primarily—and running "strats" (tactical plays) that Justin, the team leader, has devised. Brandon's handle is TANK.

Where Brandon is quick and almost feline in appearance, his brother, Justin Holt, looks like a former football player. He's bigger and fleshier than his brother, and his features seem as if they have sagged from some originally higher, tighter arrangement. He wears a gigantic gold watch hanging on his wrist and an equally bold high school signet ring. Justin seems simultaneously worried about taking up too much space and anxious that his presence isn't big enough.

Justin has been a videogame fanatic since he was seven and first discovered Nintendo. He's just never found anything else he likes to do more. He dreams of leading a top clan, like Frank Rivera. It has begun to dawn on him, however, that this may not happen. Since graduating high school, Justin has been working at a Nextel store, selling mobile phones, and earning extra money waiting tables at a local pizzeria in San Antonio called Luciano's. As an adult with adult responsibilities, Justin no longer can find the time to practice the twelve hours a day he says are necessary for true excellence. His parents are hardly sympathetic. In fact, Justin had to do some serious lobbying so that his brother Brandon could come to the CPL this year.

"They didn't want him to get all into gaming," Justin says. "They think it takes away from his childhood."

Justin and Brandon's parents both work at Dominguez State Jail in San Antonio. Their mother is a drug counselor there, and their stepfather is a prison guard in Cell Block K—"the worst in the whole prison," Brandon boasts.

Unlike his brother, Brandon has no interest in becoming a professional player. "To compete, you have to love, love, love the game," he says, "and I mean *love* the game." For him it's more about the exhilaration. He likes to feel his adrenaline pumping. "It's just really fun," he says. "It's kind of exciting to kill people."

**PHYSICALLY, JOHN CARMACK** is a slight man, with a narrow chest, skinny legs and arms, and alabaster white skin. If you were a bartender, and it was dark in your bar, you'd probably card him. He has pale hair he wears pulled back in a ponytail, and a tight little mouth, as if he were perpetually sucking in his lips. He is known to live almost exclusively on Diet Coke and pizza.

One of the first things you notice about John is the kind of metaphors people use to talk about him. People describe him as a "machine" or a "technical powerhouse" or a "workhorse and not a person." "He's a robot." You hear it over and over.

"It's not that he's truly unfriendly," says David Kushner, author of *Masters of Doom: How Two Guys Created an Empire and Transformed Pop Culture*. But then Kushner fumbles to explain it properly. Carmack is known for turning back to his computer while the person talking to him is still midsentence. He doesn't say hi to employees in the hall, and he's not big on effusive praise. "It's really not personal," says Kushner, who had to move to Dallas for several months to be available whenever Carmack actually felt like talking. He obviously wants to make it clear that Carmack isn't a dick. Rather, it's just that Carmack doesn't value human relations the way other people tend to. Carmack does have a value scale, but programming is far higher on it than human interaction. It's as if he is so hopelessly, irrevocably analytical that there's no room whatsoever to be emotive.

Carmack grew up in Kansas City and Raytown, Missouri,

a restless, unhappy kid of divorced parents. He didn't speak a single word until he was a year and a half, when he surprised his father with an entire sentence. ("Here's your loofah, Daddy," he said.) At his Catholic school, he tried to argue other kids out of what he saw as their ghastly irrational religious beliefs. He also developed a love of explosives, rockets, and bombs. In fact, he even did a brief turn at a juvenile home for breaking into a nearby school with a couple of other boys and a chemical concoction he'd made. The school was home to a couple of Apple II computers the boy had coveted. The psychiatric evaluation that followed reported, "Boy behaves like a walking brain with legs." He loved comic books and *Lord of the Rings* and Richard Garriott's *Ultima* games. After taking a course on the Radio Shack TRS-80, Carmack tinkered with the machine until he knew it inside and out. He programmed until he could get it to do things that no one, not even the professors at the college he attended for one semester, could do. Like Romero, he started making and selling games before he was eligible for the draft, let alone able to drink legally. When he finally moved to Shreveport, Louisiana, it was the first time Carmack remembers ever having been really content; it was the first time he was programming, or talking about programming all day long.

**NEAR THE INTERNET** radio booth doing a live feed, there's a bit of a commotion. It's CliffyB, and he's in full form, brandishing his early George Clooney look. He's got a silver chain around his neck, a natty leather jacket over his shoulder. He moves slowly, with studied casualness. Alan Willard, a friend and level designer with whom CliffyB shares an office at Epic, is in tow as well, lurching a step behind. It's only natural for Epic to be represented here. Epic is run by Jay Wilbur, formerly of id, and it's one of the most successful spin-offs out there. It's a Dallas company, even if it's headquarters are in North Carolina. One of the Children of *Doom*.

Cliffy is going to give a workshop on what to expect from the next *Unreal* installment, due out around Christmastime. Cliffy is happy to do it for the "kids." He also wants Angel to consider *Unreal* for future CPL events—the exposure would be unbeatable—*and* he's heard *Entertainment Weekly* is going to be here taking photographs. Cliffy hangs out, saunters about the basement, and signs a few autographs, before heading upstairs for some lunch.

Over their meal, Alan and Cliffy are bitching about a recent *Nightline* episode on *Grand Theft Auto III*. The show took the same old, familiar "videogames are bad for you" stance, Cliffy and Alan say. It's not that they think videogames are beyond reproach, but they do feel that Ted Koppel let them down. "If entertainment has to be socially redeeming," Cliffy says, "we wouldn't have rock 'n' roll. We wouldn't have the Fox network." Alan sighs in agreement.

Alan's been in the Army—he ran away from home when he was a teenager and signed up—and in his opinion first-person shooters don't teach kids to be killers. They don't make you any better at *killing,* he argues; rather, it's *teamwork* they make you good at. Tactical, combat-oriented teamwork, that is. "First-person-shooter games are really just training people to like the Army," Alan says good-naturedly and without a hint of irony.

It turns out the Army has been a source of some interest for Cliffy and Alan recently. Epic has a fantastic business model borrowed from id, which calls for the company to license its *Unreal* graphics engine to other companies. Their most recent client is the U.S. Army Game Project, which has just released its first product, a first-person shooter that the Army will use as a recruitment tool. The *Unreal* engine, which was modeled after the *Doom* engine, is fueling *America's Army Operations,* or *Ops* as everybody calls it. The game has proven extremely successful with game reviewers and FPS enthusiasts, who were thrilled at the opportunity to download an AAA-caliber videogame at no charge. Michael Capps, *Ops*'s lead designer, will be at the Hyatt on Tuesday to speak with the cyberathletes about the Army's game. The Army is even considering becoming one of Angel's CPL sponsors.

"The Army needs recruits," Cliffy says, in a what-can-you-do tone. "They need young people. And the people here playing these games *are* the right people to be recruiting. Just to be here you have to know how to build a computer, strategize, and work with other people."

Cliffy does think, however, that the Army's new slogan, "An Army of One," is stupid. "I have a better one," he says. "'Join the Army, get to use lots of cool weapons and blow people's brains out.' That would be much more effective."

**IN DALLAS PEOPLE** knew that things were going horribly wrong for John Romero far before *Time* and *Entertainment Weekly* did. In January 1999 the *Dallas Observer* ran an inside look at the company, concluding: "The place where the designer's vision is king has turned into a toxic mix of prima donnas and personality cults." *Daikatana,* Romero's supposed "game to end all games," was to use the *Quake I* engine, licensed from id, but when the *Quake II* engine came out, it once again surpassed anything that had come before. Ion Storm had to completely recode *Daikatana* or risk releasing a game that was graphically obsolete before it even hit the shelves. Delay after delay ensued, and when the game was finally released in 2000, it was a total flop, both commercially and critically. Telling hardcore gamers you're going to make them your bitch is fine as long as you then proceed to do it. But having failed to pull it off, Romero was immediately reduced to the status of poseur.

Romero lost control of Ion Storm. With Stevie "Killcreek" Case, he left the company and began making games for cell phones in relative obscurity. He cut off his trademark black locks, and sold his Ferrari for a canary-yellow Hummer. Stevie was his advocate, trying to make deals for the home-based company they'd founded with id original Tom Hall. But as soon as the name John Romero came up, all negotiations would fall apart, Stevie said. His name was hopelessly smeared. Nobody wanted anything to do with him.

In 2001, John Carmack became the third person inducted into the Video Game Hall of Fame.

**AT 11:45 ON** Wednesday morning, Frank Rivera is midway through the lunch rush at Chili's. The final round of the Cyberathlete Professional League's international summer tournament is to be held at 12:30 p.m. sharp. Frank is stressing. Hard. Finally, he can't take it anymore. He grabs his manager, tells him, "I got personal business," and leaves. He makes it from the airport to the Dallas Hyatt in twenty minutes, a trip that usually takes forty-five.

The championship round is held in the same place the rest of the tournament has taken place, a roped-off section, maybe eight hundred square feet, of the Hyatt basement. This is the territory of Frank Nuccio, the CPL's commissioner, a man no bigger than a tall child, with large brown eyes and a photographic memory for all things concerning the CPL. Nuccio is the technological wizard behind Munoz's effort to create a first-person-shooter Oz. It's his job to make sure all the competition PCs, provided by the CPL, are running, and running identically. He takes his job seriously, without being abrasive, and stands guard as the kids troop in and out, their own keyboards and mice, customized and covered with stickers, held tightly under their arms.

The competition area holds maybe fifteen discrete tables, each holding six PCs and representing a single team. For three days, the area has been awash in a roar of commands shouted out in at least ten different languages. The kids get pumped as they play: sweat pours down their faces, they grimace, swear, bark into their headsets, grit their teeth. "Nien! Nien!" from the German teams. Something that sounds like "Flasha! Flasha!" from the Norwegians—it's their captain, who is shouting for his teammates to deploy flash grenades to blind and stun their opponents. Under the tables, feet tap, twitch, bounce, stomp, and grind into the floor. In between rounds, the teams huddle together, sometimes criticizing each other angrily, sometimes encouraging each other with loud cries of "Come on! We can do it! Let's GO!" Commissioner Nuccio says this is the difference between the teams that win and the teams that lose: winners encourage each other; losers blame.

There have been two big surprise losses by Wednesday. Both American hopefuls, Domain of Pain, and Desire. Disciple. Dedication. have been knocked out. The American kids are bummed. The 3D loss in particular has the crowd bewildered and hurt. DoP at least came in a respectable fourth place. (Steve Grempka will take home a couple hundred bucks.) But 3D lost to a little-known Australian team called F0, placing only seventeenth. And 3D is a very serious team. Their players have been in Dallas for a week, holed up together in a hotel practicing eight hours a day. Schroet Kommando may have Intel as a sponsor and Andreas of the rough blond hair and exposed abdomen as a manager, but 3D has Web2Zone, a growing chain of LAN cafes, and Craig Levine, a kinky-haired, walleyed, and enthusiastic NYU business major from Long Island, managing them. The 3D guys have matching jackets with each player's name on the back alongside the logos of their sponsors. They have plastic Cross pens that hang around their necks with the 3D logo embossed on them. Craig Levine says when they give interviews in online chat groups or on Web radio broadcasts, hundreds, sometimes thousands, of people call in for them. These guys even have a couple of girls draped over their arms. "We're like the Tiger Woods of gaming," Craig shouts over the din of the basement. There's a sense in the lobby that "if 3D could lose, anyone could."

As Craig ushers his team out of the basement, reminding them to stay focused on what's to come rather than what's just happened, there are only two teams left in the competition. It's Swede against Swede. Norwegian dream team Spacebar was knocked out Tuesday—they "crossed their legs" when it came down to the final wire is the word in the basement—and the Americans were squelched like bugs on a windshield. Up for the title are Schroet Kommando and GoL.

When Frank Rivera arrives, the crowd around the competition area, now totally cleared except for the two final teams at opposite tables, is ten or twelve people thick. The Holts are watching, Brandon with his sunglasses up on his head, Justin in a floppy green-and-white chef's hat. Angel is there. Commissioner Nuccio. Stevie "Killcreek" Case. Beverly the Quakemom watches from her computer in the back of the room, although her son and husband have deserted her to watch the match up front. Lee Rakestraw remains in back with Beverly. His computer on a stick managed eleventh place in the BYOC contest.

The room is unusually quiet as the match starts. The only sounds are those of the SK and GoL team members beginning to cry commands and encouragement to one another through their headsets. In the second round, GoL starts to pull ahead. With a spray of bullets from a virtual AK-47, they have left not one but three SK players lying facedown in the tawny-toned piazza. The room erupts into shouts of "Raped!"

SK is clearly nervous. You can see it in the way their faces twitch. They're wiping their palms together between plays, moving their mice spasmodically, with little jerks and pulls. Then, Emil "HeatoN" Christensen, SK's virtuoso sniper, retaliates with a neat shot to the head of one of GoL's players. "Owned! Owned!" echoes through the crowd. The room becomes a sea of people all making the same oval shape with their lips and raising their fists in the air. "Owning" somebody is not as good as "raping" someone, but it's the next best thing.

GoL takes the first match, 13 to 1. Frank Rivera shakes his head. There's talk of whether SK is going to "drop their pants and show what they're made of," or just let GoL take them down. In a corner of the competition area, SK's nineteen-year-old Tommy "Potti" Ingemarsson is trying to marshal his troops. The crowd listens in but, unfortunately, he's speaking Swedish. Still, most of the people there don't need to know the language to know what's being said. He's psyching them up, getting them ready to go back out there and face the enemy.

By the end of the third round, Schroet Kommando is raping everything in site. HeatoN is on a tear. He's a tall, heavyset white kid with spiky blond hair dressed in an oversized SK T-shirt. As he plays, he breathes in huge amounts of air and puffs out his cheeks to enormous proportions, looking like a marathon runner on his last legs, or like Louis Armstrong holding a high note. HeatoN is thought by many to be the best shooter in the world. "Every move you think you're going to make, he already knows it," says Frank Rivera in admiration. "It's like he built the game himself or something."

A few more minutes and it's final. Schroet Kommando takes the match 13 to 9.

Pandemonium breaks out in and around the competition area. The Schroet Kommando guys have both hands raised in the air, their mouths wide open, heads thrown back in the full-on international victory stance. They're screaming. Manager Andreas is running from player to player. He executes a Pete Townsend leap in the air, his legs bent back behind him. The GoL players have their faces to the ground, necks bent forward with dismay.

The media swarms in, news cameras, reporters. CNN actually did show up. *Entertainment Weekly* is indeed doing a story on the event. Potti gives a postgame victory speech. He looks exhausted and elated. He has longish brown hair and a weak chin, a gold chain around his neck. He says it was a "very tough match," and he thanks the CPL for making all this possible. "Without them," he says in just slightly accented English, "this would just be something people did in their spare time."

Frank Rivera is knocked around in the crowd. He's awed. It was a terrific match. He wishes he'd had time to set up his PC to record it—he's trying to build up his Euro demo collection. Will I ever be this good? he thinks. Will I end up having to join the Air Force? Serving burritos at Chili's for the rest of my life? It's hard for him to keep these kinds of thoughts from flitting across his mind.

"People! People!" Angel is once again shouting over the din, trying to get everyone's attention. It's an Ed McMahon moment. Angel is holding a giant cardboard check that's just about as tall as he is. The crowd quiets down. The check, bearing an enormous facsimile of Munoz's own signature, is written out to Schroet Kommando for $25,000.

The Holt brothers, like everyone else in attendance, are in awe. Brandon, the younger boy, is almost dizzy from all the Bawls he's consumed. Justin imagines what it would be like if it were him up there, reaching out to grab for that big-ass check. What do you do if the one thing you're good at, the one thing you love above all else, seems to recede farther and farther away the faster you try to move toward it? It's not like the old days, in the midnineties, when all you had to do was pack a bag and move to Dallas and you were in, part of something new and exciting and friggin' awesome. He wonders if there's a point in even trying.

Frank Rivera shakes himself to be free of the flutter of melancholia hovering around him. He knows he has to be disciplined about his own morale, as well as that of his teammates. No negative thinking—that's his rule. You *will* succeed, he tells himself with military-like discipline.

The Schroet Kommando players grab the giant check and hold it over their heads, screaming over the whir of TV cameras and the whoops of the audience. And Frank Rivera is right up there in the front, cheering them on. "They're from Europe," he says, "but they won. They were the best team."

**ABOUT A HALF AN HOUR AWAY,** in Mesquite, in the same black-box building that started it all, John Carmack sits at his desk, staring into his computer. The CPL isn't even on the distant horizon of his thoughts. *Doom III* is one year from its release date, and all of his energy is focused on its engine, his twenty-third. The industry has been rustling with rumors that *Doom III* will be John Carmack's last videogame. People have been whispering to one another that he's gotten so wrapped up competing for the X Prize—a $10 million award for the first person who can get a manned rocket into orbit and back twice in two weeks—that he's lost interest in making virtual rockets. Indeed, he's been conferring with a group of volunteer engineers, who have taken to calling themselves Armadillo Aerospace. He's been reading books on rocket science and launching models of increasing size in fields outside his home in Mesquite.

John Romero is also staring into his computer screen. He's scrolling through his e-mail. Stevie's suitcases are on the floor behind him. She's got an interview in L.A. this week with the Game Channel, which is looking for a host for an in-house show it's producing. Romero still gets lots of e-mail, both fan and hate, and he still tries to answer it all. As author David Kushner says, "John Romero was id's number one fan."

Wireless gaming has become quite the hot topic since John left Ion Storm and is thought by many to be the next big wave in the videogame industry. Suddenly Stevie is inundated with requests for meetings; perhaps Romero will have the last laugh yet. For now, he's content to roam around Dallas in his yellow Hummer with the DVD player he's had installed and build his tiny games for Europeans to play on their digital phones, knowing it was his energy and enthusiasm that breathed life into the genre that became the first-person shooter. As long as John Romero is making games, he'll always be okay.

**AS THE KIDS** pack up their computers and step out of the super-cooled Hyatt and into the crushing heat of Dallas in July, Angel collapses into a chair at the CPL's registration table. All around him people are repacking coolers, wrapping cords around their elbows and over their thumbs. Screens of naked women and anime characters flicker off, as PCs are shut down, one after another. Out by the valet-parking podium, the next week's batch of Mary Kay ladies in their pink-and-purple horse-ribbon pins are casting curious looks at the bedraggled kids pouring out of the hotel. The kids are blinking in the sun. Their clothes are a bit looser than when they arrived, their skin pastier, their expressions dazed from several days without sleep, several days caught up in the excitement of an entire reality enclosed by the walls of a corporate hotel. Angel watches them go, shouts good-bye, hugs a few.

Angel is pleased. The tournament went well; he's begun negotiating with CompUSA to open up CPL game rooms at stores around the country; there are the amateur leagues he's founding to feed kids into the CPL; and a real estate broker has an old factory in Irving for him to see that could possibly be converted into his cherished Cyberstadium.

As he stumbles out of the basement and into the dizzying sunlight, suddenly eager for a change of clothes and a long shower, Angel can't help but think to himself, through the grime, and through the exhaustion: *this is only the beginning, only the beginning.*

# 5

## Will Wright and the Model of Everything

Before you meet Will Wright, you hear about him. "That guy is like Stephen Hawking. You couldn't make me talk to him," whispers an audio engineer at a videogame conference. And indeed, finding yourself at the other end of his glaring stare is a nerve-racking experience, and it happens every time he looks at you. Will might be hanging out in a corner of a videogame conference, trying to mind his own business, and people brave enough will approach him. They have favors they want to ask, advice to seek, conferences to which they want to lure him. Will responds to each assailant the same way—he turns his entire six-foot narrow frame and peers down at the person. And then he waits. He doesn't say anything. He just stares, like a computer waiting for input. It's enough to cause enthusiasts to falter, reporters to wince, and executives to laugh nervously.

"Hey, Will, I'm working on a first-person-shooter game

that is going to have an entirely new artificial-intelligence-driven enemy system," says an industry veteran who's arranged a quick introduction in the lobby of a hotel. He explains his ideas smoothly. He's a confident guy, good looking, a couple of game companies under his belt. Will listens, head cocked to one side, pursing his lips and peering at the guy. When he finishes, Will tilts his head the other way and glances up at the hotel lobby ceiling. *"Hmmm,"* he says. "That doesn't sound very fun." And he refocuses his gaze on the guy. The industry veteran starts sputtering a little, his expression looks a bit rattled. People are usually pretty impressed with his ideas. He keeps going, explaining how it will make the game do this and do that. Will listens. He waits for the guy to finish. *"Hmm,"* he says. "Sounds like a money sink to me."

Finally, Will gives the man a business card, and suggests he check out an artificial intelligence conference at Stanford University. Will's sidekick, a programmer named Don, who is slightly cross-eyed and talks as if he'd blown out his ears playing rock 'n' roll at the age of three, nudges Will with a wild laugh and congratulates him, at the top of his lungs, on pawning the guy off on "a bunch of old professors who've been grappling with the subject for twenty years!" Don laughs hysterically, his waist-length carrot-red hair swinging from side to side as he does so, and Will chuckles mildly into his chest.

**WILL WRIGHT GREW UP** in Baton Rouge, Louisiana, where he lived alone with his widowed mother, an amateur magician and local actress. He was a scrawny kid, adorned in a pair of metal-framed, aviator-shaped glasses—the same style he still wears today—and in possession of a preternaturally curious mind. First it was toy models that caught his attention—first, airplanes, ships, and tanks built from plastic kits, then eventually, designs of his own. By the age of nine, he had at least thirty planes hanging from the ceiling of his room and dozens more piled around the sides.

Toy models were followed by urban planning, the NASA space program, Harry Houdini, World War II history, robots, and science fiction. In the second grade, Will saw *2001: A Space Odyssey.* The idea that the world could change so much in such a short time, the realization that by the time he was an adult the world was going to be a radically different place than it was when he was seven, blew his mind. It seemed immensely interesting and attractive to contemplate, Will recalls. He imagined hopping on a Pan Am flight and heading to the moon.

At sixteen, Will left home and headed not for the moon but to Louisiana Tech University. The good grades of his high school years soon dissipated into a chaotic collection of As and Fs, depending on whether he found the subject interesting. He earned a pilot's license and learned to race rally cars, which required building your own automobile and then driving it over hundreds of miles of previously unseen terrain.

After a couple of years at Louisiana Tech, Wright transferred to the New School for Social Research in Manhattan and rented a little apartment at West Ninth Street and Sixth Avenue, above the original location of the famous Balducci's market. There he spent most of his time building robots out of scrap parts he found at shops on Canal Street and playing with his computer, where he had discovered the most amazing thing: His computer allowed him to build models, but unlike those of his childhood, these could be dismantled, evaluated, and rebuilt almost instantly. He could observe how the behavior of his models changed depending on what values he assigned various parameters. Instead of simply building models to hang from his ceiling—although he still did that, including one called Spiderbot that crawled around the walls and sometimes banged him on the head if he wasn't careful—Wright was now able to build models that were also *simulations.* They changed over time and were able to serve as simplified representations of real-world situations. They were dynamic rather than static. Discovering the power of computer modeling changed Will Wright's life profoundly.

Will released himself from higher education on his own recognizance when he was twenty-one. He'd met a girl, the sister of a friend from back home, who was moving to California's Bay Area. It seemed an unlikely match. The "girl" was eleven years older than he was, an artist who was fleshy where he was bone thin. She was a woman attuned to the nuances of people, whereas Wright tended to be deaf to their particularities. Will asked if he could move in with her, and although some people questioned her choice of a partner, particularly one with such an obviously dim future, she told him he could come with her on the condition that he leave her alone to work on her art.

In Oakland, in 1984, Will made his first videogame. It was called *Raid on Bungeling Bay*. The player had control over a helicopter, which he navigated over a series of small islands, with the prosaic objective of blowing up factories and bridges from the air.

To this day, Will refers to *Raid on Bungeling Bay* as a "stupid shoot-'em-up game." What did interest Will about the game, however, was a virtual-world editing tool he'd built in order to design the islands, factories, and bridges that constituted the game's various levels. He found he had far more fun creating the game world than blowing it up, and this gave him an idea. During the mid-1980s, the market was glutted with what people call "twitch games," games that required serious hand-eye coordination, quick reflexes, and a resistance to the induced stress of lightning-quick blings, beeps, and flashing colors. Will imagined a game that would be more laidback—and more complex. He kept playing around with the editor from *Bungeling Bay* and found himself turning what had been a design tool into a game on its own. He called the game *Micropolis*.

*Micropolis* was in essence a simulation of a city, complete with as many of the real variables of city life as the computers of the day allowed him to include. There were issues of traffic, crime, pollution, water supply, and housing. (The game was also rife with odd references to llamas, because, well, Will is quite fond of llamas.) The point of the game was to see how well your city evolved based on the decisions you made. If you wanted clean air for your inhabitants, you had to make sure factories weren't polluting the city. If you wanted the city to grow bigger, you had to build roads or public transportation. It was a simple exercise in cause and effect. If you failed to build housing, or open enough companies to give people jobs, you'd end up with a tumultuous city of riots and homeless people. *Micropolis* allowed Will to translate his enthusiasm for complexity—the seemingly endless array of possibilities that computer simulations offered—into a videogame. Will, like his friend Shigeru Miyamoto, thought of a videogame world like a garden: the quality of your blossoms in spring will depend on the hundreds of tiny decisions you make year-round.

Broderbund was not pleased. What they saw in *Micropolis* was an interesting idea that wasn't finished. They kept waiting for Will to add criteria for winning or losing. But this was one of Will's very favorite parts of the game. There was no winning. Success depended on what the player wanted out of the simulation. *Winning* and *losing* were defined by the player rather than the designer. If the player wanted to have a poverty-riddled city with bad drinking water and no fire department, that was his or her choice. A rioting population did not mean you had lost, it merely represented the consequences of the choices you had made playing the game. For Will this made the game more of a personal experience. For him, it made the game *better*.

*Micropolis* sat on a shelf in Will's office for a couple of years. Then one day, Will went to a pizza-and-beer party hosted by two guys named Jeff Braun and Ed Kilham, who were also interested in making videogames that were a little bit different. Will told them about his modification of the world editor from *Bungeling Bay,* and they came out to his office in the Oakland hills and played *Micropolis*. Once they got started, Braun and Kilham didn't want to stop playing. Another guy who was hanging around at the time, a writer named Michael Bremer, suggested renaming the game *SimCity* and its inhabitants Sims—it was, after all, a simulation turned into a game.

Will and his three new partners released *SimCity* on their own in 1989, under the company title *Maxis.* The llama became the company's mascot, narrowly beating out the Boston tree fern and the beef tapeworm. And *SimCity* quickly became the best-selling computer game of its time. *Newsweek* devoted an entire page to it, marking the first time the magazine had ever offered coverage of a computer game. *SimCity* mesmerized college students and computer geeks around the world, who watched their cities grow and shrink, struggle with financial crises, health warnings, and overcrowding. *SimCity* also captured an audience of people who hadn't played videogames since leaving the arcades of their youth.

*SimCity* became the "smart person's" game. And Wright's creation soon became a high-profile example of a new wave of videogames that would come to be called "God games." In God games, players were not so much a part of the game world as masters of it. Some of the brightest stars of game design got their start creating God games. Fellow Hall of Fame inductee Sid Meier released *Civilization,* and London-based designer Peter Molyneux came out with *Populus,* adding variety and innovation to the new genre. People commonly noted that the games were like model train sets come to life. Others called them sandbox games, because the player is like a child peering in at an ant colony, watching what happens if he adds a pile of leaves, a dollop of Jell-O, a finger, even a large rock.

**IT'S FEBRUARY 2003,** and Will is at the DICE summit in Las Vegas, having dinner at the Bellagio Hotel and Casino with Philip Rosedale, the founder and CEO of Linden Lab, creator of the massively multiplayer online game *Second Life.* Rosedale has a BS in physics and can talk about the kind of stuff Will likes to talk about. They touch on Copernicus, Network Theory, the Santa Fe Institute, Newtonian physics, chaos theory (the movie *Groundhog Day* is Will's favorite example of chaos theory), emergence, advances in biological and evolutionary research, and of course, the power of modeling and simulation. Philip drinks sake, and Will drinks water.

"Hey, this is fun," Will says to Philip. "I'm not really a people person, but if I'm here, exchanging ideas, I like it. *Hmmm.* I guess you could say it's really possibility spaces I'm into."

Will explains the idea of "possibility spaces" by recounting the time he saw *Indiana Jones and the Temple of Doom* (which he loved) as a young adult. When Indiana ran down the corridor filled with traps, Will found himself thinking, What would happen if he fell into that one? Or that one over there? Wright explains that he felt constrained by the narrowness of the possibility space in the movie. It made him feel claustrophobic because there was only one path through the space of myriad possibilities available for Indiana Jones—e.g., "this stone" or "that stone," "save the girl," "don't save the girl"—that could actually be experienced by the audience. Which leads Will right into the very nature of what he sees himself doing as a videogame maker. "Storytelling is based on empathy," he says. "Games on the other hand are based on agency, causality." Games are about exploring possibility spaces, whereas traditional art has been about exploring a particular trajectory through that space.

Philip is barely touching his sushi; he's enthralled at the sheer privilege of taking Will Wright out to dinner. The conversation turns to modeling and simulation. For Will, these are not just principles of good game design. Instead, he believes that modeling and simulation suggest something pivotal about the future of science.

"The quest to build a simulation is a scientific quest," Will says, between bites of yellowtail and mackerel sushi (his favorite.) "Experimenting to test a hypothesis used to be the way to do science, but simulation is the new way." He pauses, looks up at the ceiling, chews, swallows. "Here's a little bit more accurate statement," he says: "Simulation is quickly replacing experimentation as the central test of a new theory."

There is nothing novel about humans making models and running simulations. In fact, some argue the ability is one of the defining characteristics of human intelligence. Say you run into a dog in the street. Based on what you know of the world and of dogs, you build a model in your head of the situation.

You have a concept of what the dog is and what his relationship may be to you. Then the dog growls, and you begin, in Will-speak, the "reverse engineering" process. Others might call it simply trying to understand the situation. Is the dog protecting his master, warning you to get off his property? Does he have rabies? Then you begin the simulation process in your mind, considering possible courses of action and their outcomes. What will happen if I run? Put out my hand? Throw him a stick? And your actions will likely be based on what was the most successful outcome of the simulation you ran in your head based on your model of the dog and the situation.

What is new, and what truly excites Will, is the idea that now we can marry this abstract human ability with the powerful computational jaws of a PC.

"It's an amplification of our intelligence," Will says, "of our imagination really. Basically, scientists used to build these dynamic models in their imaginations, and they would sit there and they would imagine, or they might do a long math chain. But it was running to the limits of the abilities of the imagination. Now we have the ability to build elaborate models on the computer that no one person could ever fully understand using their own imagination." Meteorologists already use simulation technology to do weather forecasts, car manufacturers use it for crash testing, and seismologists are on the verge of being able to use it for earthquake forecasting. "Calculus has been reigning supreme for centuries," Will continues, "but now computers allow for far more complicated modeling. Originally people were shocked at mathematical disciplines like calculus, but simulation uses math as a plumber."

There are so many practical uses for computer models, in fact, that after *SimCity* hit, Maxis began getting requests for simulations from outfits as diverse and far-ranging as the Australian

Tax Board, the Canadian Railway System, and the Environmental Protection Agency. Maxis's simulation division built *SimHealth* for the Markle Foundation in New York, which modeled the entire national health care system, and one for Chevron called *SimRefinery,* which helped orient employees on how refineries worked. John Hiles, who used to run the simulation division for Will, now works for the military. He's building a model aimed at predicting the behavior of terrorists.

When they're finished eating, Will and Philip take a stroll along the Bellagio's promenade. Will leans forward on his elbows against the barrier that separates him and the rest of the tourists from the water show in the Bellagio's mammoth manmade lake. Elton John music is piped out to the promenade from speakers hidden behind well-planted foliage. Will and Philip watch as streams of skyward-bent water burst forth across the lake, accompanied by a series of great echoing booms. The audience gasps and cheers. *"Hmm,"* says Will, lighting a Marlboro Light, "Is that a sound effect or just the natural result of the water coming out of their spigots?" Philip isn't sure, but Will stays to watch the next show and concludes that indeed the sound is a natural boom. This seems to please him.

"Really, for me," he says, "the games are just an excuse to do science."

**WHEN *SIMCITY* WAS RELEASED,** it was such a hit that, for the first time, Will had a steady source of income. His partner, Jeff, was able to pay off his credit cards. Maxis moved out of Jeff's apartment and into an office suite in Moraga. And Will began working on something he alternately called *Project X, Dollhouse, Home Tactics: The Experimental Domestic Simulator,* or *Jef-*

*ferson* (as in the Jeffersonian idea of the right to pursue life, liberty, and happiness).

*The Sims,* as the game came to be called, introduces players to a social simulation. You generate characters and choose the parameters of their personality as well as their physical appearance. Gameplay consists of maintaining your character's happiness levels, as determined by social interaction with other Sims, cleanliness, productivity, and so on. Listening to music and hanging out with others makes your Sim happy. Forgetting to allow it to use the bathroom, on the other hand, makes it very unhappy. Failure to clean up your dinner dishes will result in flies congregating in the kitchen, which will eventually dishearten even the most laid-back Sim. Skip work, lose your job. Do well in a career, however, and you can earn the cash to buy a bigger house or to remodel your existing digs. At first blush, the game may appear to be nothing more than a digital dollhouse—*Dollhouse* was actually the working title until test marketing revealed a less than enthusiastic response from men—but *The Sims* is actually nothing less than an attempt to build a model of human interaction, a study of what people need to feel fulfilled.

When *The Sims* came out, the media made much about the fact that the game seemed to be a very culturally specific representation of suburban America. Certainly any game that tries to cater to something other than the *Dungeons & Dragons*–inspired daydreams of nostalgic game designers is worth noting—the success of games like *Grand Theft Auto III, Pikmin,* or *Thirteen* are similar victories for those who long for a broader palette. But Will Wright is not particularly interested in suburban America. In fact, Wright doesn't think of the Sims landscape as a model of American suburbia at all. Rather, when the

Maxis team realized *The Sims* would have to be released simultaneously in fourteen different languages, from Thai to Italian, they knew they needed to create a generic culture simple enough that people all over the world could recognize its important features. They chose what Will calls "American television culture," which he describes as a "kind of pseudo-American sit-com-like world." *The Sims* takes place within a culture of Americana, a culture and society that never really existed, not even in America, but one with which people all over our media-saturated globe can identify.

Will was reading *Understanding Comics* by Scott McCloud at the time he created *The Sims*. The book theorizes that cartoon characters are so appealing and can be so powerful, because, with their vagueness, their often exceptional simplicity, the reader has plenty of room to superimpose his or her own concepts and cultural values. This makes the reader feel more connected to the character than if it were more realistic and nuanced. The experience, primed by the reader's own imagination, becomes richer and more real than if it were drawn with greater detail. *Understanding Comics* is the reason why *The Sims* is anything but photorealistically rendered and why the Sims speak in what Will calls Charlie Brown–speak. You don't actually ever hear what the Sims are saying. All you hear is an undulating *wa-wa-WA-wa-WA,* conveying some of the emotional content of what is being said, without delivering any of the semantic content. Consumers certainly haven't felt gypped by the approach—*The Sims* quickly replaced *Myst* as the most successful PC franchise of all time, turning Will Wright and Maxis into a veritable money tree for publisher Electronic Arts.

• • •

**A FEW WEEKS AFTER** his dinner at the Bellagio, Will is at the Game Developers Conference in San Jose. (He's on the same schedule of gamemaking gatherings as CliffyB and the rest of the field.) On the first night of the gathering, Will is in the Fairmont lobby, trying out what he calls his Zen jokes on unsuspecting colleagues. One joke goes like this: A man goes into a café and orders a doughnut and a cup of coffee. The waiter says, "Sorry, we're out of doughnuts." So the guy says, "Okay, I'll have a doughnut and a cup of tea." The waiter says, "No you didn't hear me, we're out of doughnuts!" And the guy says, "Oh, that's right, sorry, I'll have a doughnut and a glass of milk." The waiter says, "What the hell is the matter with you? I just said we don't have any doughnuts!" And the guy says, "Oh, right, right, sorry, okay. I'll just have a doughnut."

Another of Will's Zen jokes is a one-liner: What's between a duck? Answer: His leg.

Although Will and Don, respectively, chortle and guffaw over these little inanities, Will is surprised when others don't find them funny. Will says his Zen jokes, like his games, are meant to force a different part of your brain into activation. They're meant to sneak around the daily functioning part of how you think and, by not delivering the information you're expecting, jolt the disengaged part of your brain into action. It's not unlike the outgoing message on his answering machine, which answers, "Hello," pauses just long enough for the caller to identify himself, and then says, "Hello, hello," pauses, and then says, "Oh, sorry. I forgot. I'm not in right now." If you point out to Will that there could be something cruel in these jokes—that the laugh is entirely at the listeners' expense—he'll tilt his head to the side and say, "Yeah, I guess. I guess they could be construed as mean-spirited. Huh, I hadn't thought of that." And you can watch him integrating this data into his own mental model of the universe.

After dinner, Will, accompanied by Don, goes for a stroll along the empty downtown San Jose streets. Don, who forgot to get a pass for the event, has gotten in everywhere because he's with Will. Will is wearing his usual black K-Swiss sneakers, jeans, and zip-up jacket. Don is wearing shorts and a tie-dyed T-shirt with a picture of each of the Beatles on it, their faces distended by his protruding belly. He's got a backpack over his shoulders and a doggy bag of leftover macaroni and cheese in his hand. Both of the men's glasses are dirty and their noses shiny with the perspiration of a long day filled with seminars and run-ins with colleagues. Neither of them have tickets to Alan Yu's annual VIP party at a local club a few blocks from the convention center, but they figure they'll tag along with a reporter who has a pass. Who's not going to let Will Wright in a VIP videogame party?

Inside, Will hangs back by the doorway. Parties aren't really his thing. But when a mysterious bag of papier-mâché eggs wrapped in bright tissue paper comes to his attention, he lights up. He and Don examine them carefully, turning them over, holding them up to the light, shaking them excitedly. Don works at one of Will's side businesses, the Stupid Fun Club, where they build robots for TV shows like *Battlebots,* and he immediately starts imitating how he imagines the robot on which he's currently working will react to the eggs. Since he seems unable to modify his tone of voice, he starts to scream his impersonation. "EGGS! EGGS!" he screams, making stiff robotic motions with his arms and legs. Will chuckles into his chest.

A careful poke at one of the eggs reveals bright purple, orange, and yellow confetti inside. Will is absolutely delighted.

And it's just in time, because like a small buzz turning into trembling vibration, people have become aware of his presence. Someone approaches him about speaking at a conference in Australia. Will insists on pouring a bit of the confetti into the man's hand before discussing the invitation. "Here, have some of this," he says. The man puts a piece into his mouth and smiles. He's game but a little confused. As he begins his address again, Will bores into him with his eyes. "It's really hard," Will says later, "I have to say no so much these days." But he gives the man one of his cards, and the man departs, gagging a little on the confetti but pleased at the square piece of paper he has in his shirt pocket. Will then begins to move about the room, tapping on people and handing them bits of confetti. "It's an old Mardi Gras tradition," he says. "I'd better go pass this around to everyone." It's early March now, so Mardi Gras is in full swing back in Will's old hometown, and the drunken phone calls he's been getting from relatives have left him a bit homesick. He notices that many of the people to whom he gives the confetti put it in their mouth. Will wonders why this is. Was it the way he poured it into their hands? The color? The shape of the confetti? The fact that it came out of an egg? Don isn't much help: he's still busy doing his impersonation of his robot receiving eggs, which draws more than a few scornful glances, until people realize he's with Will, and then they laugh as if it were the cleverest impression in the world.

Someone asks Will if this is really an old Mardi Gras tradition, and his mouth twitches slyly. "Ahhh, no," he says, but he keeps distributing the confetti anyway.

Will soon gets lost in the crowd. A group of Japanese designers have gathered around him beneath a tree in a tented area of the party. They're pushing against him so eagerly that his back is up against the tree, and his hair in its branches. Will is a good foot taller than any of them. The trees in the tent are strung with lights. They cast a red glow over Will's face, and you can see him peering down into the men's faces, puckering his lips, jiggling his last few eggs in the palm of his hand.

Will has just barely escaped the Japanese when a young man from Spain approaches him for a photograph. He says he has one question. Will offers him some confetti, and the man proceeds to ask why in the four years since its release *The Sims* has not had any real competition. Will stares at him. "Well it took us a lot more than four years to develop," Will says. The Spaniard becomes somewhat flustered. It's a conversation stopper certainly, a completely logical, coherent answer, directly addressing the question, but having absolutely nothing to do with the kind of conversation the Spaniard was hoping to induce. He walks off, red-faced, his hand filled with confetti.

Will is completely polite, gracious even—he'll turn the full power of his stare onto anyone who places themselves before it—but he is like a deaf man when it comes to hearing what people are actually trying to say. Will says it hadn't occurred to him that, while being scrupulously attentive, he was actually failing to give people anything near what they wanted from him. "Yeah, I uh, I guess he *was* sort of a black box," he says about the Spaniard. Now that he thinks about it, Will says that's pretty much what he sees when he goes into a room full of people: clusters of information-spitting black boxes.

Meanwhile, Don is outside the party, tripping over the street curbs, accidentally banging his napsack into passersby, and screaming at a middle-aged man, a former Marvin Minsky pupil and denizen of the famed Xerox PARC in Palo Alto, who now makes educational software. It turns out he's an old friend of Will's. Don leads him to Will, and they begin talking about emergence, a concept that's been around philosophy circles for some years, and that Will believes is one of the most important and profound properties of the universe. He talks about the Japanese game Go to explain it. "Go is one of the clearest examples of emergence you'll ever see," he says, puffing on another Marlboro Light. "It's the ratio of the complexity of the rules to the complexity of the strategy. Go has incredibly simple rules and incredibly complex strategy." As a child, Will was an avid Go player. "I've always kind of thought of Go as this incredibly beautiful thing for that reason. But it was only later that I was like, oh, the reason I think it's so beautiful is because it has this incredible ratio between simple rules and complex strategies—and this is something that is reflected in things as diverse as economics and DNA."

Will and his friend agree it's a travesty that public schools aren't teaching emergence. Will suggests that, since his local school board doesn't want to add a new topic to the curriculum, they get rid of an old one. Will's vote would be geology. His friend suggests geography and says he is working on a project that will teach four-year-olds calculus without using numbers. Will warns him, however, that if you try to give kids something they think is educational they won't touch it. He says the only way to reach kids, to make them want to engage with something, is through the commercial markets. "You know it only gets you so far when a teacher holds something up and says, 'Here kids, we're gonna do this,'" Will says. "Or the parents bring it to the kid and say, 'Here, I want you to play Math Blaster, Johnny,' as opposed to the kid saying, 'I want that, I want that, so-and-so is playing it and it's really cool.' When the kid is plying it from you, when they're choosing to spend their discretionary time on it, they're engaged. Otherwise, they're just humoring you." Will stamps out his cigarette. His friend looks somewhat discouraged.

Walking back to the Fairmont Hotel, where Will is staying, Don starts talking about a locksmith class he took in which he learned to pick locks using only bristle from a hairbrush. In his free time, Don sometimes lets himself into big hotels or other institutions and goes exploring through the building's infrastructure, crawling along the tops of ceilings, shimmying up pipes, finding what he can find. His inspiration: the Tech Model Railroad Club.

Will also carries a lock-pick kit with him, left over from his childhood obsession with Harry Houdini. He says lock-picking reminds him of code breaking, another interest, except that lock-picking is mechanical. When he was twelve, Will had devoured everything Houdini had written, like how to dislocate your shoulder to get out of a straightjacket. He'd poured over pictures of Houdini's original lock-pick templates. "Houdini developed this whole science that didn't exist before," Will says. "He had to invent all of it because no one else had really done it before." Will was also inspired by Houdini's total dedication to what he did. "It's incredibly painful to dislocate your shoulder, you know," he says.

**THE FAIRMONT LOBBY IS,** as usual during the GDC, packed. A reporter asks Will what he sees when he looks over the crowd of people. Will turns, studies the bar area for a while. "Nodes," he says. "I see nodes." He gestures to a group of three or so people by the bar. "There's a cluster," he says. He predicts that the two nodes will become one because one of their members he pegs as a "strong link," a term from network theory. He predicts the strong link will eventually bring the two together, forming one larger node. Just like cells squiggling about under a microscope, forming, attaching, breaking apart. Will believes the same basic principles that allow a molecule to exist can be used to understand all parts of the world, from biology to sociology. On a lark, the reporter asks Will if he closed his eyes would he know what she was wearing. "Uh, I wouldn't know what I was wearing," Will says.

Of all his games, Will plays *The Sims Online* the most—he likes to download player-created wallpapers, hairdos, and other items: "It's gotten to the point now where I surf the fan sites everyday and download cool things the fans have created, which is really ironic in a way! Because now it's the fans out there that are entertaining us, the developers, with their creations! This is something I never would have foreseen five years ago." Will's own character in the *The Sims Online* is a red-track-suit-wearing, blond-haired, dance-crazy captain of something called Das Love Boat. His wife, Joell, says Will particularly likes to go to online dance parties and let the captain boogie with other Sims.

Once, when Will was participating in an online Q&A session with fans of *The Sims,* someone asked him if he was actually a robot. "I don't think I'm a robot," Will replied. "I'm not sure I could tell if I was, though."

**ONE FINE SPRING** day in 2003 not long after the Game Developers Conference, Will pulls his BMW M3 to a stop on a dead-end street near the University Avenue exit off Route 80 in Berkeley. Here, in a warehouse that also houses the offices for a company that produces an upscale line of children's clothes called the Sweet Potato Factory, Will has built the headquarters of the Stupid Fun Club. His wife thought of the name. It's supposed to sound like a bad Chinese translation. Will gets out of his car, lights a cigarette, zips up a leather jacket, which has a CIA insignia sewn over the left breast—a gift from the agency for some consulting work on simulation technology—and strolls over to the club's entrance. Will has very skinny legs and is a very fast walker. Even when strolling, he moves faster than most anything without wheels. He has a way of walking, where his torso remains upright, while his legs become a blur of motion. Surpisingly, for a skinny guy with a shiny nose, white tennis shoes, and pants pulled up to his waist, Will has a pretty good tough-guy stance as well. Weight evenly distributed, leaning back just a tad, Will puffs away at his Marlboro Light.

Will got the idea for the Stupid Fun Club when his friend Mark Thorpe, who did the special effects for *Star Wars* and *Raiders of the Lost Ark,* started an annual event called Robot Wars. Will won the first competition with a robot named Juliebot. The next year, he won again with Kitty Puff Puff. Instead of shooting projectile weapons or some other heavy-handed mechanism to disable competitors, Kitty Puff Puff had double-stick reinforced fiberglass carpet tape wrapped around her with magnets tucked in. When competitors got too close, they would stick to the robot, who would then punch holes in their sides with a steel spike that emerged on contact. (The next year, Thorpe made a rule against double-stick tape.)

Thorpe's Robot Wars was eventually co-opted by a TV takeoff called *Battlebots,* which became a big hit. And while Will feels bad for Mark, he's a regular competitor on the TV show. So is Will's daughter, Cassidy, as well as Lisa, the daughter of his other partner, Mike Winter. In fact, Lisa's "bot," as they call them, was so popular on the show that McDonald's put a picture of it on their take-out bags and she got to go on the Jay Leno show. This year, Will is entering the competition—which, he points out, he rarely wins anymore—with a robot called Misty the Wonderbot. As of December 2003, Misty's record was 10-2-0.

To enter the Stupid Fun Club, you have to hop over a three-foot-high concrete ledge that once must have been a loading dock. The space inside would make a Manhattan real estate agent swoon. It's about three thousand square feet, with twenty-foot ceilings. Chests of tools are everywhere, movie lights sit in a pile on the floor. Power tools make moving through the space like working through a maze. There's a corner covered with mirrors where the club members can watch their bots compete from a safe distance while still judging the merits and drawbacks of each.

In the back of the space is a young guy in an Atari T-shirt working on some animation on a computer. A small stage about waist high sits nearby, adorned with odd stick figures and a little toy village. This diorama is ringed by movie lights. Will has been trying to put together a TV show, which he describes as "a cross between *The Thunderbirds* and Kurosawa, or maybe *Hello Kitty* meets Kurosawa." The show's main character is a robot that one day rolls into a feudal Japanese village. The focus of the show is how the people in the village react to the robot. The idea is that the robot, being a robot, has no real personality of its own. "It's kind of a *Being There* type thing," Will explains. "The robot is very neutral, so everyone reflects their own personalities onto it. Everyone wants to interpret their own human emotions and desires through it."

Will bends down and peers into one of the stick figure's one-foot-high homes. "It's really about studying sentient psychology," he says. "The robot is a tool . . . a kind of microscope into the human psyche."

The other show the Stupid Fun Club is developing is a

reality show, wherein a big robot on a steel gurney is taken around Berkeley to talk to unsuspecting citizens. The robot is intentionally unsophisticated. There has been no attempt to make it look like anything other than a robot with, Will adds, "bad robotic conversational abilities." It's about three feet high and three feet wide, with a metal neck and a video monitor sitting atop it. It rolls through the streets of Berkeley, apparently autonomous, although really controlled by some member of the Stupid Fun Club, and its interactions with people are filmed.

"You know, origin of life, nature of intelligence, that's basically what I'm into," Will says, "the human psyche. That's the most complex thing in the universe. It's like the ultimate puzzle."

As to whether he cares passionately about things or is simply passionately curious, Will requires less than a second before responding. "Oh, B, definitely," he says. "It's a compulsion to understand."

Will is interested in how the human psyche is going to handle the advent of AI into society. He believes that slowly all the machines around us are going to become more "intelligent," that it will happen slowly, like the proliferation of ATM machines and other convenience technologies that were uncommon at first but eventually became ubiquitous. "Oh, yeah, I'll be having conversations with my toaster," he says.

A lot of science fiction, as Will is well aware, is about this very thing: the question of what happens when nonhuman entities appear to develop humanlike intelligence. As for the underlying issue of danger that often accompanies this scenario, Will himself is not worried.

"I'd love it!" he says about the idea of having artificial intelligence be part of his daily life. "I mean, I would still basically view them as elaborate washing machines. The 'Does it have a soul and all that' question, I don't really subscribe to that. But what's going to happen when we're faced with these things that *appear* to have humanoid intelligence? To me, that's going to be the weird part. I don't know what's going to happen, but I think it'll be very strange. We're going to be tempted to project our thoughts and processes onto [the AI]. You know, [our primate ancestors and] we have been evolving for millions of years to be highly attuned with others in our thought process. I mean, it's almost like telepathy—the way we can read body language, in one little glance, convey so much. It's because our brains, our circuits, are similar. But when we have robots that are interacting with us on that level, we are not going to be able to turn all that essential mapping off, that empathy. So we are going to be trying to apply all that empathy to these machines that are in a vastly different cognitive space than we are. So that interests me."

When Will saw the film *2001: A Space Odyssey* for the first time, his little-boy self was struck by the notion that our increasingly intimate relationship with technology does not always pan out the way we expect. But he is completely nonplussed by this possibility—once again his curiosity overrides concern. "Once these things are intelligent to some level, we're not going to be able to begin to understand what might motivate them, or what aspirations (if any) they might have," he says. "Anyway, I don't see how we're going to maintain control over them beyond a certain point. At some point, they're going to become their own thing. We might end up having some diplomacy with them. I don't know, but at some point I'm pretty convinced we'll lose control of it."

Will's biting into a warmed-up burrito at a food court down the road from the Stupid Fun Club when he makes this last statement. It's the kind of thing you'd expect would make a man choke on his beans. But Will seems completely comfortable with the notion. "I think it's inevitable," he says. "It could be scary, yeah." He pauses in his chewing, head sideways, his eyes canted skyward. "If it happens, it could be final proof that human intelligence is actually an evolutionary dead end," he suggests before his eyes move back to the burrito before him.

Will's latest videogame project is code-named *SimEverything*. It was inspired by physicist and astrobiologist Enrico Fermi. He describes the concept for the game as follows: "What's a simple simulation that would describe all of life as we know it?"

In Will's new game, which he's been working on as a pet project since 1998, the player starts with a universe full of gases—say, methane, carbon monoxide, hydrogen, nitrogen. As you play, you begin to induce chain reactions: stars are born, planets cool and spawn unicellular creatures, which in turn become multicellular. Nonsentient beings become sentient. Primitive tribal communities become societies. At each stage, there is a set of parameters that defines each level of organization. For planets, there's gravity, chemical composition, how much radiation each receives, and so on. Based on these parameters, the computer generates a plausible ecosystem. Then the ecosystem generates a whole set of plausible creatures, and so on. For Will, creating a generative system is one of the primary challenges of building this game. "I mean, we could brute-force this," he says, "and end up with kind of a standard, more traditional, clunky model. But it would be very brittle and it wouldn't surprise anyone. If we made this hugely complicated thing that simulated all this stuff, it would be a failure."

Will wants the game to exhibit what scientists revere as *elegance*—Will wants to employ the smallest number of factors required to generate the largest number of meaningful possibilities. Wright's crafting the game in such a way that, instead of throwing legions of artists at it, designing every little factor, the program itself generates the graphics, which, if successful, will be a huge accomplishment in game design. "To me, it becomes almost a religion," he says. "What is the simplest set of rules I can imagine that would allow me to possibly simulate the complexities of an emerging universe."

At his desk in Walnut Creek, about twenty-five miles northeast of San Francisco, a prototype of *SimEverything* is running on his computer. There's a funny, six-legged creature taking shape on the screen. In Will's game you can zoom in and focus on a particular life-form, like the proto-insect above, or zoom out and see the entire galaxy, watching different life-forms take over spaces, get taken over, adapt, or die. When you're all the way zoomed out, 20 million years can pass before your eyes in a few moments. Zoom all the way in, and you can watch the reaction of one organism to another in a tide pool. Will punches a key on his computer and the screen is filled with interstellar gas. Will turns up the temperature with one of his planet-tuning controls, and stars begin appearing, colored circles of semi-stability amidst a sea of swirling gasses. Will explains that most of the stars will only last for a short time before becoming supernovas. He explains that when that happens, the supernovas will heat the surrounding gasses, causing a pressure wave ahead of them, almost like a forest fire. This in turn will increase the rate of new star formation. Will then starts watching for patterns of temperature and pressure inside the galaxy. All the way zoomed out, he watches waves of hot and cool gas ripple across the virtual universe, fascinated by the large voids and bubbles that emerge. The heat from the stars actually begins to pressurize the gas so much that more stars form around what soon becomes a galactic disk. "What in fact we're seeing here is the birth of a new galaxy," Will says. "One hundred thousand light-years across."

*SimEverything* can also be played at the "life level." Will drops a single-celled being onto a little planet in a small region of the galaxy. The time-scale of the simulation is still set on fast-forward, so you can watch the species actually spreading across the planet. He points to a yellow spot that appears on the screen—"That there," he says, "that's just achieved the next level [of complexity] of life." Then, as they come in contact with a radiation zone, the propogating organisms begin to die off. Will says life isn't going to spread fast in a radiation zone. "Oh, did you see that blue," he cries, pointing at the screen. "That was intelligence! So one of those species finally achieved intelligence and now they spread very fast. See, they're colonizing the galaxy. You know, with starships. So this is kind of showing a reasonable estimate of how life spreads through the galaxy."

Sometimes, when not discussing the nature of *Everything,* Will Wright can be induced to talk about the nature of videogames. He knows that all games, from an evolutionary point of view, are an educational technology, allowing children to experiment in a safe environment with the often complex relation between cause and effect, choices and consequences. Once, Will gave a talk to a class of twelve-year-olds about *The Sims,* and he was struck that the first question asked was whether you could kill your Sims. He was not, however, horrified, or even offended. He says the kids were doing the most natural thing in the world: trying to intuit the boundaries of the possibility space they were given—"That's a kid's job," he says. As for what videogames ultimately foster, chaos theory is the first thing that comes to his mind, which he describes as the idea that seemingly small actions can have enormous consequences.

But if you probe him further, the conversation will inevitably swing back to the generative work he's doing on *SimEverything.* Will believes that the biggest "differentiating factor" between the medium of the videogame and any other will be videogames' ability to learn our desires. There's already the "push" technology that made such a splash in the late 1990s—Amazon.com recommending books to you based on previous purchases; Tivo "knowing" what TV shows you might want to watch. But Will believes the work being done at the forefront of videogame development will allow for something far deeper than just push technology. "I think one thing that's unique about videogames is not only that they can respond to you, but down the road they'll be able to adapt themselves to you," he says. "They'll learn your desires. There will be the ability of the game to watch what you do, to learn about you, and then customize itself to your preferences. It'll build up a personality profile on you, you know, based on the tens of hundreds of hours you spend interacting with it. You might not even be aware that this stuff is being customized to you. You'll just happen to know that you really enjoyed this game. But the reason you enjoyed it was because it personalized itself for you.

"In some sense, it may become so connected to your personality that you might consider it a real invasion of privacy to have someone even see your game. It might be that games become deeply personal artifacts—more like dreams."

Although Will says that his games are an excuse to do science, he refuses to think of himself as a scientist. He knows the work he's doing is not bound by the stiff rigor of academic science. But he also knows the technologies that are growing out of his companies have the potential to profoundly affect our future. And the decision as to whom he gives or sells his work is based on sheer intellectual interest. In 2003 the Stupid Fun Club plans to participate in a Department of Defense competition for the development of an autonomous vehicle. "You just press the start button and it has to get to Las Vegas by itself," Will says. Intellectual interest aside, one can't help but wonder whether Wright thinks there is an attendant responsibility with being able to create such things. Ask him why he thinks the DOD is sponsoring such an event, and he doesn't even blink. Rather, he kind of stares at you as if the question were so dim-witted as to leave him hungry for something heftier. "Well I think that should be pretty obvious," he says. "They want to be able to build land-based cruise missiles." Like a computer, Will does not attempt to understand the intent of your question. He seeks only to respond to what he is specifically being asked.

Besides, these days he's spending a lot of time satisfying yet another obsession: the Russian space program. He's even begun collecting parts from the training models of the space station Mir and other Russian spacecraft. His collection includes control systems computers, navigation panels, and even a Russian space hammer. He knows John Carmack of id Software is competing for the X prize, and he hopes to be present when Carmack launches his.

"You can always look at technology and say, 'Oooh, it could be used for evil purposes,'" he says. "But the deeper responsibility I feel is 'Ooh, this could actually be useful for something and it's not being used in that way.' It's the lost opportunities that I worry about."

With that, Will Wright gets up from his desk and gets back to work. He's got phone calls to make, people to see, an appointment to keep in the never-never land of simulated, waking dreams.

# 6

## Virtual Worlds and Alternate Lives

David Reber is a thirty-year-old ex-Navy serviceman who works as a merchandiser for a Best Buy in Petaluma, California. He spends his day attired in a pale blue Best Buy polo shirt and khakis, making sure the daily shipments of computers the store receives are transferred from the trucks outside to the displays inside. He says he's the kind of guy who "gives 150 to 200 percent" at work and is "all over the asses" of those who don't, even though he's not their boss.

At the end of his nine-hour workday, David gets into his Grand Am and, because the car needs a new engine, avoids the freeways and drives the long way home through the suburban-shopping-mall parking lots and the country roads of Petaluma back to his house on a small cul-de-sac off U.S. Route 101. His house, which he rents along with two other guys his age, is standard suburban California ranch style, with a gaping garage as big as the house itself, wall-to-wall beige carpeting, three bedrooms, a bathroom, and a flat-screen TV in the living room.

When David gets home, he heads straight for what he calls his "command center." This is his bedroom—a small room with black curtains over the windows to keep the light out, a single-size bed, a Lara Croft calendar, a picture of himself at seventeen in white Navy duds, and a Namco clock. There are four speakers, one suspended from each corner of the room, and a big subwoofer sits beside a custom-built computer beneath his desk. David has spent more than $2,000 upgrading his computer and getting his satellite speaker system just the way he wants it. All the equipment is to facilitate David's metamorphosis from working stiff into a leader of Freedom's Hope, a guild of forty people on the war-torn virtual planet of Rubi-Ka. On weekdays, he plays four or five hours a day, on the weekends, more. "My one roommate is always trying to get me to go out biking or hiking on the weekends," David says, "but I'm like, 'No, I want to play! I've got a guild meeting! My friends are online.' My other roommate, he's a manager at Electronic Arts, he never harasses me about playing sixteen hours a day."

Like many players of massively multiplayer online games, David is an old *Dungeons & Dragons* fan. With a weight of three hundred pounds by the time he was fifteen, and as the sole caretaker of a prescription-drug-addicted mother while his father was off starting a new family, David took to the role-playing game immediately. He liked the logic of the rule-based game, the eloquence of decisions based on a dice roll, and he liked the escapism. He enjoyed making up characters and inventing backstories for them and working as hard as he could to make sure all of his actions were consistent with the character he'd created.

After high school and his stint in the Navy, David—about 150 pounds lighter—managed a Namco arcade, where he made change for the kids and teenagers who frequented the place; sold computers at a CompUSA; and worked for an Internet start-up in the Bay Area that folded after about six months.

One day at the start-up, he heard some of his officemates talking about a massively multiplayer online game they were into, *Anarchy Online.* David told them he didn't like to play online games because he didn't really like other people and would far rather play alone. But one of his coworkers was quitting the game—his wife was threatening to leave him if he didn't—and offered to sell David his game software. David "gave it a whirl" and found that life on Rubi-Ka was a lot more interesting than real life, or RL, as gamers call it.

Rubi-Ka is a beautiful planet, with forests of hulking trees, sunsets that put L.A. to shame, fashionable cities, and intriguing citizens. On any given day, creatures, rare and odd, scuttle through the long grasses of the planet's marshes; birds with wingspans the width of a grown man cruise the treetops; and flowers of brilliant oranges and muted taupes with buds like starbursts bloom beneath mountain ranges.

There are more than 150 different genera of flora and fauna on Rubi-Ka, and within each genus there are multitudes of species. In its cities, the residents of Rubi-Ka gather in pubs and shops and public squares. They talk, argue, fall in love, form friendships, seek adventure, and make plans for the future. Indeed, the citizens of Rubi-Ka are nothing if not engaged in their planet's well-being. There have been terrorist attacks on major cities, but there have also been peaceful protests, doctors organizing to stem the civil war that constantly simmers across the planet, and neighbors uniting to demand clean water. And when that sun sets, with ruby stripes crisscrossing the wide-open sky, it's almost impossible not to be impressed.

The entire planet, of course, is an illusion, a technological oasis that exists on a set of servers in Oslo, Norway, where Funcom, the company that designed Rubi-Ka, maintains the computers that keep the world running, twenty-four hours a day, 365 days a year. The characters flitting through town centers or camping in the wild are what gamers call *avatars* or *toons,* the virtual representations of thousands of people who sit at their computers in Tokyo, Oslo, South Korea, and Petaluma, all playing together in a single giant virtual sandbox.

When David Reber logs on one day in the summer of 2002, it's as his alter ego Twinke, a female Meta-Physicist, Level 165. Twinke is a Caucasian human in a long multicolored coat with blonde pigtails up high on her head. She's running through Rubi-Ka's capital, Tir, with her two virtual pets—one, a demon designed for inflicting damage, and another, which looks like a large, diabolic balloon, which can heal her. As she is about to leave the city for a tour of the countryside, Twinke is stopped by a lost *newbie,* or *newb* (as new, unfamiliar, or lower-level players are called). Twinke stops in her tracks and turns to face the newb. Her name is Clandestinee. *Follow me,* David types onto his keyboard, and he runs the newbie through a forest, across the main square of town, past other teams that are running toward them, and leads Clandestinee to the nearest Whompa, as the science-fiction subway stations of Rubi-Ka are called. (They're named onomatopoetically after the sound the huge machines make as they are engaged.) David waits as the newb drops him a quick curtsey and darts off into the Whompa.

Twinke is not at all like David's other avatars. Besides being female—almost 50 percent of male players play female characters—it's her personality that sets her apart. David also has a level 124 Nanomage named Brisbanevi whom he plays as greedy and cutthroat as he plays Twinke generous and kind. "Twinke is very friendly," David says. "She will help you do anything. She doesn't care what it is. And she'll never ask you for money. That's just who she is. Twinke, she is nothing like me. Then there's Brisbanevi. He *is* me. He's negative. That's me. That's who I am—in a word—a negative person. I'm the person who hates the world, and that's what Bris is."

David spent part of his Navy career on a nuclear carrier outside Baghdad while the first Gulf War, Desert Storm, raged around him. He still has nightmares from the sounds of bombs going off, and from the fear and rage he had a hard time controlling, even though he wasn't in the battles himself.

Although David originally made Twinke just as a side character with which to have some fun, by the summer of 2002, he has almost entirely given up playing Brisbanevi in favor of Twinke. "I've been screwed over a lot of times in this world," David says. "But I didn't want to be like that. I wanted to show the world, or the world of Rubi-ka at least, that there are good people out there, who are not out for blood, for lust, for money, always having to get something for something."

David says that, ironically, Twinke has been his most financially successful character on Rubi-ka. Like in RL, the virtual worlds of massively multiplayer online games have economies that ebb and flow, undulating under the pressures of scarcity, inflation, and people who cheat the system. As in RL, there are items to buy, and owning rare items—strings of code that take shape as weapons or cloaks or high-speed planes—confers a kind of status that only the most elite and wealthy citizens of the virtual planet can afford. Twinke once sold a piece of Cyborg Death Armor worth one million credits for only 200,000 credits to a player she'd never even met before. Twinke, David's experiment in kindness and generosity, now has a total worth of about 400 million credits. Brisbanevi is only worth about one million.

David has built an elaborate backstory for Twinke and Brisbanevi, twins, which involves the murder of their parents by a corporation, and the siblings' coming of age in the violent cities of Rubi-Ka. When he's logged into the game through the Internet, David role-plays the characters as he imagines they'd behave. He's found that role-playing as Twinke has made him feel good. He's found himself enjoying her generosity of spirit, her openness. Role-playing Twinke has even made him "less of a dick at work," David says.

Later that night, Twinke runs into the newb Clandestinee again. She's bald except for a long ponytail on the top of her head. She has orange facial tattoos and is wearing a long black cloak. This time, when David checks her stats—called *conning,* from "consider"—he sees that she's jumped twelve levels since he showed her where the Whompa was earlier in the day. Clandestinee is chatting in front of a coffee bar in West Athen called the Cup. She now has an attack pet of her own, named Hate, and a healing pet, named Love. (It is the lure of increasing one's talents, abilities, and possessions through achievement that keeps players logged in for so many of their waking hours.)

Twinke bows to the newbie ever so slightly. *You had quite a night,* David types. They stand together for a moment. The sun is just rising above the city walls. It is raining slightly, a morning mist.

*It's raining,* the newbie says. *I didn't know it did that.*

*It does everything here,* Twinke responds. They stand together in the rain. David can hear its faint pattering from the speakers in the four corners of his room in Petaluma. Through the doorways of the city, Twinke and Clandestinee can see the forest growing saturated with rich color as the light becomes increasingly diffused by the rain. Twinke feels proud of the little planet as she senses the disbelief and the thrill of the newbie beside her. David remembers what it felt like at first. The utter awe. The sheer and utter awe of a planet through which time and space flowed according to a simplified set of physical laws, a planet where the sun rose and set, rain fell, wind howled, and storms raged—and on which one could become whomever one chose.

**NEARLY EVERY ACCOUNT** of role-playing games begins with the 1954 publication of J.R.R. Tolkien's *The Lord of the Rings*. It was the depth of the world Tolkien created that attracted so many would-be gamers. There was a feeling of completeness and total internal consistency. The species, subspecies, languages, maps, factions, and history that made up Middle Earth made it feel like an alternate universe—even if it was only on the pages of a book. The influence of *The Lord of the Rings* on the videogame medium in general and role-playing games in particular cannot be overstated.

Some historians might start their role-playing time lines even earlier, with H. G. Wells, who, besides pioneering science fiction, also published, in 1915, the first set of rules for amateur war games. Young Winston Churchill was an avid war game fan.

The culture of war games in the United States, however, really exploded in the early 1960s, as companies like Avalon Hill began producing games for popular use. Diehard enthusiasts, replaying the Battle of the Bulge or the Napoleonic Wars in their basements, began adopting the *characters* of the emperors and generals whose armies they were commanding. Players started coming to games in full costume, adjusting their language, their thinking, and their demeanor to accommodate those of the leaders they impersonated. The games were becoming as much about role playing as about rolling the dice. And when *LotR,* as gamers refer to *The Lord of the Rings,* was finally released in the United States in 1966, it was like tossing a lit match into a cauldron of oil.

Around that time, two guys in Lake Geneva, Wisconsin, named Gary Gygax and Dave Arneson, had become so enthusiastic about the genre that they had begun work on a medieval warfare game of their own, called *Chainmail.* The game was not only an attempt to provide a rule set for war-gaming with medieval miniatures (small lead figurines, meticulously painted and zealously guarded by their owners) but also an attempt to incorporate the high fantasy of epic poems like *Beowulf* and the mythological beasts they contained into a realistic model of combat.

Gygax and Arneson were not unlike David Reber, except that, rather than accessing their alternate lives through an Ethernet port on a computer, Gygax and his friends huddled together in his basement, moving pieces around on a sand-covered table and imagining themselves in fifteenth-century Poland or thirteenth-century France. Eventually the campaigns in Gygax's basement became more detailed and even evolved their own story lines. Dave Arneson and others took turns setting up each day's scenario, describing the backstory, giving each player a goal, and refereeing disputes. The role would come to be known as GM, or Gamemaster. Gygax and Arneson got so good at what they were doing that they self-published *Chainmail.* But as the focus of their campaigns shifted further away from the historical and more toward the fantastic and as they began to eschew the battlefield tactics of an army for the adventures of an epic hero, *Chainmail* became a supplement to, rather than a sourcebook for, a whole new kind of game.

In 1974, Gygax and Arneson published a new game based on the fantasy role-playing campaigns their group had been running. The game was *Dungeons & Dragons*. And David Reber was not the only one to be turned on. By the late 1970s, the explosive success of *D&D* had established role-playing games as a staple element of American youth culture, catapulting the genre into a lucrative niche of the entertainment industry.

At about the same time that David Reber was developing his role-playing skills, programmers Will Crowther and Don Woods designed a game called *Adventure. Adventure* was like a game of *D&D* except instead of a human "dungeon master," as Arneson had been, setting the scene and controlling the action, a computer was put in charge. All of the dice-rolling and myriad statistical data that composed each element of the game world was handled by the PDP-10. *Adventure* was followed by *Zork*. The game confronted players with lines of text like "you are entering a dark room," "there is a passageway to your right," "a troll bearing a large axe is approaching." And in response, the player would type "turn left" or "cast stunning spell on troll" or "look out window."

But it wasn't until 1978 that two undergraduate students at Essex University in Colchester, England, Roy Trubshaw and Richard Bartle, both big *Zork* and *Adventure* fans, found a way to use an early campus time-sharing computer system to let many different people, all at different physical locations, play the same text-based adventure, all at the same time. MUD1, as it was called, for "multiuser dungeon," looked very similar to computer games like *Zork* and *Adventure,* but now when you "entered a dark room," there might be another player already in that room. Players found that what made it impossible to log off was not simply the *D&D*-like adventure but the presence of other "real" people in the world with them. As MUDs sprang up around the United Kingdom and the United States, other programmers would add new features and functionality to the game system. MUD communities began to evolve. Each MUD served as the locus for a specific community, each bound together by the enjoyment their members derived from spending time together in an alternate world. Friendships and governments formed. The communities experimented with democracy, anarchy, and totalitarianism. They role-played duels and hung out in personally customized strings of text that described living rooms and castles and furniture, speaking to each other across huge geographical distances with their fingers, a keyboard, and their imagination.

**BY THE END** of the summer of 2002, Twinke has been named commander of Freedom's Hope, one of many player-run clans on Rubi-Ka that oppose the hegemony of Omni-Tech, a giant interstellar corporation that hoards the mining rights to the planet. David, from his "command center" bedroom, has managed to recruit the newbie Clandestinee as a full-time guild member. In fact, Clandestinee has become such a dedicated player that his wife has begun grumbling about the hours he's spending on the computer. Twinke and Clandestinee keep in touch throughout their days on Rubi-Ka, running missions together and helping each other out as needed.

Friendships developed online often cross over into RL too. David advises his new friend to explain to his wife that

Rubi-Ka is an important part of his life, that this is where he socializes, where his friends are. He urges the wife to have patience. While not married IRL ("in real life"), David knows that marriage between avatars is a commonplace event in massively multiplayer online games. (And there are numerous stories of players who meet online and eventually fall in love and marry in the real world as well.) "I've been hit on," David says. "Twinke has been proposed to. But I can't go the marriage route. That's a little too far. I'm in a futuristic game, but, you know, getting married is just a little too far in a videogame for me. I haven't crossed that reality threshold yet."

Twinke's latest effort as leader of Freedom's Hope is to establish a bank of valuable items that only clan members can access and use. He has begun collecting empty *implants*—virtual biomechanical devices that hold valuable *nanoclusters*—that add to a character's abilities. The implants Twinke collects are so sophisticated they can't be bought in Rubi-Ka stores. They are obtainable only by conquest. David reckons Twinke has at least a hundred of them.

This kind of hoarding is one of the things the game developers in Oslo who created Rubi-Ka detest. Players hoarding materials can bog down the virtual economy and create huge problems for the massive, real-life databases and hardware required to keep track of them. In one of the very first commercial massively multiplayer online games, *Ultima Online,* based on a franchise created by gaming legend Richard "Lord British" Garriott, developers were stunned and horrified to find that within months the entire landscape of Britannia had been devastated, all the sheep they'd built had been slaughtered, and the valuable weapons and pieces of clothing hidden around the world had found their way into collections in avatars' homes rather than being recirculated through the world and its economy. ("Why do you have all the crap you have?" retorted *Ultima Online*'s creative director Raph Koster crossly when a writer from *The New Yorker* asked him why players were hoarding items so obsessively.)

Virtual worlds, which are really just graphical MUDs, are all full of monsters and creatures that drop valuable items, or "loot," as players call them. In today's games, in order to ensure the rarity of powerful items dropped by certain key mobs (short for mobile objects), virtual world designers often resort to something called *spawn timers.* These timers prevent a new copy of a given mob from appearing at its designated location in the game world until a sufficient period has elapsed since that mob was last defeated. It's an attempt to maintain balance in the world. The more rare or powerful an item is, the longer the spawn timer will be.

Since players are feverish about their desire for "phat lewt" (powerful items of treasure), they will often "camp" at the site where a given creature spawns and wait until the next copy of that creature "pops." It is not unheard-of to find several guilds, all camped near a particular mob, all waiting on spawn timers of up to eighteen hours, just for the chance to secure a single prestige item for a single member.

And even if, after eighteen hours, your mob spawns, your group survives, and you get credit for the kill (usually determined by which group did the most damage to the creature), there is no guarantee you will get your item. A given prestige item may drop only once in a thousand kills. Given the time, number of people, and coordination required to kill such mobs, the value of some "über" items is nearly incalculable, even in virtual currency. Such items are fantasized about incessantly by players, and acquiring one can confer a level of notoriety most people never achieve in real life.

David Reber certainly has a long wish list of things he'd like for Twinke, but he draws a firm line when it comes to acquiring goods without working for them. Because they are such enormous, complicated, and dynamic undertakings, all online game worlds contain bugs in their code that, eventually, players learn to exploit like loopholes in a legal system. They find a monster that, through a mistake on the part of the programmers, generates a valuable item every fifteen minutes instead of every fifteen hours. And they camp outside it, killing the monster over and over so that they can sell the item over and over, ballooning their wealth to buy elite equipment and status gear. Or they find a bug that allows them to duplicate items. David hates exploiters, as they're known, since they are an affront to the primary ethical principle of virtual communities—namely, that everything acquired or awarded be done so on a principle of merit. Everything gained must be something earned.

David draws an equally firm ethical line on the cottage industry that has sprung up around MMOs on eBay. Rare items, valuable pieces of virtual property, and high-level characters can be found on eBay selling for thousands of dollars. There are virtual currency traders who make real-world livings selling the credits or gold pieces of a game world for actual dollars. One Rubi-Ka citizen, a Level 197 Nanotechnician, figures he was making about $1,000 a month selling credits from Rubi-Ka on eBay or playerauctions.com until an exploit at a guild bank caused the currency rate to drop from $20 U.S. per million credits to $1 per million credits. At one point, the Nanotechnician—actually a twenty-nine-year-old former military corpsman in Pennsylvania—had two characters running simultaneously on two different computers so that he could blitz twice as many missions. (Blitzing is when you dispense with the niceties of role-playing and team-building and just go for acquiring as much stuff as you can in the shortest amount of time possible.) Now, it's hardly worth the time. "By the way, you ever tell anyone about the money, I'll call you a liar," the Nanotechnician warns, "'cause they'll kick me out of the game."

"I refuse to buy things on eBay for my characters," David Reber says. "I think that is wrong. I think that is cheating. Buying credits, buying characters, buying items. Anything like that. I'm just totally appalled that Funcom allows it to continue."

David is not alone. Most players of virtual worlds don't like it either, for the same reasons they hate exploiters—it destroys the illusion of meritocracy. People join virtual worlds to enjoy time away from reality, and they resent anything that threatens to import real-life status into their virtual oases. Game worlds are supposed to be places where everyone starts at the same level with the same advantages and disadvantages. No one knows what you look like, what sex you are, what your parents do for a living, or whether you're wheelchair-bound. Rising in a virtual world, they insist, is supposed to depend on your talents, skill, and perseverance. One of the best parts of virtual worlds is that they are supposed to diminish the "accident of birth." Players have been known to gang up on suspected eBay-bought characters, refusing to team with them, hurtling items and obscenities after them as they pass, and where possible, mercilessly killing their characters over and over.

The companies that own these virtual worlds—from Funcom to NC Soft to Sony Online Entertainment—don't like such behavior either. For one thing, online game publishers know their customer base very well, and given the large initial costs of developing a successful virtual world, they are loath to upset them, and thus they zealously guard the integrity of their virtual economies. But even more important is that while the players of online games feel that items they earn in the game world belong to them—it was *their* time and effort after all that caused the items to be generated in the first place—the companies who design the game worlds insist that every virtual sword, apartment, and suit of armor, and even the characters and their identities, belong to them. This is becoming such a thorny issue of intellectual property, in fact, that in November 2003 the New York Law School and Yale Law School's Information Society Project sponsored a forum to discuss "what happens when real-world law and virtual-world creativity collide." Legal scholars from Yale, Stanford, and the University of Miami hashed it out with world builders like Hal Linden and Raph Koster. "What will be the effect on a new generation raised inside these worlds?" the organizers asked. "Are these new video 'games' more violent and lawless, or are they the new public spaces where young people will learn to become citizens? How will virtual worlds and the ethics that evolve there change attitudes about real-world society?"

**AS IS OFTEN** the case in real-world politics, one of David Reber's least favorite people on Rubi-Ka is not an employee of the Omni-Tech corporation he has sworn to destroy but a leader of a rival rebel clan. His nemesis, Commander Redruum Baccarella, is the leader of the Clan Anarchist Syndicate, one of the more notorious role-playing clans on Rubi-Ka. Redruum can often be found hanging out in one of the many pubs and nightclubs on the planet, holding court with members of his guild. Redruum has red tattoos around his eyes and the posture of a young Rudolf Nureyev. When asked if the name of his guild is a take on Anarchosyndicalism, the system of political beliefs espoused by Noam Chomsky, he replies: "I don't believe I've heard of that man."

As he sits in a coffeehouse in a rebel-held village called Old Athens, Redruum's officers and guardsmen bring him reports on enemy movements. He commends them for their outstanding work and turns to look as each new player approaches. Sometimes, when there's nothing much going on, Redruum and his followers will dance in the bar. The designers at Funcom have coded several animations that players can direct their toons to perform, including the Village People's "YMCA" dance, a tango, or even a short ballet. Their movements are fluid and complete with miraculously on-tempo hip thrusts, waving arms, twirls, and little leaps. Some players are even able to transform their avatars and those of others into tigers or little hedgehoglike creatures called *leets* that growl menacingly or roll around playfully on their backs. (MMO designers are incredibly self-referential as a group—the leets, for example, are named after a common term in MMO-speak, which is a synonym for "elite." The hidden joke here is that leets are actually among the least powerful of the denizens of Rubi-Ka.) There is also almost always music in the bars of Rubi-Ka, and on weekend nights, there are special guest DJs, guys at home spinning their sets by streaming them over the Internet.

David Reber has his reasons for disliking Commander Redruum. He thinks Redruum is only out for his own advancement and fame. While Twinke and Commander Redruum both lead guilds that fight against the corporation, David doesn't like Redruum's tactics. He thinks Redruum is a warmonger.

"He does not think about what is going to happen when he goes and attacks Omni headquarters," David complains, sitting on the edge of his bed in his darkened room. "Do you think they're not going to retaliate? Do you think they're not going to attack one of our cities? People are going to die. Even though it's only a game, still, people die. Twinke hates Omni because of what they did to her parents, but she wants a peaceful solution because she's tired of all the death. She's tired of the killing."

David once got so fed up with Commander Redruum that Twinke challenged him to a duel, according to the PvP rules established by the game designers. PvP stands for "player-versus-player combat," and PvP is a hotbed of controversy among both gamers and world builders. In *Ultima Online,* for example, designers like Raph Koster and Rich Vogel were horrified to watch as powerful elite players hung out by the doorway through which new players emerged and killed them as they entered. "These games bring out the best in people, but they also bring out the worst," Rich Vogel says. Elites and überplayers were also luring n00bs—a derogatory term for newbies—into remote areas, killing them, and looting their corpses. Players who were in the world as blacksmiths and bakers, who wanted only to hang out in their virtual towns, socializing and role-playing, found themselves victims of attacks by raiding player killers. Both Raph Koster and Rich Vogel had joined the *Ultima* team after long backgrounds in text-based MUD communities, which tend to be noncommercial, player-governed affairs. Raph, who likes to wax philosophical on the subject of virtual worlds, has written long papers on the rights of avatars. As true believers in these alternate communities, they wrestled with the PvP issue seriously.

"For me the issue of player-killing was about whether people were going to have freedom of choice in their actions or whether we were going to impose codes that prevented them from doing bad things," Raph says. "At the time, I argued that if we removed the choice, people weren't going to learn diddly-squat. We can do the experiment of removing violence, but what will we learn about ourselves by doing that?"

But what he and Rich were learning was that size, and a corporate boss, change everything: MUD communities were small enough that peer pressure was an effective tool to keep people in line. Once you're dealing with hundreds of thousands or even millions of people (as many online worlds, particularly in Asia, do), you need something more, Raph discovered. Newbies getting killed before they had a chance to start playing meant newbies quitting the game before they had a chance to start paying subscription fees. Bestowing free will on humans was a choice God made when he created the world, Raph says, but in the case of virtual worlds, the market trumped even God.

As a result, today's virtual world designers have resorted to systems of "consensual" PvP, where players can still slaughter each other to their hearts' content as long as all parties involved agree to the carnage. In the case of *Anarchy Online,* there are entire swaths of the planet where avatars can engage in large-scale battles and dedicated arenas that allow individuals and small groups to test their mettle against one another. But there are also areas where an avatar can go about his business in guaranteed peace.

**WHEN TWINKE AND REDRUUM** entered the PvP Arena in Tir City, they first established some ground rules. "Self-buff only,"

David demanded, and Redruum agreed, meaning that neither player could benefit from power bestowed on them from outside help, like fellow clan members or observers.

It was a long fight. Guild members of both clans stood on the sidelines to watch and cheer. At one point, Twinke lost half her health. Redruum complained that the battle was going to last forever. But then Twinke unleashed her pet demon on him and cast a spell that left Redruum momentarily paralyzed. Acting quickly, Twinke finished him off before he could recover. As Redruum lay in the dirt of the arena, Twinke walked over to his corpse and spit on his body—the same "emote" technique that allows characters to dance and sing.

Despite losing to Twinke in the PvP Arena, Commander Redruum was to become one of the most prominent citizens of Rubi-Ka that summer. One day in August, after meeting with other guild leaders, he hopped on a ledge above a towering building in Tir City and called for a virtual revolution. There were about fifty avatars gathered around him and a guard of the Clan Anarchist Syndicate in their uniform of sandy brown armor. Using the "shout" command so that everyone in the city could hear him, Redruum called for the overthrow of the Council of Truth, a United Nations–like entity set up by Funcom as part of their ongoing story line. For a time the Council had been a major vehicle through which Funcom guided and encouraged roleplay and interaction on Rubi-Ka. But the tides of the people had turned against it, and Redruum was leading the assault.

(Watching, of course, was Twinke, who stood behind Commander Baccarella shouting, "Redruum sucks, Redruum sucks," and then mooning him using the /moon emote as Redruum began his exhortation.)

"Let's take our destiny into our own hands!" Commander

Redruum cried from his boulder platform. His speech was rife with references to the Roman Republic and statesmanship, and a senate composed of guild leaders. "Sure our enemies have vast armies, technically superior weapons of war, and a nearly unbreakable budget—but do they have a cause? Do any of them have the drive that fires our hearts? They are all employees, puppets dancing for the profit of their masters." It was a strident and fiery speech, one that John Seppelfrick, the player who created Redruum, would hardly have occasion to make in real life. A mild-mannered twenty-three-year-old network administrator from Aurora, Illinois, Seppelfrick enjoys playing softball and is in a local bowling league with his father.

The call for the overthrow of a developer-established institution—represented by a needle-nosed building in the center of Tir—caused a stir never before seen on Rubi-Ka. Community Internet boards—many built and run by players—were ablaze. The phrase *coup d'état* was thrown around. Long articles were written delving into the minutiae of the game's story line to justify or condemn Redruum. "I, for one," wrote one outraged virtual journalist, "say enough of this madness. Redruum, the career terrorist, the madman, has gone far enough this time. . . . Fellow clan-members, let yourself be heard. Ignore the terrorist Redruum and his misguided lackeys' call to arms. We fight for justice, not to put criminals into power!" Others wrote: "The time has come for action. The time has come to take matters into our own hands. The time has come to show the Council of Truth"—the offending organization of the designers in Oslo—"we will no longer stand idle as they do nothing in our conflict! Unite with us as we take the first steps."

The Funcom world builders, constantly monitoring the activity in the game, were watching the action along with the players. Gaute Godager, one of the founders of Funcom and a developer of *Anarchy Online*—as well as a former psychologist, and a well-known *D&D* dungeon master in his hometown—knew who Redruum was even before his call for revolution.

Although it's tempting to think of virtual world builders as playing God, Godager laughs at the very notion. "I am much more like a politician than God," he says. "It is like a tennis match, where we throw the ball to them [the players] and make them react, and then they punch it back at us, and we react to what they're doing. But we can't put on the mantle of God and smash them, because that would not make for any fun."

Like good politicians, Godager and his team listened very seriously to Redruum's complaints. And then, much to everyone's surprise—Commander Redruum included—Funcom pulled down the Council of Truth. When Redruum is told that Gaute Godager is actually aware of his existence, John Seppelfrick in Aurora taps the *s* on his keyboard so that the avatar Redruum takes a modest step backward. "Really?" he types. As gamers rarely use punctuation—it slows down their communications—that lone question mark betrays the magnitude of his excitement. *"Hmmmm,"* Redruum writes. He is a leader, after all, not someone to let his feelings of personal pride take over. "Tell Mr. Godager I think he is doing a wonderful job," he says, "and if at all possible I would like to talk to him someday."

**FOR ALL THE** turmoil and excitement on Rubi-Ka, by next summer, David Reber is ready to jump ship. There's a new MMO coming on the market that has the gamer community abuzz. It's *Star Wars Galaxies*. In a mark of vindication for their medium, LucasArts is turning to a virtual world to carry on the *Star Wars* legacy. Like hundreds of thousands of other MMO-ers around the world, David has been following the game's development since the end of 2000 when *Star Wars Galaxies* community relations manager, Kevin O'Hara, started the game's first official Web site. It opened to 500,000 registered users—all people who wanted to follow the world-building team's progress and to give their input as to what the game ought to be like. MMO gamers are an opinionated lot. If the citizens of Earth were half as interested in their planet's well-being as virtual citizens are in theirs, we would live in a vastly different world.

Reber's friend from *Anarchy Online,* Clandestinee, has actually gotten a spot in beta testing for the game, a coveted position. The first five hundred people were handpicked by O'Hara from 350,000 applications. O'Hara was besieged with virtual-world badges of honor—"I was a level 65 scout in *EverQuest*!" "I've been playing MMOs since *Meridian 59*!" "I lead a guild of 200 on *Anarchy Online*!" Spots in beta went for as much as $500 on eBay. Although Freedom's Hope is staying on Rubi-Ka, David Reber knows some of the other big guilds are planning to send out sister groups to colonize Tatooine, Naboo, and Corellia as soon as the game opens; he's not thrilled about this. It's that issue of meritocracy again. By the time *Star Wars Galaxies* is getting ready to go live, MMO players have taken to complaining bitterly that if you don't get into a virtual world on the ground floor, so to speak, you're out of luck. People complain there are no good plots of land left in *Ultima Online* on which to build a home; that *EverQuest* has become so über that newcomers don't stand a chance. Virtual worlds are supposed to be new frontiers, rife with all the opportunities that make frontier life worth living. But when the über and the elites become the aristocracy, what's the point? Living on a virtual world as a plebe can be as depressing as being one on planet Earth.

***STAR WARS GALAXIES*** was created by what was supposed to be the dream team of world builders. Around the time that LucasArts was looking for someone with whom to entrust their most precious of properties, Sony had just increased its stake in the virtual world business by forming Sony Online Entertainment in San Diego, California. Between 2000 and 2003, Sony invested heavily in a future that included the building and renting of virtual worlds as a viable business plan. *Star Wars Galaxies* was to be the crown jewel in Sony's new role as king of the massively multiplayer game.

Sony tapped Rich Vogel to produce the project because he had pulled off the launch of *Ultima Online* under the tutelage of Richard Garriott. True, it was a disastrous launch, landing its subsequent owner, Electronic Arts, in a multimillion-dollar class action lawsuit filed by players. But in a field this new, such things are easily overlooked by eager employers. The number of people with any experience at all in building and running virtual worlds could have fit into a one-bedroom apartment. Besides, troubled launch and all, *Ultima Online* now boasts a fearsomely loyal population of about 300,000 people, each paying $14.95 a month for the privilege of being virtual citizens. *Ultima Online* had served as a kind of proof of concept in a market that was hardly viewed as a sure thing.

Rich Vogel, who is thirty-six years old and stoop-shouldered like a man who's been carrying a heavy burden for a long time, put the rest of the team together. He brought Raph Koster with him from *Ultima Online,* as well as a dozen artists, modelers, and programmers. Although many of the sixty-five-person team earned their stripes on *Ultima Online,* there are also people on the team who were former architectural designers, and even one who was a scientist at the Hubble Space Telescope project.

The *Star Wars Galaxies* team was built around three disciplines: design, art, and programming. (The team also included all the producers and middle managers necessary to make sure that the three disciplines were communicating sufficiently with one another.) There's a lot of coordinating to do, because while Kevin O'Hara is working with the community of future players, and Artie the conceptual artist is brainstorming about how lampposts in the city of Dee'Ja Peak should look, the programming team is working as if their lives depended on it to construct the world-building tools that will allow the designers to actually implement their vision of this world. The development team is headquartered in Austin, Texas. Sony, which is providing the back-end infrastructure, is in San Diego. LucasArts, which has final approval for every single detail of the game, is in Northern California. All told, it took four hundred people working around the clock for more than two years to build this virtual world.

**DAVID REBER FINALLY** managed to land a spot in beta testing during phase three. By June 26, 2003, the day the game goes live, he's ready to take this new world by the throat. He's gotten a day off work in order to be there at the precise moment the portals of this virtual amusement park—as Rich Vogel describes it—swing wide. As David sits at his desk, black shades drawn, subwoofer ready to give him the full bass-filled experience of the new world, the *Star Wars Galaxies* teams are running their final "smoke tests." The testers, in their windowless, clockless room, are running their avatars through the world one last time—Are the banks working? Is the commodities market open for business? Are the chat channels running? Kevin O'Hara is making sure the appropriate EULA (end-user license agreement) will greet players when they log in. Is there a trademark indication on every mention of *Star Wars*? One by one the results of the smoke tests come back to Rich Vogel.

At 8:59 a.m. in Petaluma, David Reber checks to make sure he's got a full cup of coffee by his side. His hands hover over the keyboard. At the exact same time, Rich Vogel, in Austin, acknowledges the successful smoke tests and picks up the phone. He dials up Mike Thompson, Sony's head of database operations in San Diego. He gives Mike the go-ahead, and Mike punches in the final command, six letters that set an entire universe in motion: *C-O-M-M-I-T.*

David enters the registration area as his clock strikes nine a.m. What he doesn't know is that he's only one of about 75,000 people doing the exact same thing at the exact same time. LucasArts hasn't even started its PR campaign for the game yet, and Vogel and his team were only expecting about twenty or thirty thousand registrants. Sony's billing infrastructure crumbles under the onslaught. David Reber bangs his fist against his desk in Petaluma. Every time he tries to register, he gets disconnected. Rich Vogel is tight-lipped in his office. He's dedicated his life to virtual world building and he's got more experience than almost anybody in the business. He knows the one thing that other members of his team may not entirely realize: building a virtual world may be maddeningly hard, but running one the size of *Star Wars Galaxies* may not even be possible.

At ten a.m., David gets an announcement asking him to be patient. It feels like a betrayal. He's angry, and were it not for the fact that the game's official messageboards are down, too, he'd be posting in them right now, telling this development team what he thinks of them. This is a *life* he's waiting to start after all.

At the same time, in his office two doors down from Rich Vogel, under a Kermit the Frog poster and a clock that tells time backward, Raph Koster is answering e-mails from irate fans. Raph has been a celebrity among virtual-world aficionados for almost a decade. As a hardcore MUD-er before joining the *Ultima Online* team, Raph has been writing and speaking on the subject of virtual communities for a long time. He's made himself so available that some players are contacting him directly when they find the official avenues of communication closed. Like David Reber, they're furious that the world they've been waiting so long to inhabit is not open. It's like arriving at a community center on the hottest day of the summer and finding out the pool has been drained. Online players are quite sensitive when it comes to what they perceive as fair and unfair, elevating matters of entertainment to issues of justice and desert. Right now they feel snookered, lied to, and frustrated, and they don't hesitate to use any means at their considerable technological disposal to express it.

It takes the *Galaxies* team two and a half hours to fix the registration problem. Suddenly David finds himself, after so many attempts he's lost count, actually making it through the account registration process. He enters the keycode that proves he paid $60 for a copy of the game, creates a user account, and gives Sony his credit card number and permission to charge him $14.95 a month for the duration. He lets out a little celebratory *"woot"*—the interjection of choice for pleased gamers.

Meanwhile, in Austin, associate producer J. Allen Brack lets out a similar cry of truimph. The team watches as the number of successful registrations starts rocketing. As J. watches, the numbers on his computer monitor climb steadily, reaching fifteen thousand registrations within an hour.

**DURING BETA TESTING,** David Reber played on a server called Ahazi, and although all traces of players' existence was wiped from the server when beta testing ended, it's Ahazi where Reber chooses to create his first *Star Wars Galaxies* avatar. He played as a Rodian artisan in beta, and that's the character he's going to create for himself now. He is particularly excited, however, by the profession he's chosen for his character.

*Star Wars Galaxies* is offering something new to MMO players in its profession system. Though it's now a staple of the genre for players to have many kinds of professions from which to use, Raph Koster initially scandalized people by offering "trade professions" with *Ultima Online*. Trade professions allowed people to become productive, respected, and sought-out members of their virtual communities not only by slaying ogres and trolls and hobgoblins but also by adopting trades like baking, blacksmithing, or tailoring. At the time, Raph got nasty e-mails asking, *Are you kidding? Do you think I'm going to spend $14.95 a month to sew clothes?!* But the trade professions became so popular that they've since become one of the core features by which customers judge the quality of a game world.

For *Star Wars Galaxies,* Raph has again upped the ante. Along with his world-building team, he has created a group of "social professions." In *Star Wars Galaxies,* players can be a functioning part of the society and the economy by becoming musicians, dancers, and personal trainers. Now, Raph gets nasty e-mails asking, Y*ou want me to be a Wookie hairdresser? That's ghey!* (Online gamers often use *ghey* instead of *gay* to distinguish between the "lame" and homosexual connotations of the word.) But Raph is not easily put off by criticism. He's "an idealist on a virtual crusade," he says. "Just making a game about killing Orcs would be immoral." So the *Star Wars Galaxies* world is a delicate ecosystem where warriors come to cantinas to be healed of "battle fatigue" by musicians; hairdressers get paid to spiff up other toons' appearances. Entertainers dance for tips. The profession system nudges people together who might not otherwise naturally gravitate that way—even in a virtual setting. In *Star Wars Galaxies,* it is hoped that hardcore warrior types will brush up against would-be artists, and gunslingers of the Han Solo variety will come begging to artisans for the weapons they need to fight with, and to chefs for the food they need to eat.

David Reber has known from the beginning that he's going to be an artisan. Artisans can train their way up to become master architects. And if beta testing is any indicator, architects are going to make a lot of money very fast in *Star Wars Galaxies*. Almost everything of value in the game is player built—another departure courtesy of Raph—and so David figures, why shouldn't it be he to whom all the guilds come for their association halls, cantinas, and homes?

Late in the afternoon of his second day in *Star Wars Galaxies,* David gets a *tell* from Clandestinee, who is now playing a toon named Ninz Honda. (*Tells* are how players send private text strings to one another no matter how far apart they may be geographically in the virtual world.) The two friends meet near the city of Mos Espa on Tatooine. David Reber has named his Rodian Brisbane. He's not playing the same hard-boiled Brisbanevi of *Anarchy Online,* but neither is he going to be the generous altruist Twinke was. David quit Rubi-Ka in a huff of ill-hidden hurt feelings, complaining that he'd always been there for his guild members but that few were there for him. He's also furious that upon leaving the guild, he wasn't invited into the überguild Storm. (Freedom's Hope was a well-respected guild, but it was not über.) Although Sherry Turkle, a professor at MIT who has written about identity-building in MMOs, might say it is at just such a moment that the very point of role-playing emerges, David has spent his life being disappointed by those around him, and it was not an experience he was anxious to re-create. He left *Anarchy Online* with many of the same feelings that plague him in real life—feelings of betrayal, loss, and loneliness. He feels burnt by the kindness he allowed himself to exhibit through Twinke. Things are going to be different in *Star Wars Galaxies,* he tells himself.

By the time Brisbane and Ninz meet, Brisbane has acquired a turban, a gunman's duster, armored boots made of the bones of large herbivores, leather pants, and a red shirt. He is carrying a blaster. Ninz, who is a blue Rodian with two Mohawk-like rows of spines growing out of the top of his head, is impressed. David has nearly mastered the artisan profession in a single day, and he is already preparing to become an architect, the next step on his profession tree. He is beside himself with joy at the wide-open frontier before him. In an e-mail to Ninz, he cries that he's finished with women forever. *Star Wars Galaxies* has everything he'll ever need, he says. And, oh, he wants Ninz to go into business with him. He has an idea for an architecture and resources company called Dewback Industries. "It will have the world in its grasp," David says. He appoints himself CEO and puts Ninz in charge of resource development, security, and personnel.

**WITHIN A FEW WEEKS,** David is a Master Architect, one of the first on his server. He sends a slightly hesitant Ninz out on daily scouting missions to find the materials such as precious metals and animal hides necessary to keep the firm humming. David also instructs Ninz to keep an eye out for aluminum, as the prices for good-quality aluminum on the commodities market are insanely high. Every Weaponsmith, for example, needs it, and Ninz can mine several hundred thousand units before a site goes dry, and then sell each unit for about a hundred credits.

Ninz is having a hard time explaining to his wife why he "has" to do these things. "David is making me" isn't cutting it anymore. She begins to understand why there are so many *EverQuest* Widows support groups, where spouses of avid online gamers gather to commiserate about their husbands' (and, in some cases, wives') incredible dedication to lives that, though virtual, can become all-consuming.

From his room in Petaluma, David becomes seriously engrossed in the business of Dewback Industries. He begins to keep Excel spreadsheets that track every item the company makes: the materials required, the costs of those materials, retail cost of items produced and their profit margins. The success of Dewback Industries has been one of the few counterweights to what's been a tough time for David Reber in RL. He's run into trouble at Best Buy because a computer glitch in the corporation's employee monitoring system has marked his register as coming up short twice, which in turn triggers a computer-generated notice to his manager who is forced to put him on unpaid probation, despite admitting that David is one of the few workers who actually understands the technology he is selling and that he's the last guy to be stealing from the company. David e-mails Ninz that a visit to the doctor reveals he's developing an ulcer.

Maybe it's the pain in his stomach, but David fires the company's first employee, Anir—in RL, a twenty-eight-year-old coworker of David's—after about two weeks in operation. Reason: lack of commitment. It was a unilateral decision to cut out Anir, but David explains the situation to Ninz and hopes he doesn't mind too much. Ninz doesn't. He's noticed that organizations in virtual worlds are often run in what seem to be strikingly antidemocratic ways, but he also knows that this is mostly due to the difficulties of running a community whose citizens are only part-time members. Besides, Ninz is enjoying his travels through this new world. Each planet feels unique—there are the forests, grass plains, and mudflats of Talus; the bubbling lava pits and sulfur pools of Lok; the deserts of Tatooine.

Like Will Wright, Raph Koster is highly interested in urban planning, and so the cities have been designed carefully to reveal something about the societies that built them, each with its own etiquette and culture. The city of Keren on Naboo is laid out in a graceful arc, with the bank in the center of town and gracious, wide streets leading in and out of the city. For Tatooine's Mos Eisley, infamous as a hive of villainy and murderers, Raph and his team designed a city of dead ends, convoluted side streets, and lots of creepy dark places for encounters with AI pickpockets and other unsavory characters. Every city contains an infrastructure that includes a cantina, hospital, bank, common space, a shopping area, and some traveling facilities.

**AS THE WEEKS** go by at the Austin development team's headquarters, unshaven faces, bleary eyes, and poor eating habits have become a way of life. Every day it's been something, if not multiple "somethings." One player figured out that the /launch command, meant to set off fireworks, can actually launch just about anything. Banks, guildhalls, lampposts, nonplayer characters go flying into the air and then disappear. And of course everyone who sees this follows suit, and soon the air is filled with flying objects. The mining facilities that people have spent hours building: gone in the blink of an eye. Thank god they can't launch each other, the development team groans (which isn't to say they didn't try). One of the producers had to find the programmer who wrote the code and get him to close the loophole, and Kevin O'Hara had to placate the people who were freaking out because their storage facilities have been sent flying through the air.

Associate producer J. Allen Brack has found an exploiter in a network of caves filled with killer bats. The player has realized that, although they look continuous, the caves were actually designed as separate cells. The bats can't cross from cell to cell, so the offending player has positioned himself at the boundary between two cells, shooting bats, racking up experience points, and assuming no risk. "This is my area! Go find your own!" he shouts at J., who donned his own avatar, a female Zabrak, in order to speak with the player.

Raph is getting a little nervous about a phenomenon he calls "The September That Never Ended." It's a phrase from the days of the early Internet. September always meant hundreds of thousands of students getting access to T1 lines for the first time and an accompanying onslaught of newcomers into people's precious online communities. The newcomers would crash the established ways and trample over carefully established etiquette. They'd tend to either get bored and leave, or adapt and stay. But when the full Internet boom happened in the midnineties, it was the September That Never Ended; the equilibrium could never be restored. Raph knows that as virtual worlds move from the everyone-knows-everyone days of the old MUDs into this brave new future of the corporate-owned virtual amusement park, the same thing could happen.

That's why, as much as it goes against his nature, he has come to agree with Rich Vogel on a three-strikes-you're-out policy for virtual citizens who don't play nice. In *Star Wars Galaxies* you get one warning after inappropriate behavior, which can range from killing another player in a non-PvP zone to blocking up a forum with posts of "you suck, you suck, you suck" to sexually harassing a Zabrak. After you get three marks on your file—the new virtual worlds keep records of every step a player takes through the world—you're out. Raph has even given talks to other world builders advocating random raids based on modern-day RL police tactics as the most effective model for maintaining stability in virtual worlds. It goes against his disposition, but Raph cares about the success of virtual worlds as much as anyone alive today. He sees them as alternative communities of the future. Any youth marketer will tell you that *community* is simply a buzzword, used today to sell everything from cell phones to mouthwash. But Raph's been hawking his vision of community since the Reagan era.

"The *point* of these games is to bring people together," he says, "to give them the experience of working together, working in groups, forming communities. Giving to community. Fighting for their communities. Defending their communities. These days, these are not experiences given to most humans, frankly. Most people never get the sense of 'this is our place and we're going to make it stand for something.' Most people don't have a sense of societal engagement. I think these games can give them that."

Raph grew up traveling the world with his mother, who worked for UNICEF. She was Puerto Rican; his father, a Midwesterner of Irish decent. He spent several of what would have been his high school years swimming and lounging in a hotel pool during the ousting of Baby Doc in Haiti. Other years were spent in Peru and the Philippines. One of the tenets of Raph's life philosophy is the possibility of empathy between people and groups of people. He believes in "building bridges."

It is absurd to Raph that people won't accept high technology as a mode of communication, as a mode of facilitating anything *Real.* And he means it with a capital *R,* the way the rabbit in *The Velveteen Rabbit* was made Real through the love of a little boy. Raph is not some *Wired*-obsessed, bring-on-the-hive-mind futurist techno freak. In fact, he'll argue to exhaustion that the invention of the printing press had a greater impact on society than the computer. But he also believes that what is now denigrated as merely virtual will one day be considered real and authentic in important ways.

"I'm saying the human interaction of communities is what makes them real," Raph says. "There are a lot of communities in real life that are artificial, that are just aggregations of people who don't really have a shared interest, a shared stake in things. Can you name eight of your neighbors? We're very disconnected from one another. But one of the things that happened with the Internet was a new kind of tribalization, where people are finding themselves online, saying, 'Oh, here's my *real* community.' "

**BY THE END** of August, *Star Wars Galaxies* has 275,000 inhabitants. That gives it more citizens than Birmingham, Alabama, or Anaheim, California. And *Star Wars Galaxies* has been in existence for only two months. Brisbane and Ninz have erected a workshop on Tatooine among an extemporaneous collective of player crafters. Ninz continues to survey and scout while

Brisbane crafts. After managing to sell several houses of increasing size, Brisbane has secured the word of a major guild leader that his members will purchase only through Dewback Industries. And a single guildhall sells for more than half a million credits.

Before they'd been on the virtual world for a month, Brisbane and Ninz were easily multimillionaires. Once Brisbane made Master Architect, it was fait accompli. The market was theirs for the taking. Other players, slower players, are eager to buy houses for status, harvesters to advance their own characters, and raw materials to make weapons. Brisbane, true to the character of the Rodian as described by the *Star Wars Galaxies* handbook, is mostly out for himself. He's gruff but fair, still generous and helpful, but not open to the kind of hurt he felt on Rubi-Ka.

Ninz himself quits the game after several months of hardcore playing. His wife definitely had something to do with it, but Ninz had also started having the nagging feeling that he was missing out on something else: he had to admit that the lack of real-life accomplishment had gotten him down. Which would be fine with Raph Koster. Raph says the ideal player plays until he's gotten what he needs out of the game and then returns, new skills in hand, to RL.

David Reber has no intention of quitting. Brisbane has met a girl, another player. Brisbane and the girl have been running missions together, and they are even considering meeting in RL. Besides, David has another goal etched into his mind now. He wants to be a Jedi knight, something so difficult to accomplish that Kevin O'Hara's chat rooms have been bogged down for months with complaints. But by early 2004, Brisbane has mastered twenty-nine of the thirty-two available professions in the game, a feat that certainly qualifies him as über. Being a

Jedi is the most elite profession ever created in any MMO, and David is on the verge of achieving it.

It's a long and arduous process, but David firmly believes that if he's only given a fair shot, he can channel the Force as well as anyone.

# 7

## Smartbomb

On a rainy day in October 2003, at the annual conference of the Association of the United States Army, Dr. Michael Macedonia is wandering through Hall C of the Washington, D.C., Convention Center, checking out the latest wares from the hundreds of companies that do business with the U.S. Army. Lockheed Martin, Boeing, and United Defense are there, showing off tanks the size of mobile homes, 40-mm grenade launchers, thirty-round semiautomatic submachine guns, and the latest in war-gaming simulations.

Macedonia is a beefy, big-faced man packed tightly into a black suit. He wears his black hair scooped up and away from his face in a Ronald Reagan–style pompadour. The son of a prominent Army man, Macedonia grew up everywhere, from Kansas to Paris, France. He moved so much, in fact, that he calls his alma mater, West Point, the closest thing he has to a home. He's played many different roles in his life in the Army, from project manager on automated electronic warfare system development to fighting in the first Gulf War. Macedonia is prone to slapping people on the back and telling jokes with a booming laugh that he lets loose regularly. There's something defensive and sad about his eyes, though, that makes you think of a little boy trapped in a grown man's body.

Today, Macedonia is the chief scientist and technical director for the Simulation, Training, and Instrumentation Command (formerly known as STRICOM, and now known by the acronym PEO STRI). As such, Macedonia is the equivalent of a chief technical officer in a private-sector company. He helps the Army invest in technology to train its soldiers, an increasingly important part of Army philosophy since the 1970s when, as Macedonia recounts with a laugh, "We trained soldiers for six weeks, taught them how to polish their boots and fire their weapons, and then we sent them to Vietnam where they got killed."

A self-proclaimed "total geek," Macedonia may have dedicated his life to the Army, but his heart belongs to a world inhabited by science fiction, computers, and videogames—these are the things that make his gaze relax and his voice loosen. After serving in the first Gulf War, Macedonia even thought about leaving the military altogether to pursue his dream of starting a massively multiplayer online game company. His PhD from the Naval Postgraduate School, after all, was in networking military simulations, which, as he says, "is basically the same thing." When he couldn't get funding for a start-up game company, Macedonia decided to stay in the Army. Fortunately for him, the U.S. military is now undergoing some of the biggest changes in a century, and he may just get the opportunity to fulfill his science-fiction-fueled videogame dreams anyway.

Macedonia stops by a particularly loud tent in Hall C, where a movie-sized screen is showing digital animation of jungles, urban terrains, and deserts. Little digital enemy soldiers bob and weave their way to the foreground. A row of *real* men kneel before the backdrop with slightly modified Javelin M2 grenade launchers on their shoulders that recoil, boom, and let off smoke just like real Javelin M2s, but without actually shooting bullets. The spokesman for Cubix, the defense contractor that built this training simulation, the EST 2000, says to think of it like an old arcade game. But instead of blowing plastic frogs off their lily pads or plastic cowboys off their horses, you're learning to aim at and kill "enemies." The men in khaki kneeling before the big screen are having a blast, which is good, because Cubix built the thing to be fun. Macedonia stops to laugh with the men, and he shakes his head at the noise, and the smoke rising from the Javelins, and the sheer marvel of it all.

The wares of other companies also delight him. There's Topscene, a "mission rehearsal system" that used satellite images, aerial photographs, and data provided by intelligence agencies to create a 3-D visual database of Afghanistan. Before actually attacking that country two years ago, pilots played Topscene on computer consoles to help them identify targets, recognize landmarks, and learn where to expect roads and where to expect only mountains.

MultiGen-Paradigm is showing off its software tools for 3-D modeling of geographic locations. The set of tools is not unlike the ones used by the *Star Wars Galaxies* team in creating the virtual terrain of *Star Wars.* But these tools are used for modeling real locations, not imaginary ones. Before President Bush's February 2003 attack on Baghdad, fliers stepped into the training replicas of their fighter cockpits, and thanks to the software of MultiGen-Paradigm, saw a digitized version of downtown Baghdad out their windows as they practiced flying and dropping bombs.

It all reminds Macedonia of one of his favorite books, *Ender's Game,* by Orson Scott Card. It's the near-future story of a worldwide, undisputed U.S. military superpower that has realized children are the best fighters around—as long as the fighting seems like a game. The book follows one particularly brilliant six-year-old named Ender who is handpicked to enter the national military academy where, day in and day out, the students play "the game." It's a virtual reality simulation to prepare them for an expected alien attack. At the end of the book, however, it is revealed that the most crucial practices were not practice at all, but were actually real battles, making unknowing killers out of the children soldiers.

Although this might raise a few eyebrows among nonmilitary types, Macedonia talks eagerly about the lessons to be taken from the book. He explains that it was a source of inspiration for lots of people in the military when it came out in the eighties. "I've always been fascinated by what you could do with a six-year-old," Macedonia muses.

As Macedonia wanders the halls, a little robot named the Talon is making circles around admirers in the main hall. The sergeant in charge of the thing is fiddling with a suitcase-sized remote controller to show his audience how to maneuver it. The Talon is the prototype of a drone, a hunk of metal with heavy-tread tractor wheels that can be transformed into a M203 grenade launcher or a machine gun, or simply sent out into the field as a surveillance device. In the suitcase, there are multiple video displays showing what the Talon sees, three joysticks for controlling its motion, and numerous switches and buttons for making it run through its paces. It looks impossibly complicated, but the sergeant assures his audience it's not. "If you can play Nintendo," he says, "you can operate this."

The retired Army engineers in their gray suits shilling for Lockheed Martin and United Defense seem puzzled. As they show off their multimillion-dollar simulation training tools, you get the sense they're beginning to fear for their jobs. There are changes afoot. Ed Payne is debuting SIMWAR, Lockheed Martin's tool for teaching commanders how to train their brigades, which he's worked on for the past seven years. But across the plush carpet aisle from him, where the Talon is making its circles, are two military-funded *videogames,* one for recruiting, *America's Army,* and one for training, *Full Spectrum Warrior.* Ed Payne doesn't know what to make of this. SIMWAR shuns the elaborate graphics of the videogame in favor of icons—blue boxes to represent artillery supplies and so on—in a style directly reminiscent of traditional war games. It's hard not to see, however, that while it may be doctrinally correct by Army standards, SIMWAR is not nearly as engaging as what's being displayed across the carpet aisle. And that's just the point. Young ROTCs with bright cheeks, tucked into their stiff, green uniforms, are lining up to play *America's Army* and *Full Spectrum Warrior,* just like people lined up to play Willy Higinbotham's *Tennis for Two* nearly fifty years ago. They're a little glassy-eyed and utterly delighted, like you can imagine the children who followed the Pied Piper into the ocean might have been.

**MACEDONIA EXPLAINS WHAT** everyone in today's military knows. And indeed, it sounds remarkably like a science-fiction scenario. But it's not. When the Cold War ended, the United States was left standing, the sole superpower in the world. The generals who ran what was now the most powerful military on earth woke up and realized that the kind of war for which they'd been preparing was obsolete. The entire paradigm of war—huge companies of men ready to fight to their death on predefined, well-marked battlefields—vanished. The tectonic plates of geopolitics creaked and chafed against one another, and in one of those systemic changes that happen every so often, shifted into a new configuration. The generals knew that now the enemy was not the Russian Bear, but little groups from across the globe, aligned primarily by their distaste for the United States.

Political and military leaders got together in their war rooms to strategize. They warned one another that without a new strategy, their way of life would not only cease to spread across other lands, but also could be threatened right here at home. They dubbed this period Transformation, and they gave it a capital *T* to make everyone understand how important it was. The military had to be transformed from a lumbering force of bodies with guns into a lean and nimble, technologically enhanced institution capable of fighting at a moment's notice on any terrain on earth. The future of war was going to be near-continuous, asymmetrical, spur-of-the-moment engagements. In endless meetings, papers, and conferences, the military and political leaders spelled out their plans. Transformation: it would create what they dubbed the Future Objective Force, the last remaining super military power on earth.

Then they did just what characters in science-fiction novels do when they're placed in such situations. They sought out the wise men, rounded up the finest technologists the world had to offer. In this particular case, that meant the best of the best from the communities of virtual reality, computer graphics, simulation and modeling, artificial intelligence, and entertainment. What is in your dreams? the generals asked. What is possible that has never been possible before? For its Future Objective Force, the U.S. needed new weapons, new training devices, and a new kind of soldier. And the military didn't care where the ideas came from. The technologists were drawn from within their own network of think tanks, larger academia, and from entertainment corporations. And they envisioned for the leaders all these things, and particularly a new soldier, one that would be faster, smarter, and more lethal than any soldier that had come before. Him, they called the Future Objective Force Warrior.

**A PROTOTYPE OF THE** Future Objective Force Warrior, expected to be ready in 2010, is not ten feet away from the Talon, which is still making its circles in the main hall of the AUSA conference.

Showing him off is Jean-Louis "Dutch" DeGay, a member of the military PR corps. He's in a dandyish suit, and has all the flair of a natural-born midway man. You almost expect him to twirl his mustache. He gestures at the Warrior while never taking his eye off the audience, fluidly pointing out details and mentioning astounding facts and figures as if he'd been born with the information. The Future Objective Force Warrior wears lightweight, chemical-retarding fabric, has bullet-repelling breastplates and shoulder guards, and boots that redistribute his weight. There's an antenna rising from his helmet that allows him to communicate with other soldiers and his commanders on both local and wide-area networks; and there's an eyepiece that curves over his left eye through which he can view iconic graphics and map overlays on what looks to him like a twenty-one-inch monitor.

"He's an F-Sixteen on legs," Dutch says between bursts of data, "an F-Sixteen on legs." As Dutch talks, it's easy to forget that it's actually a man standing next to him and not another artificial intelligence entity like the Talon. "The soldier is becoming a platform," Dutch says. "Once he powers up, he's a platform ready to roll out."

Strapped to the Warrior's back is a lightweight Pentium-class computer that communicates wirelessly with a PDA-like device on his wrist. Like a super brain atop the soldier's own, the computer communicates with the "platform." If for some reason the soldier's vision becomes impaired—say, his infrared optical device goes out while he's raiding a building in the dead of night—the Pentium will present a virtual representation of where he is, and he can navigate by that. Through his eyepiece he sees circular target overlays around figures in the distance, and his earpiece announces by tone whether that figure is friend or foe. The Pentium calculates the distance of the figure and informs him exactly how to aim and when to shoot. It monitors his heart rate and hydration levels. And it's also stocked with games like *Full Spectrum Warrior,* being displayed at the next booth, to keep the warrior both entertained and well trained.

Some in the military dream of a robotic army, but what people like Macedonia know is that there's no need. Sure, robots can't die, but any artificial expert worth his salt will tell you that a robot capable of making the kind of decisions modern soldiers need to make is many years and many billions of dollars away. (Even today, twenty-five years after Marvin

Minsky and John McCarthy founded MIT's Artificial Intelligence lab, there still is no computer in the world that could hold a reasonable conversation with a five-year-old child. Successful artificial intelligence is far more elusive than most people realize.) The Future Objective Force Warrior avoids the AI problem by combining the genuine intelligence of a human soldier with the computational abilities of a computer, and it integrates the pair by means of videogame-derived interfaces. And because of the ubiquity of videogames in civilian culture, recruits will begin training already comfortable with the paradigm.

Soon, the PDA device on the warrior's wrist will make him a constant participant in a virtual networked environment, or what is increasingly being known, even in military circles, as a massively multiplayer online game. This is one of Macedonia's most cherished dreams. He envisions the warriors in constant, real-time communication with their battalions, even if they're in different physical locations. Just like the way the other "characters" on the screen in *Star Wars Galaxies* or *Anarchy Online* are really other people sitting at their computers, the "characters" with whom the warriors will be playing are his fellow soldiers. It's using the paradigm of the MMO interface as a communication device—an application of technology recommended to the military by Macedonia among others. The game, Macedonia hopes, will help warriors learn the terrain and customs of wherever they're stationed. And, most important, the game will keep him in the loop, in real time, with Army intelligence, an incalculable wartime advantage.

Like in *Ender's Game,* Macedonia also wants the soldier's experience to be uninterrupted by the distractions of civilian life. Knowing that in 2005 some cell phones will have graphic capabilities roughly on par with the first PlayStation, Macedonia dreams of an MMO for his warriors that they can play cell phone to cell phone, even when they're not in combat situations.

"I can have my soldiers always be part of the game," Macedonia says. "I can merge the real world with the virtual world. . . . I can have real people in real places interacting with real people in virtual places that are copies of the real world." He laughs his robust laugh. These are the things he loves to talk about. He pauses. "It does get really weird, and really kind of becomes science fiction at a certain point," he says. "It really is *Ender's Game*."

**THE ARMY HAS** always been interested in games. Generals know what kindergarten teachers know, which the videogame industry can be loath to admit: games teach. Show me the games of your children and I'll show you the next hundred years, anthropologists say. Take chess and Go. They were military simulations, albeit low-tech ones. They allowed the sons of kings and emperors to learn to think strategically; to conceptualize the battlefield; and to see firsthand, and in a no-consequences setting, the rippling effects of different moves.

It was Atari's *Battlezone* in 1980 that brought the U.S. military's gaze specifically onto the videogame. *Battlezone* was the first videogame to offer a first-person perspective. Instead of watching the action from above, the player viewed the action through the eye of a tank periscope. Thinking it would improve gunners' hand-eye coordination, the Army built a modified version of the game, changing the controls to more closely resemble a Bradley Infantry Fighting Vehicle. A couple years later, when a young designer named Gilman Louie started his *Falcon* flight simulator series, the military jumped on it. Today, the Air Force still gives customized copies of the game to every student pilot and undergraduate taking the Naval

Reserve Officer Training Courses, at the sixty-five colleges that offer the program. The Navy was delighted to find that students were playing the game at home in their own free time, and that those who played the game performed better than those who didn't when they stepped into the actual cockpit for training.

And just a few years before the Columbine killings introduced the rest of the country to the game, the U.S. Marines had already discovered *Doom.* A lieutenant from the Marine Corps Modeling and Simulation and Management Office modified the game by turning the original *Doom* characters into American Marines and "enemies." The twisted hallways and dank dungeons created by the id designers were altered to reflect real-world tactical situations—such as being trapped in a foxhole while repelling an enemy infantry assault, or attempting a counterattack through a barbed-wire-covered battlefield. Crumbling gothic passageways were replaced with bunkers, concertina wire, tactical emplacements, ditches, and hills. In one scenario, digitized foreign embassy floor plans were laid over one of John Romero's levels so soldiers could practice rescuing American hostages. The altered game became known as *Marine Doom*, and was so popular, according to the lieutenant, that when the *Doom* lab at his base shut down for the night, marines would beg to be allowed back in.

**LIKE ALL HIGH-TECHNOLOGY** industries, the videogame industry has, by default, long been intertwined with the military. The videogame industry grew out of soil the military has been tending since the 1940s, when it began pumping money into "computational devices" in an effort to beef up code-breaking and artillery-table-calculating skills needed during World

War II. William Higinbotham worked on the Manhattan Project, Ralph Baer invented the Odyssey while working at defense contractor Saunders and Associates, and the Artificial Intelligence lab where Steve Russell and his TMRC cohorts developed *Spacewar!* was funded by the Defense Advance Research Projects Agency (DARPA). Indeed, the present status of the videogame industry as a cultural and economic juggernaut has in great part been the outgrowth of military research in the fields of computing, modeling, and simulation, artificial intelligence, virtual reality, and war-gaming.

But at some point everything flipped—instead of the gamemakers taking their cues from military simulations, the military began to take its cues from the gamemakers. The offspring outpaced the parent. The videogame industry shot up in all its hoary disorder, surpassing the greatest military in the world in the fields of simulation and modeling, computer graphics, networking, and interface design. And they knew how to use these technologies in a manner that could make any kind of learning entertaining and fun.

**IT WAS THE** Chief Imagineer at Walt Disney who helped set the ball in motion for the great videogame-military merger. In 1999 word filtered down through the chain of command from four-star general Paul Kern, who had just returned from a meeting at the Walt Disney Imagineering facility in Glendale, California. Since its founding fifty years ago, Walt Disney Imagineering has served as a hub for technological breakthroughs to be used for entertainment purposes. It was Atari's Nolan Bushnell's dream job, and it has produced some of the most technologically advanced work in the entertainment industry—from theme parks and hotels to hydraulic rides to virtual-reality shows. When General Kern took his meeting, Disney's Imagineering facility was under the reins of a man named Brian Ferren, a well-known futurist, computer scientist, and member of the Army Science Board—described by Macedonia as a technological advisory group made up of "the country's wise men."

After his meeting, General Kern sent a missive to those beneath him demanding to know why the military wasn't doing the kinds of things Disney was doing. "Why can't we do the same stuff as the entertainment industry? They're doing all this cool stuff," Macedonia recalls Kern asking. He speaks in a kid's whiny voice, imitating his boss: "Why can't we be like Walt Disney?" Macedonia drops the mimicking. "I wanted to say, 'Because you don't give us enough money.' But generals, when they say these things, you have to come back with answers."

Macedonia began looking around for people to help turn some of these entertainment-fueled dreams into military reality. He turned to his former thesis advisor from the Naval Postgraduate School, Mike Zyda, who had recently presented a paper then circulating among military circles. It was called "Modeling and Simulation: Linking Entertainment and Defense."

**MIKE ZYDA IS NOT** on first glance the kind of character you would cast to play supertechnologist to the world's superpower. He's in his midforties, with a potbelly hanging over the top of his pants, and a little gray mustache that twitches above his mouth. A native of Southern California, Zyda has the speech intonation of a real-life Jeff Spicoli of *Fast Times at Ridgemont High,* smattering his breathy conversation with "cool" and "fave" and "awesome." At first you think he's trying to be funny. Then you realize he's not. After spending time with him, you also begin to realize that he actually is just the kind of guy the world's superpower would call upon in a science-fiction novel.

When he first started teaching at the Naval Postgraduate School seventeen years ago, Zyda threw away the faculty handbook that was presented to him in a binder and replaced it with a copy of Machiavelli's *The Prince.* Zyda prides himself on his ability to read people, to break down patterns of human behavior with scientific precision. Some are fascinated by people; Zyda is fascinated by what controls people. When he takes notes at meetings, he records not the subject being discussed so much as the body language of other attendees. Sweaty palms, he'll jot down. Skittish eyes.

(Occasionally, Zyda will remind you that he was born in the eye of a storm at 12:01 a.m. on September 11, 1954, as if his very birth were proof that he belongs at the center of whatever storm is currently stirring.)

Like the best pedigreed of the science-fiction wise men, Zyda has degrees in neurocybernetics, bioengineering, and Spanish literature. He's done consulting work for everyone from Paramount Pictures to the White House to the Ministry of Industrial Development in the Sabah Province of Malaysia. He's a member of the National Research Council's Committee on Scientific and Technical Challenges in Creating Virtual Reality Environments and its Aeronautics and Space Engineering Board's Committee on Advanced Engineering Environments. But it was his study "Linking Entertainment and Defense," which he presented to the council in 1997, that put him where he is today.

Zyda happened to arrive at the Naval Postgraduate School just as the military's first serious effort to build an advanced simulation-training device, or a networked virtual environment, was wrapping up. Commissioned by the DARPA, SIMNET, as it was called, was based on the work of virtual-reality pioneer Jack Thorpe. A simulation training tool for Army tank drivers, it was a cyberspace war game that could be played by soldiers in different physical locations by logging onto that new thing, the Internet. Think *The Sims Online,* but at war.

When DARPA and the U.S. Army Topographic Engineer Center sponsored Zyda to build the Naval Postgraduate School Net, which plugged into SIMNET, adding features like virtual helicopters that could be "flown" by real superior officers observing the virtual battle of their soldiers, Zyda found himself getting calls from "about a hundred different Department of Defense organizations."

"From the midseventies through the midnineties, the Department of Defense was the big driver for new technology," Zyda says. "So if you wanted to say, 'Here is the coolest new virtual world,' it would have been made by the DOD. In the midnineties, though, graphics cards got good for PCs. And as expenditures in entertainment R & D went up, that industry started to exceed the DOD."

The trouble was SIMNET had cost $140 million, and had taken ten years and hundreds of people to build. Then the military got wind of *Doom,* which was created by a team of eight people working on it for six months, at a total cost of about $25,000. And it had achieved far more than the SIMNET team had dared to dream—not only was it networked, but it was also visually stunning, fast-paced, and *engaging.* When the Nintendo 64 came out in 1996 with its incredible graphic advances all housed in a machine the size of a tissue box, people like Zyda began to get excited. Zyda imagined military tools that weren't created by a "bunch of engineers," but rather by artists. "Linking Entertainment and Defense" was based on Zyda's musing of what would happen if a little entertainment pixie dust could be sprinkled over the clanking simulations the Army was producing. His former pupil, Macedonia, adopted the same tack.

"The reason we're turning to the entertainment industry is that here at STRICOM, we have old men designing our simulators," Macedonia explains. "I'm not exaggerating. They're in their forties and fifties, and the last videogame they played was *Pong,* or maybe *Pac-Man* over drinks. And what happens is they bleed the life out of these simulations. They're engineers. They design by committee. And one thing we've learned from our psychologists here is that emotion is critical to learning, and that one of the key aspects of eliciting emotion is being able to provide a story. It goes all the way back to Homer. Look at *The Iliad* and the oral tradition—that was the way history was taught. The only way to remember all these facts was you put them into a story. A story is a way for folks to be able to understand, to absorb, and to retain. And frankly, I don't have a lot of storytellers here."

So, at Macedonia's request, Zyda, who in the meantime had grown sour on the internal politics of the Naval Postgraduate School and was eager for a road out, spent the first six months of 1999 transforming his report into a proposal for an institute dedicated to developing training simulations and combat warfare systems for the Army, but staffed by the best people the entertainment industry could provide.

The result was the Institute for Creative Technology, or ICT, a joint venture between the University of Southern California and the U.S. Army, opened at the end of a palm-tree-lined street in Marina Del Ray, California, with $45 million in military funding. The offices were designed by the same man who designed the original starship *Enterprise* for *Star Trek. Apocalypse Now* screenwriter John Milius was brought in as a consultant along with *Big Top Pee-Wee* director Randall Kleiser, special effects guru Paul Debevec, and former president of the Motion Picture Association Jack Valenti. Relationships formed quickly with videogame companies such as Pandemic, Quicksilver, and Sony ImagingWork.

Zyda, naturally, expected to get the top post at whatever school the military would decide to fund. But when the University of Southern California got the bid, Elizabeth Daly, the dean responsible for hiring the director, began to evade his queries. When Macedonia became hard to reach on the phone, Zyda grew wary. After a couple of weak handshakes from USC honchos, Zyda invited a fellow Naval Postgraduate School professor named John Hiles out to lunch with him. Hiles, a soft-spoken, rotund man who used to work for Will Wright, agreed to meet him at their favorite Chinese restaurant, the Great Wall. It was their equivalent of war-gaming a scenario. Zyda explained the situation to Hiles, and together they drew bubble diagrams of all the players in Zyda's drama, with arrows to represent relationships and possible outcomes.

Both Hiles and Zyda are at the forefront of a new movement, growing out of advances in the field of cognitive psychology, that is attempting to accurately model human behavior into a computer system. Although Will Wright likes to say, "Once you're alive, you become very hard to model," Hiles likes to insist, "Once you've been educated, you become very easy to model." Hiles believes that after about the age of five, most people are molded by their education and their societies into fairly predictable entities. Like Zyda, he is perfecting his theories with funding from the military. His most recent project, Iago, is a computer model built on information about Ramsey Yousef, the Islamic jihadist involved in the attack on the World Trade Center in 1993. The model simulates how Yousef, or someone like Yousef, might react to current events in the news.

As the waitress brought them their tea and the check, Hiles pointed to a bubble around USC's Elizabeth Daly. There's your problem, Hiles said. Based on the model they built, Hiles concluded that Daly wanted to hire someone from within her ring of personal entertainment contacts for the top spot at the new institute. Sure enough, a former Paramount executive, Dick Lindheim, was named the ICT's director.

While Zyda was left up in Monterey stewing, the Institute for Creative Technology began work on its first project, *Full Spectrum Warrior,* a commercial-grade videogame designed by Pandemic, published by THQ, and built to run on the Microsoft Xbox. The idea for *Full Spectrum Warrior* was to ship it first to the Army as a training tool, and then to sell a version to the public through the commercial markets. (While the Army itself is not allowed to profit off such a project, the companies involved are.) The game's main selling point is that it's the most realistic Army game of all time. So while kids across the world are revving up their Xboxes to play at war, soldiers around the world will be revving up theirs—placed in areas where soldiers gather, like mess halls and rec rooms—to train for war.

Macedonia is thrilled with the idea. One of the things that had so impressed the Air Force about Gilman Louie's *Flight Simulator* was that soldiers loved to play it. Like in *Ender's Game,* the idea is to make a game out of training. It was like suddenly finding homework that your students couldn't get enough of.

One plays *Full Spectrum Warrior* as a squad leader, and the objective is getting one's men in and out of dangerous situations safely. *Full Spectrum Warrior* teaches such things as stacked formation, securing of exits, what part of a room to search first when you take over a building, and why it's important to ensure no one is on a higher floor waiting to run down and ambush you. Speed, methodology, and behaving as a collective are the key lessons. Indeed, while the debate over videogames and violence has raged since the days of *Missile Command,* the military, at least, has concluded that there is no direct correlation between playing videogames and an increased urge to kill. But that doesn't mean they're not effective military training tools. For the kinds of hands-off killing preached by the modern military, homicidal rage is hardly a requirement. In fact, as laid out explicitly in the Department of Defense's 2003 study "Training for Future Conflicts," the modern American military increasingly wants soldiers who are more than just bodies with guns. It's all part of Donald Rumsfeld's vision of a world of war where American soldiers do their killing long-distance. "The transformation of the military will increase the cognitive demands on even the most junior levels of the military," the report says. Its primary finding: "In short, everybody must think."

In other words, the Army now needs people who can make instantaneous decisions, work with amoebalike coordination with their squads, and handle advanced, computer-controlled warfare systems. As CliffyB has been known to point out, that's a pretty good description of your average hardcore gamer.

The ICT's other big project is also borrowed from fiction.

Under Macedonia's guidance, they're building a real-life holodeck, à la *Star Trek*. The idea for the project, originally called the Sensory Environments Evaluation Project, is to elicit the kinds of emotions soldiers are likely to feel when going into battle. This is the domain of Jacqueline Morie, a small woman in a loose dress and with messy hair, who looks as if she'd be more at home in a Berkeley art studio than working for the Army. Indeed, before joining the ICT, Morie was an artist, specializing in large-scale installments designed to evoke emotion.

Today, Morie spends her time at the ICT in an amphitheater, surrounded by a 150-degree curved screen as high as the ceiling. Three projectors in the back of the room blend their images onto the enormous screen, which is viewed by participants wearing head-mounted displays to make it all appear three-dimensional. Participants are given joysticks with which to facilitate their character's movement. They can go forward, backward, sideways, just like in any modern videogame. Morie's aim is not to make something that is photorealistic, but rather to create a sense of what she calls "presence," an environment that *feels* real on a deep emotional level.

On the holodeck, it's dead of night in war-torn Bosnia. Put on your headset, and you're dropped into a remote village along the Vrbas River to spy on an abandoned mill complex suspected of housing enemies. The graphics are as sophisticated as 2003's *Quake III,* which is to say, they're as sophisticated as it gets. After your mission, which also includes collecting certain items missing from the American containment area, you are expected to report to your superior officer on your findings. Dogs bark, water trickles, and people you can't see murmur in the distance. Trees bend slightly in the wind; a bridge creaks and then sways as a truck rolls over it.

The tires make grinding noises on the pebbles that line the road. Beneath your feet on the holodeck, a custom-built subwoofer system rumbles at a frequency your ear cannot detect, but which increases your visceral reaction to the experience. More obvious sounds project from speakers all around the room. The bark of a dog up ahead and to the left sounds as if it is, indeed, coming from up ahead and to the left. Occasional pieces of debris fall and make clunking noises.

Morie, being convinced that smell is the most underrated of all the senses, has designed a necklace participants wear that lets off certain smells at specific times through the mission. The whole point of the exercise is to create as *real* and *immersive* an experience as possible—the same keywords videogame makers use all the time. Indeed, standing on the holodeck feels like being *inside* a videogame.

What the military hopes to achieve through the holodeck is to train soldiers for the emotional experience of their first battle. It's common knowledge in the Army that the highest casualty rates in war are among novice soldiers; living through your first battle seriously ups your chances of living through the next. It's scary being in the holodeck, partly because it feels so much like being in a war situation, and partly because it feels as if the traditional walls that separate reality from unreality, fact from fiction, are melting. Perhaps it's a little too reminiscent of the game room in *Ender's Game.*

Mike Zyda might have been left up at the Naval Postgraduate School raging at his betrayal at the hands of his former student had it not been for one fatal flaw in the dream of Transformation. Donald Rumsfeld assured the American public that actual human bodies would hardly be needed for the Bush administration's 2003 invasion of Iraq. But it turns out that even in the Future Objective Force, soldiers are needed. It's all very well to develop the most sophisticated training tools the world has ever known, but if you don't have anybody to train, there's a problem. While war-themed games fly off the shelves of stores and many a retired military man makes an income advising these videogame companies, wanting to play at war isn't the same as actually wanting to sign up for it.

The United States hasn't had a draft in more than thirty years, and no politician with any interest in staying in power is keen to reintroduce one. The mores of our time tell people to be individuals above all else and never to allow themselves to be cogs in someone else's machine. But armies are all about turning boys and girls into soldiers, which are, essentially, fighting cogs. In a world of relativism, living for the moment, and personal success as the ultimate achievement, it's hard to convince people that they ought to risk their lives in a moderate-paying job that might end in a layoff or might end in death. Recruitment has been such a problem that the military has tripled its recruitment budget, from less than $200 million in 1993 to almost $600 million in 2003. And in its desperation for Future Objective Force Warriors rather than just guys with guns, it has adopted incentives like $20,000 sign-up bonuses for recruits who can do information technology work. If the war in Iraq has taught us anything, it's that the U.S. military is woefully understaffed in the warrior department.

**COLONEL CASEY WARDYNSKI** is a small, lithe man, with steel-gray hair cropped close to his head; small, flat ears; and intelligent blue eyes that are almost hypnotic in their intensity. He's a graduate of West Point with a degree in economics and political science, and he has a PhD in policy analysis from the

Rand Corporation. Early in his career, while handling logistics and security for the movement of nuclear material around the world, Colonel Wardynski got interested in computers. The result was a program called Special Weapons Information Management System, or SWIM, which the Department of Defense, the Navy, and the Air Force adopted to keep track of the post–Cold War nuclear-weapon stockpile. Wardynski's program, which he wrote in six months, helped reduce the rate of error in accounting for nuclear materials from 50 percent to 0.2 percent. Today, Wardynski is a professor of economics at West Point and runs the office of Economic and Manpower Analysis for the Army, which means he does things like figure out how to recruit Afghani citizens to join the Afghan National Army, and fly over to Baghdad to run statistical models on manpower needs.

Colonel Wardynski is a smart man, and he grasped the same fundamental truth about videogames that first-person shooters learn. "What a videogame does," Wardynski says, "at heart, is teach you how, in the midst of utter chaos, to know what is important and what is not, and to act on that."

Colonel Wardynski believes in his work. He has the true believer's trust in the good of his country. He's a self-described patriot, who exudes both honesty and toughness, the kind of man you can imagine you'd follow into battle should he lead you there. Colonel Wardynski knew about Transformation. And he knew that the United States wasn't going to get very far if it couldn't get its recruitment numbers up. In 1999, around the same time that Mike Zyda was working on his plan for the ICT at Michael Macedonia's request, Colonel Wardynski had an epiphany.

"I realized we had to get the flow of information about life in the Army into pop culture," Colonel Wardynski says. He had realized that kids no longer had contact with people who could tell them stories about life in the Army. Vietnam was unmentionable, the first Gulf War had used a relatively small force, and veterans of World War II were dying out. That's when it hit him. "What do kids do with their time?" he asked himself. "Oh, they play videogames. Where do they search for information? Oh, on the Internet. So that's where we have to be."

With the pragmatism of a military man, Colonel Wardynski was simply acknowledging what family groups have been screaming about for years. Pop culture has become an underground education system for American children. Study after study shows that kids spend far more time engaged with media than they do at school or with their parents. In any society, people get their ideas about life, what's important, and who they want to be from the messages of their culture. Our culture happens to be one dominated by mass consumer entertainment. So that's where the Army would go. And, conveniently for the military, pop culture had come to mean videogames. Even at West Point, internal statistics showed that more than 80 percent of the student body played videogames.

The Army has been trying to reach teenagers through their devotion to the videogame for years. It's almost impossible to open a videogame magazine or log onto a videogame Web site without being besieged by advertisements for the Army. "An Army of One" ads crop up regularly in *Electronic Gaming Monthly* and *Game Informer*. Sign up for a videogame Web site, and you're likely to get pop-up ads for the Army haunting your computer for months to come. But while this attention from the military may have helped sell some military-based commercial games, it didn't seem to help with actual recruitment. It was Colonel Wardynski who realized that the mode of communication between the Army and the youth had to be the videogame itself. Like a virus in a computer, it would spread the word about life in the Army.

Wardynski had heard about the ICT. He arranged meetings with Macedonia and the former Paramount executive, Dick Lindheim, but they couldn't agree on what it was Wardynski was dreaming about. The ICT was about training. Wardynski was interested in recruiting.

A friend recommended he get in touch with a professor at the Naval Postgraduate School in Monterey, California, who might be able to help him out. There, Wardynski met Mike Zyda. By the time Wardynski got to him, Zyda had just started a new institute on the grounds of the Naval Postgraduate School called the MOVES Institute, for "Modeling, Virtual Environments, and Simulation." MOVES, which boasted people like Gilman Louie and Jack Thorpe on its board, was Zyda's revenge for losing stewardship of the ICT. The call from Wardynski was a reprieve, both a balm to his wounded ego and a delight to his intellect.

Although Zyda and Wardynski could not appear more different, they turned out to be ideal working partners. Within a few months, Wardynski had gotten Zyda funding for MOVES's first gig, the Army Games Project, from the Assistant Secretary of the Army for Manpower and Reserve Affairs. Their first mandate was to create *America's Army,* a game that would be downloadable for free from the Army's Web site and available as inserts in videogame magazines. The project was codenamed Operation Star Fighter, after the 1984 movie *The Last Starfighter,* a film about a teenager who is recruited by aliens to fight in an intergalactic war after getting a perfect score on his local arcade machine.

*America's Army* was initially slated to be the Army's search engine for star fighters. Zyda and his team had considered monitoring players' game aptitude as they played and forwarding that information directly to Army recruitment. It was certainly technologically feasible, but the team decided at the last minute that "by our cultural standards, that would just be wrong," Zyda says.

***AMERICA'S ARMY* WAS** launched on July 4, 2002, and by the time the Academy of Interactive Arts and Sciences had invited Zyda and Wardynski to speak at DICE 2003, more than 2.4 million players had registered the game on their computers. It was also well received by the industry, getting a nomination for Best Action Game of the Year (2003) by the AIAS, as well as a host of other awards. By the time DICE 2003 rolled around, the *America's Army* franchise had become an unqualified blockbuster in the gaming world.

At DICE 2003, Zyda is giving a talk entitled "Weapons of Mass Distraction—America's Army Recruits for the Real War." Zyda is "psyched" to show *America's Army* to the video-game industry. He's standing in the glass-paned corridor of the Hard Rock overlooking the hotel's network of faux tropical swimming pools and imported sandy beaches, waiting for Wardynski to get in on a red-eye from West Point. He's mingling with people like Shigeru Miyamoto, Will Wright, Raph Koster, CliffyB, and Seamus Blackley. When he takes to the stage at 11:15 a.m., he's surprised at how many familiar faces are in the audience. He hadn't expected to know anyone, but he realizes, as he looks out into the crowd, that the room is filled with many of the same people with whom he's been attending conferences on virtual reality, 3-D graphics, and modeling and simulation for years.

The words *America's Army* flash onto the screen behind him, projected against a background of red, white, and blue, and surrounded by a dusky sky filled with buzzing helicopters and camouflage-wearing digital soldiers running toward the camera. While Wardynski sits tight-lipped and serious in the front row of the audience, Zyda bobs his head along with the music and moves his mouth along with the words coming from the auditorium's speakers. He explains to the audience how the Army opened its coffers of visual and audio data to his team, sharing hours of footage of training camps and actual war carnage. Zyda explains how every detail of the digital action in the game, from the pine trees that surround Ft. Bennings to the way bodies look flying through the air, has been modeled to a T. A young woman in the audience—not a gamemaker, but a graphic artist and cell phone technologist, who is mainly here to see futurist artist (and *Blade Runner* designer) Syd Mead talk—asks Zyda if the designers had trouble dealing with such material. Zyda totally misunderstands the nature of her question. "Oh no, it was awesome!" Zyda says.

It's a tricky line Zyda and Wardynski have to walk, using the military accuracy of the game as a selling point, while simultaneously defending it as an acceptable plaything for teenagers. Wardynski is quick to point out that 41 percent of the game shows no weapons at all, focusing instead on training routines like obstacle courses, parachuting, scuba diving, and laser tag. Wardynski was prepared for controversy over a taxpayer-funded game intended to woo teenagers and young adults into the Army, and he's been very, very careful every step of the way.

"I staked my military career on this," Wardynski says. "My

reputation is everything I have. When you work for a four-star general, you only blow up once. It's not like in a game, where you get to start over."

Considering all the thought and work he'd put into making the game palatable to the public as well as the military, Wardynski was pleased by the lack of controversy it aroused. Although he'd been trained to handle skeptical, even hostile reporters, there was almost nothing in the nongaming press about the game when it was released. And when it did get coverage, it was framed more as an oddity than an outrage.

The audience at DICE is equally nonplussed. There's a question about whether the game includes people coming home in body bags (it doesn't), but otherwise the most critical question Zyda receives is a complaint that his government grants give him an unfair competitive advantage over other gamemakers who have to actually raise capital to make games.

The videogame industry, unlike the generation of culture producers before them, prides itself on its apolitical stance. There is hardly a gamemaker in the upper echelons of the industry who has not been drafted for some military-sponsored project or roundtable discussion or consulting work. Raph Koster has his DOD invitation hanging on a bulletin board in his office; Will Wright wears his CIA jacket with a chuckle. The fact that this very conference is taking place only days after the U.S. invasion of Iraq doesn't seem to make these questions any more pressing. James Korris, a director at the ICT, says it's a natural post-9/11 shift, that the entertainment industry is reassessing who's really the bad guy. Wardynski says it's just that *America's Army* is not that unique. He says that it's just part of a continuum dating all the way back to the Uncle Sam posters of World War I or the propaganda movies of World War II. And he makes no apologies.

"The Army wasn't invented by this game," he says. "We've always recruited kids. I take no issue with the necessity of the U.S. having an Army. I'm not trying to convince anyone who doesn't want to join. I believe the Army to be a noble profession, and I have no problem spreading information about it. We do have enemies. Our freedom is not secure. I want to put the idea of the Army into their space so they'll think about it."

When the talk is over, the several hundred men and a smattering of women pour back out into the hallway. "Whoa, that colonel—Kung Fu grip!" Alan Yu says as he comes out, impressed by Colonel Wardynski's cool, no-bullshit manner. Otherwise, people don't have too much to say about it. The young graphic designer, though, is near tears. "I don't even read the newspaper or get upset about the things in the news," she says. "But I just wanted to stand up there and say, 'Hello! Are you people insane?' I mean, please, tell me this isn't real!"

**FOR HIS PART,** Michael Macedonia continues to dream. He wanders the halls of the October 2003 AUSA convention eight months after Zyda and Wardynski gave their spiel at DICE, and when it turns to night, he checks out a couple of the delegation parties at a hotel across the street. Nothing much is doing. There are lots of people from Florida—"it's the simulation capital of the world!" Macedonia explains—eating satay and drinking more than they should in Hawaiian-print shirts. Macedonia puffs along in his black suit and little tasseled loafers. These are good times for him. Who would have thought that his little-boy passion would turn out to be the hot-spot nexus through which the world's lone military superpower would seek to merge man and machine into one heart-pumping, razor-sharp, computationally enhanced, new-age Warrior. Science fiction should *be* so good. And Macedonia has finally found what he always wanted, a home, in the future.

# 8

## Trojan Horses

Times Square is awash in green light. It's approaching midnight, and outside of the Toys "R" Us store, black-clad policemen are keeping a crowd of several hundred people in check. Just two months and four days earlier, the world watched in disbelief as the Twin Towers in lower Manhattan crumbled to the ground like so many sandcastles. Tonight, the crowd watches as searchlights cut through the winter sky in rolling arcs of green. It's a futuristic, sour-apple-meets-bubbling-acid green, and it's the signature color of the Microsoft Corporation's multibillion-dollar new investment, the Xbox videogame console. A plastic disc of the electric green adorns the top of every machine like a dollop of radioactive garnish.

It's the Xbox that has brought this crowd out on such a cold November night. The line runs up Broadway, around the corner onto Forty-third Street, down Sixth Avenue, and back across Forty-second Street. The turnout tonight is so good that the overflow crowd is being shunted to the World Wrestling Federation restaurant a few blocks away.

A tall, red-headed man, rattling with nervous energy, bounds across Broadway toward Toys "R" Us. It's Jonathan "Seamus" Blackley, and he's more torqued up than all the gamers and all the PR people working the crowd put together.

It's always hard to pinpoint one person's exact contribution to a product that ends up with a staff of fifteen hundred behind it, so while Seamus certainly doesn't hold the highest title on the project, nor could it fairly be said that it was his idea, the Xbox is definitely his baby. Without Seamus, Microsoft might still be releasing some sort of home entertainment product this evening, but it certainly wouldn't have been the Xbox. Seamus takes in the lights, the crowds, the noise, and he thinks to himself, *We did it, we fucking did it.*

It's a manufactured event, of course, choreographed for maximum publicity value. There seem to be almost as many PR people in cordless headsets and black windbreakers as there are customers. Microsoft is spending $500 million marketing the Xbox's launch. It sounds like a huge figure, but it will take at least that for Microsoft to barge its way into the videogame console arena, a market that has been the exclusive realm of the Japanese for more than a decade. For months leading up to this evening, Microsoft has been courting males between the ages of sixteen and twenty-six as if its success as a company depended on it. There have been ads on MTV and ESPN, sponsorship of extreme sports events. Radio stations have been giving out passes to promotional events for weeks, and marketing partner Taco Bell—found to be the restaurant of choice for hardcore gamers—is running a promotional campaign to give away thousands of Xboxes. An operation code-named MAX has launched a fleet of trucks across the country like a modern-day circus, putting down stakes in specially selected cities and erecting a thirty-five-thousand-square-foot "game space" area beneath a cold-air dome stretched across two forty-foot tractor trailers. There is but a single pitch at these events: *Xbox is on the way.*

Microsoft needs the Xbox to seem like a winner from the outset. There are few second chances in an industry as fiercely competitive as that of videogames, and there is a reason all and sundry are referring to the parade of new consoles being launched by Nintendo, Sony, and Microsoft as the "Console Wars." The domino effect of a good opening day includes an impressed media and excited gamer word-of-mouth, and a good launch can light up Web sites and Instant Messengers around the world. On the other hand, if a new game console is perceived as lame (and gamers are *very* particular customers), the loss of confidence—from both the consumers who buy the machines and the developers who build games for them—can be both catastrophic and lightning quick.

Seamus pushes his way through the crowd, his girlfriend, Vanessa "Van" Burnham, a veteran gaming and technology writer, clinging to his arm. A couple of guys in their early twenties from New Jersey are hanging around just a few feet away. The steam from a corner vendor blows the smell and warmth of hot onions and boiled hot dogs into the night air. Despite driving for an hour and a half to be here, the New Jerseyites Harry Artinian, a twenty-one-year-old Staples employee, and his buddy David Ecker won't be purchasing an Xbox tonight. For that they would have had to get in line hours ago. Still Harry and David are psyched just to be here. Hardcore gamers, Harry and David know the specs for the Xbox well. They know about the custom-built Nvidia graphics chip, which can execute one trillion operations per second; they know about the presence of an Ethernet port in the back and why Microsoft chose that over including a dial-up modem. (Not only is the inclusion of Ethernet a bet on the future of online gaming, it also represents a bet on the future of broadband entertainment in general). Harry, David, and most of the many hundreds of people standing in line are equally aware that the Xbox incorporates a 733-megahertz Intel Pentium III microprocessor, which, while considered ho-hum to PC enthusiasts, is certainly the most powerful chip ever used in a game console.

Of course, none of this technology means Microsoft necessarily stands a chance against the current console makers Nintendo and Sony. If you let them, and, frankly, even if you try to stop them, Harry and David will tell you why this is so. Even the most high-flying technology in the world is no guarantee of success in the game console market. There are a dozen stories about consoles that were ahead of their time, that were flat-out *awesome,* and about which industry journalists still write nostalgic pieces. Sega's Dreamcast console, for example, was the first 128-bit console on the market, and many gamers still refer to it as one of the best ever built. The Dreamcast was discontinued after only two years, however, because Sega simply couldn't get enough machines into people's homes and couldn't establish a library of games quickly enough to succeed against Sony's ruthlessly effective marketing of the PlayStation and PlayStation 2. Other consoles have met their demise because price points were set too high or didn't have enough marketing support, or because the machines were so difficult to program for that none of the third-party gamemakers wanted to work on them. Some of the most talented men in the industry have had sterling reputations wiped out after failing in the console market. And now that the world's most successful consumer electronics firm, Sony, and the largest software maker in the world, Microsoft, have entered the fray, the videogame market has become an arena for an entirely new level of combat. Success now requires extraordinarily deep pockets, extensive distribution and supply channels, and a willingness to take huge losses on console sales in order to establish a base of customers. Seamus and his girlfriend brush past Harry and David, who in turn watch as the couple flash their Xbox ID passes and are allowed entrée into the building. Harry and David sigh. The videogames industry is a tough business. It's cutthroat, Harry and David say. Very cutthroat.

Inside Toys "R" Us's sizeable videogame section, the Xbox top brass, a few journalists, and a horde of PR girls are waiting for the clock to strike twelve. That's when Bill Gates himself will arrive and the very first Xbox will be sold. Xbox general manager J Allard is laughing, his head thrown back, a noise that makes its way all around the room. J is the guy who was brought in to transform the Xbox from a wild idea to an actual, marketable entity. Allard was in effect the second man in the relay race to get the Xbox made, taking the torch from a reluctant Seamus Blackley. J had made his mark at Microsoft by helping convince Bill Gates in the early 1990s that Microsoft should invest in a little something called the Internet. (He even changed his first name to J, no period, in honor of e-mail addresses.)

Once inside, Seamus and his girlfriend join the rest of the Xbox crew. There are high-fives, slaps on the back, excited hand-rubbing. It's hard not to notice that J and Seamus keep their distance from each other. Although both men are mute on the subject, their distaste for one another is one of the industry's worst-kept secrets.

**TWO YEARS BEFORE** the Xbox's launch, Bill Gates and his top executives retreated to Puget Sound to discuss Microsoft's business model. A seismic shift was under way. The late nineties was a time of a burgeoning new consensus among media pundits and high-tech industry folks that the consumer world would turn its eye from desktop computers toward "information appliances." Thanks to advances in digital and mobile technology, broadband acceptance, and dropping manufacturing costs, the dream of a digital living space had emerged. It would be a place where gadgets such as personal data appliances—video recorders, phones, music players, on-demand cable and movies, and gaming capabilities—were all connected wirelessly over a single home network. And whoever controlled the gateway through which all of these gadgets gained Internet access—to shopping, news, entertainment, and the many other digital products that awaited—would have a gold mine on their hands. It would be a kind of holy-grail tollbooth through which any "content" provider would have to pay to pass. *Convergence* was the word being thrown around to describe this approaching phenomenon, and it caused many a CEO on many a continent to salivate into his pillow with dreams of new revenue streams and, likewise, caused them endless nightmares of being left behind.

There was even talk of a post-PC era. Microsoft may have enjoyed 20 percent annual growth for most of the nineties, but, as the twenty-first century approached, this slowed to single digits. The PC market, though healthy, was no longer booming, and many thought it saturated. In contrast, by 1998,

Sony's PlayStation was already outselling the top five PC makers combined. And gaming software in general was on its way to a 45 percent annual growth rate. Yet Microsoft's business model was still almost entirely PC-centric. Gates was very clear in his instructions to the executives gathered around him—Microsoft was not going to end up being just another corporate software maker.

**"WE'RE ON THE** verge of a digital entertainment revolution," J explains, a month before the Xbox's launch. "But what's the equivalent of the word processor in this revolution? What's the thing that's going to get people to buy into this revolution? Entertainment. Gaming."

The Xbox is not Microsoft's first attempt to establish itself in the videogame industy; it's just that none of its predecessors has been very successful. As early as 1983, Microsoft developed a PC-console hybrid for Asian markets—called MSX—which flopped because there weren't enough successful games available to support it. In 1994 Microsoft executives tried unsuccessfully to strike a deal with Sony to develop and publish games for the PlayStation. And in 1997 Microsoft even bought WebTV, which let people go online through their televisions, but the effort became a money-draining also-ran.

The trouble for Microsoft was that everyone, from former AOL-Time Warner CEO Gerald Levin to TCI Cable chairman John Malone to Disney CEO Michael Eisner, knew that Gates wanted into the living room. But considering Microsoft's ruthless reputation and its contemporaneous investigation by the Department of Justice into alleged unfair monopolistic practices, no one was in a hurry to partner with them. So when it was time for Sony to start working on the PlayStation 2, Gates, desperate not to be left behind in the pilgrimage to the digital living room, tried personally to convince Sony CEO Nobuyuki Idei to use a version of Windows in Sony's next-generation console. Gates was flatly rejected.

Gates then watched from the sidelines as Sony's game division exploded, by 1997 accounting for 22 percent of Sony Corporation's consolidated operating profits, and the next year, as manufacturing costs dropped, hitting 44 percent. By that time, Sony could boast 80 million PlayStations sold worldwide. One third of American households owned one. And the press was dubbing it a Trojan Horse, a gateway box atop the TV snuck into the living room as a game machine. It was all teeth-gnashingly irritating to Gates.

**IT WAS ABOUT** this time that Seamus Blackley showed up—or, rather, limped in. Seamus had spent the mid-1990s making a PC game for Steven Spielberg that was supposed to mark DreamWorks' big entrance into the videogame industry. The game, *Trespasser,* was closer to the *Ishtar* of the videogame industry than its *Jurassic Park,* however: overhyped, over budget, overdue, and roundly slammed by critics and gamers alike. In 1999, the year after *Trespasser* was released, Seamus spent his time at the Game Developers Conference hiding from other gamemakers.

Seamus is a former jazz pianist, high-energy physicist, and aerospace engineer. A six-foot-three-inch bear of a man, Blackley also has a lightning-fast tongue that bespeaks an even faster, manically churning brain. He has a tendency to slide into tangents while talking about games—"So anyway, I started flying gliders and I got really into it and I'd always wanted to fly so I thought, 'Hey,' and I read some aerodynamics texts and it was really easy compared to like crazy-ass nonrenormalized perturbatory field theories so I said, 'Okay, I'll design airplanes,'"—that can easily become non sequiturs. More often than not, however, his point is about how desperately the videogame industry needs to make room for and recognize the creative talent that Seamus believes is its lifeblood.

"*Tony Hawk's Pro Skater* sold more copies than Britney Spears's last album, all right," Seamus says. "Now, who made *Tony Hawk's Pro Skater*? Nobody knows. How did the game get made? Nobody knows. Where does it come from? Nobody knows. People believe that there's like a giant machine in Finland that squeezes these games out. I want people to know who makes these games. I want people to be fans of the people who make these games. I want people to buy games for the same reason they buy a music album—because of the quality of the creative content and not because of some licensing deal."

As a project manager at Microsoft, Seamus was assigned the task of comparing PlayStation 2 graphics with the graphics capabilities of the PC. On an airplane somewhere between Redmond, Washington, and Boston, where he'd been visiting, it came to him. Seamus knew, along with everyone else in the industry, that while programming games for the PC was in theory far easier than for a console, the sheer variety of PC hardware made it much more difficult to work with. In order to reach the largest market, developers of computer games had to program to the lowest common denominator—cheap entry-level machines. On the other hand, the proprietary technology used by console makers typically changed every five years or so, and this drove developers crazy. It could take half that time just for developers to learn how best to utilize a console's hardware resources. Seamus realized that it was just these sorts of barriers that kept game developers from being able to focus on creativity and quality. He recalled the troubles he'd run into designing *Trespasser* for the PC, and he thought about the PlayStation 2, which promised to be extraordinarily difficult to develop for because of a proprietary processor and an operating system that was anathema to game developers. Suddenly, Seamus wanted to jump out of his seat. Microsoft could, if it chose, make a console that would *kill* the PlayStation 2. It was all so painfully obvious. Of any technology company, Microsoft was uniquely suited to build a console that gamers and game developers would die for. All Microsoft had to do was design a reasonably powerful Windows-based PC that could be packaged and marketed as a videogame console. Since all of Microsoft's PC consoles would have the same hardware specifications, the nightmare of programming for myriad end-user configurations would be over, but the simplicity of writing games for Microsoft's operating system would remain. Seamus was so excited he wanted to grab the flight attendant and shake her.

When Seamus returned from his trip, he found the repercussions of Gates's Puget Sound getaway rumbling through the Microsoft hallways. Fear was growing that Sony's PlayStation was becoming a juggernaut in the living room, staking a claim that would soon be too solid to challenge. Within weeks, Seamus found a few mavericks, scattered across many divisions of Microsoft, who had also been dreaming of a great gaming console. He found Kevin Bachus and Otto Berkes of Microsoft's DirectX team, which was responsible for the suite of program interfaces that allowed computer gamemakers to take full advantage of a PC's multimedia hardware. He also found Ted Hase in developer relations. The team became known internally as the Microsoft Cowboys. A few higher-level executives, most notably Nat Brown, in systems software, and Ed Fries, the head of Microsoft's games division, backed the Cowboys almost from the outset.

Microsoft has always rewarded an entrepreneurial spirit within its halls. When J Allard was urging Microsoft executives to build TCP/IP into Windows—the protocol that allowed PCs to communicate with the Internet—it was a totally unsanctioned project, something he had undertaken on his own. So it was with the Cowboys. Seamus and his posse began, on their own, to explore whether Microsoft could realistically do something as bold as moving into the hardware business.

**THE PROBLEM WITH** the hardware business is that, as Microsoft itself had proven to the world, it's not where the big profits lie. The big profits lie in software. And the same is true of videogames. Console makers generally lose money on each console sold. But as the arbiters of which games make it to market, the owners of a console platform can reap extraordinary profits from royalties on each game sold. While a console might be sold at a loss of up to $125 per unit, the markup on games for console makers is about 15 percent. If the game is developed under the console maker's own roof, the margins can be even higher. And ever since Nintendo decided to put a "lock-out" chip in its Nintendo Entertainment System (which prevents any game not approved by Nintendo from running), it has become standard practice to include similar technology for any new platform. As a result, console manufacturers are able to command royalty fees of between $7 and $11 per game. Such potential profits provided additional motivation for Seamus and the rest of the Microsoft Cowboys to make their dream a reality.

On their own time, and while slowly recruiting others into the project, the four men began working on a prototype of a modified Windows operating system. They also began feeling out chip manufacturers. Seamus turned to his contacts in the game business, such as Tim Sweeney, who'd designed the engine for Epic's *Unreal,* and John Carmack of id, for input. Seamus wanted a machine made for developers, one that would free up their time from chasing technology and troubleshooting, so they could get down to the business of showing the world that videogames were art.

Seamus had long dreamt of the day when videogames would be reviewed in the *Arts and Leisure* section of the the *New York Times*. "The thing that's beautiful about videogames, and the thing that attracts people like me to them, is that it's this nexus between technology and creativity," he says. "And it's so powerful and beautiful. Videogames are an opportunity to use technology as a creative medium. That's why we started the Xbox project."

When Seamus was six, some relatives bought him a toy monorail system. He took out the motor, hooked it up to a battery, reversed the connections of the motor, attached a pencil to it, and freely began drawing pictures as it rotated. "Really, really what I want to do with the Xbox," he says, "is set game designers free to make their art."

Seamus knew this was no easy task. By the late 1990s many smaller development studios were shutting their doors. Game studios live from development deal to development deal and can easily be bankrupted by a single flop. To be considered a blockbuster, a videogame has to sell about a million copies. The vast majority of titles, however, never even earn out their advances. As a result, by the turn of the century, studios with only a hit or two were being swallowed like so many plankton by one of several publishing leviathans. Because most of these big fish publishers—Electronic Arts, Sony Computer Entertainment, Nintendo, Activision, and Vivendi Universal—were publically traded corporations, the pressure to create blockbuster games and get them out on time became intense. Of the roughly one hundred games a given publisher may have in development at any given time, the vast majority are sequels; celebrity vehicles; or licenses of popular movies, TV shows, and books. For example, only about 16 percent of Electronic Art's fare is original, meaning neither a sequel nor a game based on already existing, licensed properties. There is no room for the equivalent of a Miramax in the videogame industry yet, no publisher that has found a way to make huge profits from independent, less obviously commercial fare.

**SEAMUS IS THE** kind of person to whom problems seem like so many ill-arranged chess pieces. Seamus is inherently analytical and optimistic, but he is often flabbergasted by what he views as the tenacity with which the videogame industry holds on to aspects of itself that are simply wrongheaded. Seamus, as someone who cares about videogames the way a literature professor believes in literature, wants to see great videogame makers given the tools and the environments needed to hone their craft. He wants to see them rewarded by the culture. With the Xbox, Seamus thought he had found a way to do this and to keep the money wheels of American capitalism churning happily at the same time. The Xbox would provide the technical stability and power for which developers had been waiting, and Microsoft's development and publishing arm would offer a new kind of nurturing support system, both financially and artistically. This in turn would draw all the best game developers, who would create a whole new realm of games, and the Xbox would clobber its competition. This was his plan—utterly logical and utterly optimistic. Many at Microsoft were shocked at Seamus's naïveté.

On July 22, 1999, Gates and Steve Ballmer gave Microsoft

vice president Rick Thompson—much against his will—the thankless plan of building a real business model for the Xbox. Seamus and his cohort had projected a $500 million initial investment and a staff of fifty people. It quickly become clear to Thompson that Microsoft would have to spend $5 or $6 billion just to get into the game. The Cowboys had suggested losses in the first year of $169 million and cumulative profits within five years of almost $1 billion. Rick Thompson concluded the Xbox could lose as much as $3.3 billion over the course of its life cycle.

The cost of each machine alone would run from $171 to $291, depending on the price of goods at a given point in the manufacturing cycle, but market research showed the machine could not realistically be sold for more than $300. If Sony started a price war, which was certainly common among console manufacturers, Microsoft could end up hemorrhaging money. The company would have to sell nine videogames for every Xbox machine sold just to break even, a number only the PlayStation had ever reached, and even then only toward the very end of its life cycle. On top of it all, Seamus wanted to do away with royalty fees!

The analysis had nearly driven Thompson mad. If they tried to reduce the cost of making the Xbox—for example, by not including a hard drive, using a slower processor or a less expensive graphics chip—they would lose their only hope of a competitive advantage: having a stronger, faster, better machine to attract the best gamemakers. Neither could the high-speed Internet connection be lost, because that was the most vital part of Microsoft's long-term strategy. How exactly it would pay for itself in the near term, however, Thompson could not say.

The overriding reason to go ahead with the Xbox, Thompson

concluded, was the simple fact that hardcore game fans are the trend setters, the mavens, the early adopters of new entertainment technology. And they would be the ones who'd be influencing the rest of the culture when it came time to make the dream of convergence real. If the Xbox successfully landed Microsoft in the world's living rooms, it could count not only on the substantial profits of big-time game publishing, but also—or so the dream went—on one day controlling an empire of movies- and TV-on-demand, Internet and cell phone use, digital personal recorders, and all the profit streams from all the as-yet-undreamed services that would be sold along with this arsenal of new gadgets.

Seamus believed that if Microsoft was going to launch a full frontal attack on America's living room, gamers were the people to reach first, and Thompson agreed. Seamus was 100 percent correct that a top-notch game console was the best bet to capture them. Fortunately, Microsoft had $30 billion cash in reserve for just these kinds of bets.

**AT AROUND A** quarter to midnight in Times Square, while the Xbox crew waits in Toys "R" Us, Bill Gates is making a quick publicity stop at the World Wrestling Federation restaurant down the street. He shakes a few hands, gives a few autographs, gets whipped in a two-out-of-three *Dead or Alive III* fighting match with wrestling-cum-movie-star the Rock, who's also on hand to promote a new game of his own. Then Gates heads over to Toys "R" Us. There are barricades keeping the long line that snakes around the store against the edge of the building. Helicopters buzz overhead. Gates's security people are on extra alert because of last month's terrorist attacks. Microsoft thought of postponing its launch but decided against it.

Gates steps out of his car to flashing bulbs and a pulse of

press corps and bewildered line dwellers. He's surrounded by men in black suits and blinks dumbly in the bright lights, like a blind man, behind his round glasses. They hustle him into the building as PR girls shout to the crowd that Bill Gates himself is coming through.

Inside, Gates begins the handshakes and big-cheeked grinning all over again. There's the affable Xbox CEO Robbie Bach, who used to run Microsoft's consumer software division and was present at that initial Puget Sound retreat; bespectacled marketing chief John O'Rourke, who moved over from the home office division to sell the Xbox; and a sideways-grinning, shyly pleased Ed Fries, who beefed up Microsoft's game division into an eight-hundred-person publishing and development powerhouse in less than two years. Seamus gets a call on his cell phone. It's Kevin Bachus, who quit the Xbox in a fit of disillusionment, frustration with management, and fatigue, just months earlier. "I feel like my baby is going out into the world and strange men are putting their hands all over her," Kevin cries. It's loud in the room, and Seamus has to put a hand over one ear in order to hear. Everybody is welcoming Gates. Seamus can hear all the different laughs and cries of good cheer from all the different men with whom he's worked for the last two years. And of course, there's J Allard, laughing loudest of them all.

**AFTER THE XBOX** became an official project, everything changed. The Xbox was now property of the Microsoft Corporation. Seamus, Kevin Bachus, and Ed Fries were all who remained of the Xbox's original supporters. J Allard was brought in during that brutal period when a product shifts from an idea to an investment, when what's needed are no longer wild visions but practical business know-how.

J himself had been on a leave of absence, hanging out at home, playing videogames and trying to figure out what his next move was going to be. He'd already built Microsoft's first Internet server and written the now famous 1993 missive to Bill Gates entitled "Windows: the Next Killer Application for the Internet," which helped convince Gates of the importance of building Internet-savvy features into Microsoft's products. By the time Seamus and his buddies had started busting ass to make their Xbox dream a reality, J was tired and a bit burnt out. But he was also interested in the future of digital entertainment and a diehard believer in the possibilities of the Internet. As the fervor grew about convergence, he found himself increasingly thinking about the idea of the "One Box to rule them all." When he heard murmurs about the Xbox, it dawned on him: this could be it.

"I knew that if I came back it had to be for something big that I could get totally excited about. I didn't want to go to work on Windows Widget Number 14," J says. "I was playing all these games and I thought, 'These things are going to go mainstream. This is going to be a completely legitimate form of entertainment.' A lot of people say, 'Who is your competition? Sony or Nintendo?' and I'm like, 'It's *Friends,* it's Steven Spielberg.' We're competing for leisure time here."

Just a few years ago, J was a standard-issue, prematurely balding, pudgy programmer type, adorned in lightweight, high-tech fabrics. Today, he's slimmed down and has bleached his remaining hair white blond. J has adapted quickly to the vernacular of his customers—things run the gamut from "bad ass" to "sucking hard," and he refers to his boss as "one persistent mofo" rather than as "Mr. Gates" or even "Bill." In public he's all trash-talking zingers, frat-boy guffaws, and nuevo-ghetto hand gestures. But while he may have become a tad carried away with his new image, he has as vivid a vision of the Xbox as Seamus. His just happens to be a bit different.

"Twenty-five years ago, Bill Gates and Paul Allen founded Microsoft by looking around and seeing how technology was changing the workplace," J says. "They said, 'If we can get a quarter every time somebody does work, that's a damn good business, because we know the world is going to keep working.' For twenty-five years that was the mission—changing the way people worked. Today, you look around you and say, 'Holy shit, technology is going to change the way people play—forever!' And you say, 'If we could get a quarter every time somebody plays'—and we know people like to play more than they like to work—'that could be a really good business.' I mean we could grow another Microsoft here. I mean, once you lock up the nine-to-five, you start worrying about the five-to-nine. The next twenty-five years are about changing the way people play."

**ONCE ALLARD WAS** on board, Seamus had to fight even to remain on the project. At first, he fought bitterly with J about the technical specifications of the Xbox's innards, and he had to convince a hostile Rick Thompson that he was worth keeping around. But Seamus is something of a force of nature—a loud, booming presence that is hard to ignore and hard to keep down. And Seamus had gone *otaku* on their asses.

In Japan, *otaku* is a term for one who is obsessed. Translated into English, the word means something like "maniac." But with the rise of the digital generation, *otaku* has come to stand for a Japanese youth phenomenon wherein encyclopedic information about some very narrow, even obscure, topic is a prize in itself. He who knows the most about a single subject is coolest. You can be a goldfish *otaku*, in which case you must know everything there is to know about every species of goldfish that's ever existed, despite never owning one. You can be rock 'n' roll *otaku*, airplane *otaku*, and you can very nicely be videogame *otaku*.

After burning through several other more official-sounding titles, Seamus finally embraced the term he felt fit him best and he became the Xbox's chief evangelist, an ambassador between Microsoft and game developers around the world. It became his personal mission to convince every game designer from Los Angeles to Tokyo to Sydney to London that they *needed* to make games for the Xbox.

In the year before the Xbox's launch, Seamus traveled to Japan thirty times. He took with him a prototype of the Xbox and some demos he'd had friends of his make that showed off the kinds of things that could be done on Microsoft's machine. Reflections glittered, eyes glinted and gleamed, snow held footprints, and light danced off shiny surfaces. There was a demo of an Amazon woman named Raven who did high-flying martial-art moves while a giant robot copied her in tandem. Kevin Bachus, who'd been named director of third-party publishing (third-party titles are games made by studios that are not owned by the console maker), traveled with Seamus, nailing down business deals after Seamus gave them Xbox religion. In meeting after meeting, Seamus and Kevin explained: If Nintendo's GameCube was about toys, and the PlayStation 2 was about simple entertainment, then the Xbox was going to be about art.

**IT'S ALMOST MIDNIGHT** now at Times Square. The first person in line, a twenty-year-old named Edward Glucksman from New Jersey, is introduced to Bill Gates. He demolishes Gates in a round of *Fusion Frenzy* and then gushes that he's always wanted to grow up to be just like him. The shelves of Toys "R" Us are filled with Xboxes and games to go with them. Ed Fries is proud of the titles. There was one other chink in the armor of competitors, and Ed worked the spot like a surgeon going after a lodged bullet. Nintendo was known for squeezing their third-party partners so tight they could barely eek out a profit; Sony was known for a kind of rampant corporate arrogance. *Empowering* became a key word in the Xbox lexicon. Treat the developers right and they will come, became the motto.

Ed is particularly proud of a sci-fi first-person shooter called *Halo,* made by Bungie Studios, in which Microsoft acquired a stake in 2000. It's a new property, but Ed hopes it will become one of the Xbox's franchise pillars. (Under Ed, about 58 percent of Microsoft's publishing portfolio was devoted to original material.) Another big title is *Munch's Oddysee* from Oddworld Inhabitants, which everyone who's seen it admits isn't quite perfect but is worthy of being lauded for its creativity alone. There are also ten Electronic Arts titles in the launch library and a decent second-party racing title called *Project Gotham Racing*. (Second-party games are those where the developer is partially owned or exclusively tied to the console maker.) *Dead or Alive III,* from Tecmo, makes Seamus particularly proud, because it was thanks to the relationship he forged with Japanese gaming god Tomonobu Itagaki that Microsoft got the fighting franchise onto the Xbox.

As the clock strikes midnight, the doors are flung open, and the crowd surges in. The area fills up with red-nosed fans, shivering first from the cold and then from the sudden blast of heat. People are grabbing Xboxes and armsful of games. The registers begin making a real racket. Each console is selling for $299, each game for $49.99. Bill Gates is beaming. Toys "R" Us CEO John Eyler is also beaming—videogames have become big business for more than just those in the game industry. Videogame sales now account for a hefty portion of Toys "R" Us's revenue. And toy stores aren't the only ones trying to tap the surging revenue of the games industry. Everyone from Wal-Mart to Blockbuster to Barnes & Noble now counts on videogames to bolster their financials. In 1999, for example, Barnes & Noble acquired videogame retail chain Babbage's, renamed it GameStop, and by 2001 watched game sales outpace book sales by a substantial margin. "Most remarkable is the phenomenal success of GameStop," wrote Barnes & Noble chairman Leonard Riggio in the company's 2002 annual report. In a year full of disappointing news of sales goals not met and a troubled retail market, Riggio reported that sales from GameStop increased by 20.7 percent compared with 6.4 percent for the Barnes & Noble chain.

***CHA-CHING, CHA-CHING, CHA-CHING.*** As the din heightens and the room fills up, Seamus takes his girlfriend, Vanessa Burnham, by the hand and walks over to where Gates has retreated to a corner. Seamus has got one more thing up his sleeve. "She seems nice," Gates says, pointing at Van. Seamus agrees that indeed she is.

"Maybe she could help you get your act together," Gates jokes.

"Something has to," Seamus replies. At this point, they have drawn some attention from those nearby. Gates reaches into his breast pocket.

"You ought to marry her," he says.

"You think?" says Seamus.

"Absolutely," says Gates, and produces the diamond engagement ring Seamus had given him the day before. As Seamus drops to one knee, and his girlfriend agrees to become his fiancée, the entire store bursts into cheers. John Eyler is the first to congratulate them, followed by Gates and the rest of the Xbox team. They kiss in front of a wall of stuffed white-and-black panda bears, serenaded by the music of the cash register. Seamus charges out the store's back door, new fiancée hanging on his arm. It's the best night of his life. *I did it,* he thinks. *I fucking did it.*

**FIVE MONTHS LATER,** in Los Angeles, it's E3 2002, and Microsoft, with an established console on its hands, is having its Xbox bash at the Park Plaza Hotel. The street that fronts the entrance to the hotel has been closed by the police. Signature green Xbox lights are circling the sky above the hotel. Inside cages, contortionists painted Xbox green fold their bodies into different *X* shapes as people arrive. In the VIP lounge, J Allard is sipping a cocktail out of a martini glass. He's wearing his new orange-tinted rectangular glasses. Tonight is a special night for J because it marks the first public Xbox event of which he is the central figure, the host. Only six months after its launch, Seamus left the Xbox project, blowing out of Microsoft with blustery cries of starting his own company to make games the *right* way. In fact, other than Ed Fries, there are no original members of the Xbox team still on the project.

"The next thing we have to do," J muses, "is extend beyond the couch. Because every once in a while Johnny gets grounded. And if Johnny gets grounded, he can play games in his room, but he can only play alone—so let's go online."

That little Ethernet port on the back of the Xbox is destined to become a portal through which gamers who pay a monthly subscription fee can play against their friends over the Internet while talking to one another on wireless headsets. It's a move the whole industry is watching. While the movie industry has ancillary avenues for sales—like foreign distribution, rentals, and cable TV—the videogame industry is still searching for the equivalent to buoy its business. Many eyes are on Xbox Live, since it marks the first big trial of both online console gaming and the subscription-based model that will support it.

Of course, for J, Xbox Live is part of a dream that starts with online gaming and ends with a braid of interactive media, service subscriptions, and retail portals slid into the American home on the back of a broadband network connection.

"The Xbox is the Trojan Horse that gets them [Microsoft] into position to become a home-entertainment hub," industry analyst Bob Sutherland told *USA Today* shortly after E3 2002. "This is all part of their long-term strategy to create a lifestyle where you end up spending more with them every month."

J's dream starts with you. Here's a taste: You're watching a football game on TV. Your favorite quarterback gets injured and you learn he's out for the rest of the season. "Oh wait," you cry, because you realize that he's your fantasy league quarterback. Immediately an icon pops up on your screen and says, "Time to Change!" You pick up your universal controller and toggle over to your *NFL Fever* game, which you've also been running, and the videogame renders in real time what happened to the quarterback. You then game out the play along with the members of your fantasy league team, all hooked up to their Xboxes back in their own houses.

You're about to run a play when the phone rings. Another icon pops up in the upper right-hand screen and says, "Do you want to take a call?" You press another button on your controller, and now you're talking to your mom through your headset, your game on pause. ("Or, you can just ignore mom, dump her into e-mail," J says.)

You get back to playing your game, send an e-mail or two, and hop onto a messageboard. There you see an offer for an AFC champions T-shirt that you like.

J counts off on his fingers. "It has [your] size, remembers your billing info, knows [your] home address—so you buy it." He spreads his hands wide. "It's inevitable. It's just a matter of who's going to capitalize on it."

**SEAMUS APPROACHES THE** Park Plaza Hotel with big steps. Seamus's new venture is to operate like an independent movie studio—finding talent, putting game teams together, funding them, and finding distribution. Seamus has been giving interviews on CNN and to the gaming press that this company won't force impossible-to-meet deadlines on its clients, and won't be rehashing tired franchises.

"In order to continue to grow and become a mainstream medium that is serious not only as an art form but as a driver of culture—all of those things everybody wants it to be—you have to get into a position where you can take serious risks on new properties that are going to turn the audience on," Seamus cries. "Those are the products that draw excitement to the industry."

Seamus knows that in a market-driven society, this also means building a business model that is profitable and sustainable. That's the trick. The independent film business took off when people started making movies for a fraction of the cost of the Hollywood studios. But there is no real way to make a console game on the cheap. And with the budget of console games soaring to between $5 and $10 million, it's getting harder and harder to convince publishers—or even developers themselves—to take a risk.

Although Seamus believes he's done the right thing, the first few days of E3 are rough for him. There's a sadness and a kind of defensiveness hovering about him. He's asking people if they're going to "their Xbox thing," meaning the bash at the Park Plaza Hotel.

The doors of the hotel are flung open against the dark evening in a dazzling blast of light and music. In the lobby, the ceilings are soaring, and a sweeping staircase flows up to the balconied second floor. Flitting in and out of circling lights are dancers dressed as fairies with green gossamer wings. Seamus enters with everybody else.

"It's like the audience is so hungry for anything new, but I look around and even the most successful titles are sequels," Seamus says. "The industry got into the commanding position it's in now because of the creative ideas and the crazy risks that people were willing to take and the new kind of stuff that people tried out, but game developers have stopped thinking like game developers."

In the VIP lounge, guests recline on oversized pillows under Arabian-style tents. There are tables piled high with exotic fruit, spiced rice, and pastries. There are belly dancers, snake charmers, and fairy-like girls swinging from golden swings with boas around their necks. An Electronic Arts producer can be heard from inside an erected tent asking a fortune-teller: "Am I gonna get lucky tonight?"

Upstairs, superstar trance DJs Sasha and Digweed are spinning. The members of Garbage are getting ready for their set. Seamus takes a deep breath. He steps onto the stairs with an arm outstretched to start shaking hands with all the people he knows streaming up and down the vast staircase. While J Allard may have gotten named one of Bill Gates's most likely successors in *Business 2.0,* Seamus has been named one of the most connected men in the world of technology by *Wired* magazine. Seamus sure seems to know everyone. He runs into Lorne Lanning of Oddworld, one of many who champion his ideas. They're about halfway up the stairs, talking to each other while lesser luminaries eye them. More and more people are pouring in. Seamus stands firmly on the stairs, weight distributed evenly on both feet.

It's getting darker outside and more crowded inside as the party gets rolling. As people circle through the different rooms and patios of the hotel, they return repeatedly to the lobby and the massive stairway ascending almost out of view. They gape in awe at the spectacle it makes. The fairy girls are shifting from step to step, in and out of the green searchlights. Seamus stands alone on the middle of the giant staircase now. He's greeting people as they make their way upstairs, welcoming them to "*our* party." The Xbox may have crushed his heart, but it's still his baby. And all around him, the fairy girls twirl and shimmer in the green light.

# EPILOGUE

## GDC 2005

Things have been going well for Epic over the last couple of years. Jay Wilbur and Alan Willard have just returned from back-to-back trips to Singapore and Hong Kong, showing the Epic engine to the many new game companies that have sprouted like so many mushrooms in a *Mario* game. The Singapore government is even considering subsidizing the purchase of the Epic engine to help jump-start its nascent gaming industry. The Singapore government seems to know as well as anyone at the 2005 Game Developers Conference that development teams—not to mention budgets—are getting bigger, and megapublishers like Electronic Arts, Microsoft, and Sony are desperate to fill hundreds of new coding, animating, and level-designing positions. Outsourcing to developing countries is a big subject of conversation among the gamemakers in 2005.

Alan is exhausted even before the conference has really started. He's logged twenty thousand frequent flier miles so far this year in his travels for Epic, and his daughter is now two and a half years old and getting harder and harder to leave behind. Besides, Cliffy's new franchise—the one of which he's been dreaming since 2002—will debut at E3 this year, which means the Epic team is expanding and working overtime in preparation for juggling two franchises instead of just one.

Alan isn't alone in feeling overworked. Quality-of-life issues within the industry have become a hot topic. The International Game Designers Association is circulating a white paper with shocking revelations such as the fact that free pizza at crunch time can't always replace vacation time—especially for designers over the age of nineteen—and that the eighty-hour crunch weeks most games go through before shipping may not be the best way to keep teams happy and motivated.

Rich Vogel, of Sony Online Entertainment's *Star Wars Galaxies,* is about twenty feet outside the Epic suite, at one of the many tables set up on the second floor of San Francisco's Moscone Convention Center. "We eat our young in this industry," he says, shaking his head. He should know—*Star Wars Galaxies* was in crunch mode for almost four years. Christmas 2003 was the first holiday through which he and his team didn't work since starting the project in 2000.

Will Wright sits in on a roundtable discussion on the subject. The conversation moves from just quality-of-life issues to the fact that while the videogame itself has moved into the mainstream, making a videogame can still be a pretty haphazard affair. Even industry veterans like Will aren't sure how to move their teams most effectively into the new era. There are complaints at the session about the common problem of managers who aren't really qualified to be managers—they're just designers who've stepped up because there's no one else to promote—and questions about how to even think about quantifying productivity. One person asks for advice about handling small offices that have been occupied for weeks straight and have grown so smelly people can't concentrate.

This year is the first that the GDC has been held in San Francisco, and although there was initially a lot of excitement about the change of venue—surely the move to San Francisco from San Jose mirrored the industry's own journey into the big time—the enthusiasm turns to grumbling once the event actually gets started. People are complaining there's no Fairmont Hotel this year. Specifically, they're frustrated and sad that without the San Jose Fairmont's sunken lobby to serve as conference headquarters—a watering hole through which everyone from the highest profile designer to the newest-hire tester came to socialize—they're not having the kind of informal chats and exchange of ideas they'd come to expect from GDC. They say the feeling of community has been shattered. In San Francisco, there are four or five hotels at which the gamemakers are congregating, and no one is sure where to go. There's a lot of scrambling up and down the streets of San Francisco's South of Market district, while shouting into cell phones and sending text messages, and a lot of "Oh fuck it" and hopping into cabs to go to one of the city's many restaurants and bars.

This is also the first year that longtime GDC honcho Alan Yu isn't running the show. He stepped down in 2004 to take a spot at Electronic Arts, which means no more of his annual "suite party." His replacement, Jamil Moledina, former editor in chief of *Game Developer* magazine, is trying to replicate the event at a nondescript hotel called the Argent, but the party doesn't have the same feel.

Some of the industry's luminaries, like Seamus Blackley, are giving and taking meetings in the Argent lobby and barely even setting foot in the Moscone Center. Others, like Shigeru Miyamoto, Lorne Lanning, John Romero, and John Carmack, aren't even in attendance. Despite the best efforts of Moledina, that feeling of equality and brotherhood that marked former gatherings seems fractured. "It just feels like Hollywood now," complains one designer, speaking over the din of noise at a Sony-sponsored bash across the street from the convention center.

Indeed, this year there are far more suits—or at least blazers over jeans—than shirts with flames licking up from the bottom. There's still the occasional man in a top hat or some other proud mark of geekdom, but the crowd is far more homogeneous than in past years. Colored dreadlocks have replaced greasy ponytails; cheap buzz cuts have become gelled spikes. They've gone mainstream. And while they're delighted that their strange brand of entertainment magic has been accepted, it's an adjustment; they're no longer just observing each other, but are also now being observed by the culture at large. So there's a lot more thinking about appearance among the gamemakers, about who they ought to be or wish they were, rather than who they are.

It's easy when you're at GDC to forget that those who choose not to attend actually still exist. But if you keep your ears cocked, you're sure to hear rumors pertaining to almost anyone about whom you might be curious. One of the most joyously spread rumors at this conference is about John Romero and Stevie Case, the rock-star couple of first-person-shooter culture. The two split up in the spring of 2003. Stevie is now married to a director of product development at THQ's wireless division, and they have a ten-month-old baby, who, Stevie says, "rocks her world." With an infant, she doesn't have as much time for gaming but is still managing to spend some time playing *The Urbz* on Nintendo's new handheld device, the Nintendo DS, as well as *Halo 2* and *Burnout 3* on Xbox.

As for John, he left Monkeystone, the company Stevie and he had built, to take a job at Midway. The big rumor fluttering from lips to lips at GDC is that he's taken a "child bride" from Romania. Of course, truth is rarely as exciting as rumor, but indeed, Romero has tied the knot, and yes she is young, and she is from Romania. (She has a name, too: Raluca.) They married on January 26, 2004, and John has been spending a lot of time commuting back and forth between her hometown of Bucharest and his new home in San Diego. Romero is currently very excited about both the new game he's working on—a remake of the arcade classic *Gauntlet*—and the impending reunion of Judas Priest.

Rumors also swirl concerning Romero's ex-partner, John Carmack. The highly anticipated *Doom III* was in some ways a disappointment to gamers as well as to the bean counters at id. And it is increasingly understood within the industry that, to quote one game journalist, "Carmack has always viewed the actual gamemaking as a pain in the ass." It's always been the technology that turned him on.

Carmack did not win the X Prize, although he continues to experiment with real-life rockets—and many believe that, had he won, he would have been out of the game business faster than one of his space capsules could have shot up into the clouds.

People don't even expect to see Miyamoto-san at the convention anymore. As his managerial duties at Nintendo get heavier, he recedes further and further from the design community. Satoru Iwata, his old friend and the man named as successor to Mr. Yamauchi when he finally retired, is at the conference. In fact, he's delivering one of the keynote speeches—on the future of Nintendo, a subject that still has game developers shaking their heads. With his beaming smile, Iwata reinforces what has always been Nintendo's mantra. He explains the three things the company teams ask themselves with every game: Is it innovative? Is it intuitive? (Meaning, does the gameplay feel natural?) Is it inviting? In other words, to paraphrase Miyamoto-san, the Japanese continue to focus on innovation, whereas American designers are more market-conscious, reacting to consumer demand rather than generating it. This is widely acknowledged in the game industry. "Photo-realism," Iwata reminds his audience, "is not the only means of improving the game experience. It's just one path."

On Wednesday, the conference's official opening day—Monday and Tuesday are devoted to all-day workshops and the Serious Game Summit, a two-year-old venture dedicated to more "serious" uses for videogame technology—J Allard of the Xbox gives his keynote address. Although J gives his talk in the same ballroom where Iwata gave his, their speeches could not be more different.

J's image is projected on large screens at the side of the stage for the benefit of the hundreds of people crowded into the room. It would seem his metamorphosis has been completed. He looks as fit as any upscale professional with a personal trainer, has shaved his head, and wears a red T-shirt under a black blazer. As the public face of the Xbox, J is giving Microsoft's view of the future of gaming. The Trojan Horse is out of the closet. J's talk is, at heart, more about the future itself than the future of gaming in particular. Gaming is just one part of J's vision; it's a means to an end for him. "Look how people are living their digital lives in their digital living rooms," he crows to the audience. He speaks of the importance of the advent of affordable high-definition television and what he dubs the "remix generation."

"Forget Gen Y," he says, with a wave of his hand. "These

kids want to leave their mark on everything they touch," which leads to his pitch to the designers on how, if they're building games for the Xbox 2 (now called Xbox 360), they can add new channels of revenue by offering personalized customization to gamers. Add a new stripe to your car in a racing game, pay a dollar online—all easily facilitated by a pop-up box on the screen and a push of a button on your controller. And the transactions, of course, will be handled by Microsoft.

J also points out that today the industry has friends who wouldn't have touched them even a few years before. He has a little movie he shows with snippets of conversation from movie director James Cameron of *Titanic* and *The Terminator* fame. Cameron explains that he no longer develops properties with just one medium in mind. He says what everyone in the room already knows, that entertainment consumers of the twenty-first century don't just want movies or a CD. They want *worlds*—entire universes they can enter through movies, games, soundtracks, whatever. Cameron says that with the advances in graphics and personalization techniques, videogames will now be "lucid dreams," with the player as the star of his own movie. "Who else lets the user be the protagonist?" J asks the crowd. He is a dynamic speaker. "We're the right medium for this age!" he cries.

Seamus Blackley, J's former counterpart at the Xbox, isn't at the talk. While some say it's sour grapes, that Seamus is hiding out now that the Xbox is no longer his, he's actually at a meeting during J's talk. Since his development company folded in the fall of 2003, Seamus has become an agent at CAA in Los Angeles. He's helping build up the agency's gaming division, representing people like Will Wright, as well as independent game studios. His days and nights are now spent trying to put deals together for developers whose games may be outside the industry's ever-increasing reliance on franchises and sequels to licensed material. While J was blasting the audience with his vision of videogames as the center of the digital living room, Seamus was in one of his "agent suits" at a bank in downtown San Francisco, trying to secure funding for one of his clients.

Back at the Argent the next day, in camouflage army shorts and a zip-up sweatshirt, Seamus is not overly optimistic about the state of gaming. "These people are getting frozen out of their own futures, and they don't even know it," he says about the GDC attendees. "And those who do, they're just walking around with stunned looks on their faces."

Seamus has never been a believer in the dream of digital convergence. He is a true believer in videogames as the art form of the twenty-first century. "If there aren't good games to play," he complains, "then why am I spending eight hundred dollars to digitize my living room?" There's an unmistakably forlorn look in his eye.

And he's not the only one in despair over the state of the industry since its headlong dive into the mainstream. Game designers talk of "sequel-itis and licensing-itis."

One designer forecasts licenses milked until there's nothing left, and laments that the "urban violence of minority cultures is being interpreted by white-bread developers who romanticize what it's like to be 'bad.' "

Not everyone is so despondent, though. Back at the Moscone Center, Raph Koster, the former lead designer on *Star Wars Galaxies,* is eating slices of pale-looking pâté with a plastic fork. Since the launch of *Star Wars Galaxies*, Raph was tapped by Sony to be chief creative officer of Sony Online Entertainment. It was a big step up for him—going from working on one game to working on all of Sony's online games. It also meant the splitting up of a six-year partnership with Rich Vogel—"the twins," people at GDC still call them. But Rich told him to go, that it was too good an opportunity to pass up, and Raph agreed, packing up his bags and moving his wife and eight-year-old daughter to San Diego from Austin in the fall of 2003.

There's some irony in Sony's choice, considering that *Star Wars Galaxies* did not become the phenomenon for which the company had hoped. Although it was the fastest-growing game in North America for a time, and although it boasts 600,000 subscribers worldwide today, the fact is that *Star Wars Galaxies* has become something of a joke among the massively multiplayer gaming world: too many promises made and too few fulfilled. Even David Reber, who finally made Jedi, ended up leaving the game in disgust. According to David, *Star Wars Galaxies* failed to stem certain exploits, had a shoddy combat system riddled with bugs and always under repair, and perhaps most important, left him disappointed when things didn't work out with the girl he'd met there. He's now back on Rubi-Ka playing *Anarchy Online* as Snakeeyes, (Level 220, "Fixer") and runs with a raiding powerguild called Synergy Factor. David loves his new crew. Financial problems brought him back into sharing a house with his mother, whom he takes care of. Recently, *Star Wars Galaxies* has been seriously upstaged by Blizzard's *World of Warcraft,* which came out in November of 2004 and by March had already hit the 1.5-million-user mark.

Many in the MMO gamer community lay the blame for *Star Wars Galaxies*'s failings squarely at Raph's feet. They say his vision of player-made content and social professions—dancers, musicians, and artists rather than Orcs, trolls, and warriors—didn't cut it. They say Raph's vision of a virtual world based on socializing and the "Real" relationships that can be formed was too idealistic—and not really what gamers wanted, ultimately. But it's a view both Rich and Raph dispute. In fact, Raph says he feels more convinced then ever of the validity of his utopian virtual dreams. If anything, he is even more adamant that the importance of play, for adults and children alike, "is critical to the upkeep of civilization."

Raph likes his new job, although he misses the sheer creativity of being a hands-on world builder. To fill that void, he wrote a book, *A Theory of Fun for Game Design,* based on his readings and musings about things such as cognitive science and the nature of human interaction. And he's also returned to making games himself—small ones that he starts on Friday night and finishes on Sunday, doing all the coding, animation, music, and story lines himself. His most recent weekend game, which he made for his daughter, is called *Water Snake,* and it's about a sea serpent that sinks to the bottom if you don't feed it enough, and shoots out of the water, where he can't breathe, if you feed him too much. His daughter has Type 1 diabetes, and Raph says the game is, at heart, a blood-sugar simulator.

Rich, waiting for Raph to pick him up for lunch, is sitting on the third floor of the Moscone Center, dressed in a green soccer jersey, looking a lot fresher than he did in the opening weeks of *Star Wars Galaxies*. His eyes are no longer bleary from lack of sleep. Rich's hope is that with the release of the next *Star Wars* movie, the game will have another chance to catch new players and lure back old ones. He knows it won't be easy, though. "When people leave your game, they're divorcing you," Rich says. "They're very hard to get back."

Rich has returned to his other passion, environmental photography, to achieve some balance in his life. "And I'm very lucky," he says. "My wife and I are still together."

One floor below Rich and Raph, Will Wright is basking in the standing ovation he just received for the surprise demo he gave of his *SimEverything* game. People in the game business expect to be amazed by Will Wright, but this was something else altogether. People were queuing up half an hour before he was scheduled to appear. The yellow-T-shirt-wearing conference workers had to block the entranceway with their bodies to keep people from slipping in before seating was scheduled to begin. When they finally stood aside, people rushed in, climbing over chairs to get to the front, and lining up four deep in the back when seats were gone. The conference workers were begging people not to block the aisles, but people plopped down anyway, sitting cross-legged in the front, like kindergartners waiting for a sing-along. During all the frenzy, Will was up at the podium, his narrow head and big glasses just visible over the top of his laptop, seemingly completely unaware of the excitement buzzing about him. It was hard not to pity the speakers who were scheduled to be giving talks in the same time slot.

Will starts by saying that what he's picked up from this year's GDC so far is that next-generation games are going to be incredibly expensive and content-driven, and that small studios will be forced out of business. "I would like to offer an alternate vision of the future," he says, and gets his first round of applause.

Will has a unique gift for mixing visual imagery with mathematical diagrams and language to get his points across. Fifteen minutes into the talk, before he's even told the audience they're going to get a preview of his new game, people are holding their stomachs and laughing. He moves through the entire history of relevant late-twentieth-century technology by showing first a picture of an Apple II (complete with an advertisement boasting that it's "six times faster than a teletype"), then a picture of a disk, then a massive tanker ship, and then a field of ship crates at a loading dock. He says the real inspiration for his new game came not from how much data the modern-day computer can hold—à la the modern tanker with its thousands of crates—but from the demo scene in Scandinavia. Because people in the demo scene have no budgets and are making their games for fun, they still use algorithms to make procedurally generated content, as opposed to using massive teams of designers to design massive amounts of content. "So I recruited an elite team," Will says—a picture of a group of black-clad Ninjas pops on the screen beside him—"and I want to show the demo of our new game to this community first, because this is the community where I feel the most affinity."

This is a big departure from standard game industry procedure, which mandates demoing games at E3. It's Will's way of reaching out to a crowd that is oscillating between delight at their newfound status in the culture at large, and demoralization at their lessening status in the industry.

**WILL'S NEW GAME,** *SimEverything,* now renamed *Spore,* has come a long way since the spring of 2003.

The game begins in a drop of water. The player controls a unicellular creature that must gobble up globs of one color to grow strong enough to reproduce, while avoiding globs of another color that chase it.

In the next phase, the creature evolves the ability to leave the primordial soup and crawl onto land. The player now has the opportunity to manipulate the creature's basic skeletal form, pulling him out to be long and narrow, or crunching him up to be twisted and humpbacked. He can have a huge head and almost no body, or a tiny head and big feet. It's up to the player. And all the different variations are not designed by animators and stored in a giant database, but are generated by the computer based on the physics of the organism's skeletal structure. The generative, procedurally based nature of *Spore* is like a revelation to the audience. Not only does it have the potential to cut the costs of gamemaking considerably—the computer is doing a lot of the work usually assigned to a horde of animators—but it also means that what a player makes is unique. The likelihood is that no one's eight-legged or one-legged or no-legged creature will look the same as anyone else's.

The next phase of the game involves sexual reproduction—a big increase in complexity from the unicellular blob in the beginning of the game. The player's creature must find a partner with whom to mate. (And because Will Wright has designed the game, the mating takes place with seventies-style lounge music in the background.) Postcoital, the player gets an egg, and another chance to create an even more evolved creature. It goes back to Will's original fascination with the editing tool he made for his first game, *Raid on Bungeling Bay*. To Will, the real fun of playing games is not that different from the fun of creating them. "Really, the point of the game is to lure players into being more creative than maybe they realize they are."

Eventually *Spore* lets the player invest in bigger and bigger brains for the creatures, and then they can do things like build campfires and, eventually, cities that can look like anything from a Dr. Seuss illustration to something out of *Star Wars*. Depending on the player, the city can grow up to be militarily, economically, or culturally driven. And players have to watch out because there are other cities that, depending on their tendencies, may attack, or simply knock at the city gates, looking to initiate trade. Will zooms out the game's perspective to reveal a whole new level of organization. The city, which had been built by a civilization that had started the game as a unicellular blob, is now shown as a blip on a large planet. "Oh shit," the audience mutters.

When Will explains that eventually players can get spaceships for their creatures, and then pulls back the game-level perspective again to reveal an entire solar system, people gasp. They applaud. They look at one another with wide eyes.

Will maneuvers his spaceship to an unfriendly-looking planet, which, he explains, has no atmosphere. It's up to the player to make these other planets habitable—accomplished through the use of a "genesis tool," which makes it all happen at once, or step by step, as the player brings plants from his homeland, and so on.

Then Will zooms out the focus of the game yet again, and the audience realizes the game's scope is not just a single solar system, but an entire galaxy. The applause is tremendous.

Will sends out a search for intelligent life from his spaceship, which he explains will echo around the galaxy. When he gets a response, he cruises over to a planet, which he then proceeds, much to the audience's delight, to blow up. "There goes my reputation as a nonviolent gamemaker," he says.

As if the audience weren't already choking on the heft of Will's vision, he then explains that the whole time people are playing *Spore,* Maxis will be collecting data and making matrices based on their aesthetic choices and game style, and then feeding this data back into the game to make it even more of a personalized experience. It's the first real step in Will's vision of a game that is more like a waking dream than a game at all.

Another thing about *Spore* is that it's also a brilliant homage to the history of the videogame itself. The first stage in the primeval tide pool, where the player must gobble up as much as possible without being eaten, mimics the gameplay of *Pac-Man*. The next stage of evolution is akin to a game like Blizzard's *Diablo*—a basic kill-or-be-killed scenario. The tribal part is Peter Molyneux's *Populus;* the city-building part is Will's own *SimCity;* the civilization-building part is Sid Meier's *Civilization;* and so on.

"My biggest obstacle in building this game," Will tells the crowd, "was my own belief that it wouldn't work. So I encourage all of you to follow your ideas, no matter how crazy they may seem."

And that's when the audience explodes, jumping to their feet and applauding with their hands over their heads. "My universe just shifted!" "The world is now a different place!" "Oh my fucking God!" It's as if Will represents everything the gamemakers packed into the room feel inside, but are afraid to express. Will's never been ashamed of his obsession with dinosaurs or spaceships or science fiction—he's never tried to become *cool.* And somehow, by staying true to himself, by letting himself just *be,* his vision grows and grows. The standing ovation is as much for this as for the greatness of *Spore.*

Outside, smoking a cigarette and shaking hands with people who want to take his picture, Will agrees there might be some truth to the idea that he is an inspiration to the gamemakers around him because he follows his imagination exactly where it chooses to roam and then has more success than the rest of them put together. He thinks about it for a minute, his lips pursed. "Yeah," he says finally. "I guess I'm kind of a proof of existence."

Will isn't overly fazed by the success of his demo, though.

He's got other things on his mind as well. His obsession with the Russian space program has continued. With the help of CAA, he's pitching a TV show on the subject, and he's recently purchased the entire interior of a Soyuz-T, the standard Russian space capsule. So now, in his house with his wife, Joell, and his daughter, Cassidy, there's a five-foot-by-three-foot control panel, and a stack of boxes containing all the parts he would need to build the actual capsule, should he choose to do so. And at the Stupid Fun Club, he's been experimenting with boosting the artificial intelligence capabilities of the appliances. Now club members have to convince the refrigerator to open, the coffeemaker to brew. Each appliance has a different personality, and will remember if you haven't been treating it right. "It's kind of weird," Will says. "You walk by and you realize that they've been gossiping about you. Oh yeah—out loud. You walk by and you hear, 'Oh shit, I have to deal with Will.' It's kind of weird." He chuckles in a satisfied way.

Will's old sidekick, Don Hopkins, is at the conference too, his hair still long and carrot red, his eyes still dazed by too much thinking, smoking, and hacking. He's wearing a T-shirt with an image of Ronald McDonald holding a huge machine gun—"He's a corporate mercenary," Don says, adding his wild laugh. Don has spent the last few years hacking play sets for *The Sims,* using an editing tool Will gave him. Mike Zyda of *America's Army* approaches. "Hey I know you," Don cries. "You're the NPSNET guy." Zyda, in a greasy black blazer and carrying a backpack, admits that indeed he is.

The last year has been a hectic one for Zyda. His angst over losing the top spot at the Institute for Creative Technology at the University of Southern California has been assuaged somewhat by the fact that the school has sponsored him to open a different research institute on its grounds, called the GamePipe Laboratory. Zyda is well pleased to be done with the Naval Postgraduate School and feels vindicated by his ultimate triumph at USC. But he has mixed feelings about *America's Army* now being under the reins of Colonel Casey Wardynski. Not only is their partnership over, but it turns out that the AUSA conference in the fall of 2003 was the last time the two men have even seen each other. The game, however, has not died. Through a licensing deal with UbiSoft, *America's Army* will, at last, be available in the summer of 2005 for consumers everywhere on both the Xbox and the PlayStation 2.

Indeed, military-themed simulations have continued to rise in popularity among videogame makers—one designer dubs them "MMMFs," for "murder made more fun"—which is good news for someone like Angel Munoz of the Cyberathlete Professional League. If the 2002 summer CPL event saw attendance of 1,500 people and $100,000 purses, Angel is expecting the 2005 event to draw 1,500 just in competitors. He expects at least another 5,000 people as spectators; and the prize money for the Dallas event has tripled, to $300,000. In fact, Angel and his sponsors—Intel, Nvidia, and CompUSA—are giving away a total of $1.7 million this year to professional FPS-ers. Next Angel is taking the show on the road with a world tour, stopping in places like Istanbul and Rio de Janeiro. And his amateur cyberathlete league has jumped from 6,000 people in the summer of 2002 to 175,000 in the summer of 2005, in the U.S. alone. While his Cyberstadium remains a dream, Angel has signed a contract with a new convention center in Gaylord, Texas, just minutes from Dallas, that is at least four times the size of the Hyatt Regency. It's no

Cyberstadium, but it does, at least, allow for real food vendors (like Pizza Hut and Kentucky Fried Chicken).

With her new baby, Stevie Case is no longer on the board of directors. John Romero, however, is still chairman. And CliffyB still holds his spot.

**CLIFFY IS LOOKING** quite dapper at this year's GDC. He cruises the halls of the convention center, giving quick nods to guys who swivel their necks and whisper, "It's CliffyB," as he passes. His look for GDC 2005 is a pinstriped black blazer over a T-shirt reading BILL GATES IS MY HOMEBOY, and striped terry-cloth wristbands on each arm. Cliffy's hair is blondish this year, and while still heavily gelled, it's in a much more "natural" style. He's traded in his contacts for glasses—Calvin Klein—and his Viper for a Lexus. CliffyB is growing up.

Cliffy's new game, *Gears of War,* which runs atop Epic's new engine, is nearing completion, and is scheduled, as Ed Fries intimated in 2003, to be released the same year as the Xbox 360. Getting a new franchise approved these days, let alone for a premier launch spot with the new Xbox, is about as easy as picking the winning numbers for your state lottery. It's about as good as it gets for any gamemaker who's not Will Wright. Producers and hosts from the videogame cable channel G4, which has finally made it into more than 50 million homes since the DICE summit of 2003, continue to hover around him.

But ask Cliffy if CliffyB-dom is everything for which he'd hoped, and he'll say "no" before he has time to reconsider and back up and say how great it is. Along with growing up—Cliffy turned thirty this year—has come an awareness that there is no victory circle in life. There's just life itself.

And right now, life is a blur of hard work in the Epic offices in Raleigh, North Carolina, interspersed with travel, and media interviews, and getting his photograph taken with famous people (like Dave Navarro and Carmen Electra or the Wayan Brothers), listening to his CAA agent tell people he's the David Fincher of the videogame world. It's all been very exciting, this becoming a star of an industry on the rise. But it's also confusing. In a sense, Cliffy's not sure which life is real.

Cliffy's internal changes are reflected in his work. *Gears of War* is not even a first-person shooter. It's third-person and much slower paced, which is a big deal coming from a pillar of the first-person-shooter world.

Cliffy is giving a talk at this year's GDC, and he's nervous beforehand. He's pounding sugar-free Red Bulls and hanging out by the door asking women friends of his to use their feminine charms to lure in more people. But sure enough the room fills up, and when Cliffy takes to the stage, there's hardly an empty seat in the house.

The conference room in the Moscone Center has high ceilings—more than thirty feet—and walls covered in pale yellow carpeting. Cliffy looks small up against this backdrop. He's got a sketch pad on an easel beside him with a big smiley face drawn on it. Like Will Wright, and like James Cameron in J Allard's keynote address, Cliffy has long been interested in the dreamlike nature of games, and he brings the subject up right away. "The ultimate game," he says, "is where playing feels like being in a dream."

As the talk gets going, Cliffy warms up. He's not so different from all the men in the audience who wish they were he. He speaks their language better than almost anybody. He hums from the theme of *Final Fantasy,* acts out the voices of whatever game he mentions, and complains hotly about the truism that the game industry has yet to create its *Citizen Kane.* "I am so sick of hearing this shit," he says. "Hello! *Doom, Warcraft, Zelda*?"

Cliffy may have been tight and nervous before his talk, but soon the light of intelligence and wit shines out of him. He gets into a groove and starts going off on tangents, like one about the HBO show *Oz*—"You know that uplifting prison drama about rape and shivs and whatnot," he says—to make a point about how the human brain is hungry for stimulus. (The connection is that he learned from *Oz* that solitary confinement is used as the worst form of punishment.) His pop culture references are indeed stunning. He is a child of media, his mind twirling around the characters and genres and movies and TV shows that have made him who he is. Within one twenty-minute period he refers to Yoda, self-help guru Anthony Robbins, *Halo 2, Super Smash Bros.*—"Did you guys see that story in the paper about people who work as mascots getting beaten up a lot?" he asks the audience. "I wasn't really surprised, because, let's be honest: it's fun to pound a mascot"—as well as Vin Diesel, Jerry Bruckheimer, *Silent Hill II, Resident Evil 4,* and on and on and on. There's something almost Robin Williams–esque in his manic impersonations and raving tangents, as if he is truly inhabited by all the personalities, real and otherwise, that he has digested over the years.

At one point, Cliffy talks about driving to work one day after playing *Burnout 3,* and says that he found himself about to swerve into another car—as you can do in the game without actually dying. He says after playing *Halo 2,* he found himself seeing the world through the frame of that game. "It was cool, but kind of scary," he says. "Remember, people," and here he raises a finger at the audience, "we, as game designers, are teachers. And we're working with powerful magic here."

Game Over.

# NOTES

## CHAPTER 2

**34** *Till the day he died:* John Anderson, "Who Really Invented the Video Game?" *Creative Computing* 1, no. 1 (Spring 1983): 11.

**36** *"It wasn't something the government":* ibid.

**38** *And in 1834, London scientist:* Doron Swade, *The Difference Engine: Charles Babbage and the Quest to Build the First Computer* (New York: Viking Adult, 2001), 10.

**39** *A three-story shack of a place:* Nancy Heywood, "Celebrating Building 20," March 4, 1998, Institute Archives and Special Collections, MIT Archives, Cambridge.

**39** *But it was its very lack of style:* Steward Brand, *How Buildings Learn: What Happens after They're Built* (New York: Penguin USA, 1999).

**39** *"It is kind of messy":* Simson Garfinkel, "Building 20: The Procreative Eyesore," *Technology Review* 94 (Nov./Dec. 1991): 11.

**42** *One unofficial TMRC member:* Steven Levy, *Hackers: Heroes of the Computer Revolution* (Garden City, N.Y.: Anchor, 1984), 31.

**43** *That "You can create art:* ibid., 43.

**43** *"In short," concluded Russell's:* J. M. Graetz, "The Origin of Spacewar," *Creative Computing* 7, no. 8 (Aug. 1981): 56–67.

**57** *And every other patron:* Scott Cohen, *Zap: The Rise and Fall of Atari* (New York: McGraw-Hill, 1984), 29.

**59** *Still, while most pinball:* Steven L. Kent, *The Ultimate History of Video Games* (Roseville, Calif.: Prima Publishing, 2001), 53.

**61** *The Italian models had:* ibid., 61.

## CHAPTER 3

**71** *Mr. Yamauchi had turned:* David Sheff, *Game Over: How Nintendo Zapped an American Industry, Captured Your Dollars, and Enslaved Your Children* (New York: Random House, 1993), 20.

**72** *So when Miyamoto's father:* ibid.

**78** *Within five years:* Susan Moffat, "Can Nintendo Keep Winning?" *Fortune* (Nov. 3, 1990).

**79** *Between 1985 and 1991:* Sheff, 55.

**79** *By 1990, polls showed:* Moffat.

## CHAPTER 4

**102** *"Oh my God":* David Kushner, *Masters of Doom: How Two Guys Created an Empire and Transformed Pop Culture* (New York: Random House, 2003), 152–53.

**102** *By 1996, the medical profession:* Marc Laidlaw, "The Egos of id," *Wired* (Aug. 1996), 1.

**108** *These were unthinkable numbers:* ibid.

**109** *He had begun dreaming:* Kushner, 205.

**109** *The results weren't flattering:* ibid., 206.

**116** *"Here's your loofah, Daddy":* ibid., 18.

**116** *At his Catholic school:* ibid., 19.

**116** *The psychiatric evaluation that followed:* ibid., 24.

## CHAPTER 5

**145** *This is something:* "Will Wright on Creating 'The Sims' and 'SimCity,'" moderated chat with Will Wright, CNN.com, Nov. 3, 2000. http://cnn.com/community/transcripts/2000/12/1/wright.chat/.

**145** *"I'm not sure I could":* Will Wright chat transcript, SimCity 4 Web site, Dec. 4, 2003. http://simcity.ea.com/community/events/will_wright_12_04_03.php.

## CHAPTER 7

**201** *Thinking it would improve: Defense Horizons* (Apr. 2002): 1–8.

**201** *Today, the Air Force:* ibid.

**202** *The altered game:* cybernetic.co.uk/marine.html.

**213** *And in its desperation:* Eric Schmitt, "Soft Economy Aids Recruiting Efforts, Army Leaders Say" *New York Times,* Sept. 11, 2003, A1, A14.

## CHAPTER 8

**227** *In contrast, by 1998:* Dean Takahashi, *Opening the Xbox: Inside Microsoft's Plan to Unleash an Entertainment Revolution* (Roseville, Calif.: Prima Publishing, 2002), 22.

**229** *Gates was flatly rejected:* ibid., 13.

**229** *Gates then watched from the sidelines:* Reiji Asakura, *Revolutionaries at Sony: The Making of the Sony PlayStation and the Visionaries Who Conquered the World of Video Games* (New York: McGraw-Hill, 2000), 187.

**229** *and the next year, as manufacturing:* Takahashi, 22.

**235** *The cost of each machine:* ibid., 184.

**237** *"I feel like my baby is":* ibid., 329.

**240** *The first person in line:* Takahashi, 329.

**241** *Under Ed, about 58 percent:* Tristan Donovan, "Top 20 Publishers," *Game Developer* (Sept. 2003): 32.

**244** *This is all part of their long-term:* Byron Acohido, "Will Microsoft's Xbox hit the spot? Tech titan's hunt for treasure begins with luring gamers online" *USA Today* (June 4, 2002), 1B.

# INDEX